The Absence

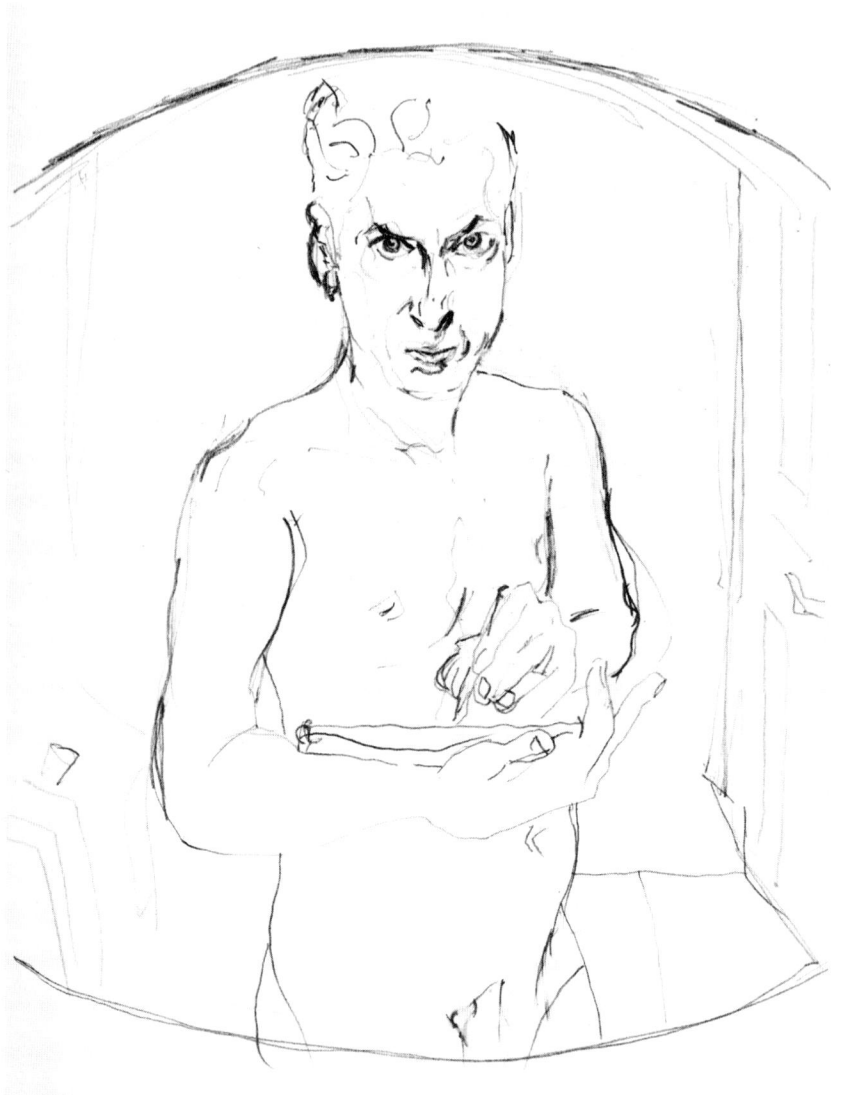

In the mirror in the bathroom
2.00 am Friday 28 July 06

THE ABSENCE

Memoirs of a Banshee Drummer

Budgie

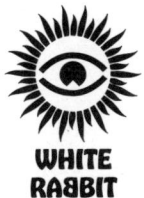

WHITE
RABBIT

First published in Great Britain in 2025 by White Rabbit,
an imprint of The Orion Publishing Group Ltd
Carmelite House, 50 Victoria Embankment
London EC4Y 0DZ

An Hachette UK Company

The authorised representative in the EEA is Hachette Ireland,
8 Castlecourt Centre, Dublin 15, D15 XTP3, Ireland (email: info@hbgi.ie)

10 9 8 7 6 5 4 3 2 1

A CIP catalogue record for this book is
available from the British Library.

ISBN (Hardback) 978 1 3996 2156 4
ISBN (Export Trade Paperback) 978 1 3996 2157 1
ISBN (Ebook) 978 1 3996 2159 5
ISBN (Audio) 978 1 3996 2160 1

Typeset by Input Data Services Ltd, Bridgwater, Somerset

Printed in Great Britain by Clays Ltd, Elcograf S.p.A.

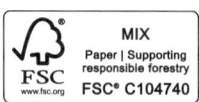

www.whiterabbitbooks.co.uk
www.orionbooks.co.uk

for
Isabella and Cosmo

Prologue

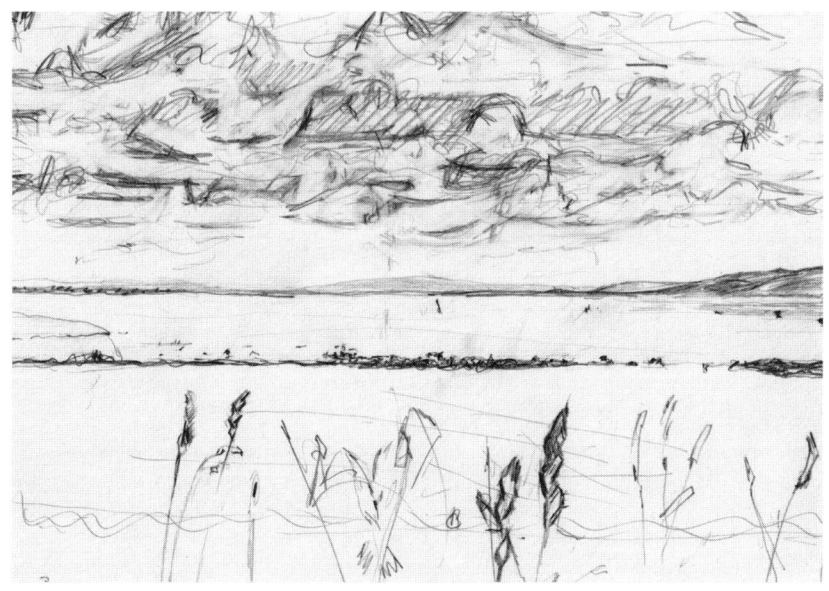

SCRAPE, scrape, scrape, blow and poofff! . . . a delicate cloud of plaster dust floats up into the air, drifts and hangs there like exhaled cigarette smoke. It's early evening. I am scratching an image of Lowe House church into ink-coated plasterboard. Dad is dozing in an armchair next to the fireplace. My mum and my sister Linda are sitting side by side. Linda is knitting a cardigan for her boyfriend Brian, and Mum is helping her with the sleeves. Mum puts down her needles and says quietly to Linda, 'I won't be doing any more knitting tonight, I'm a bit tired.'

These are her last words.

I hear coughing and Linda's voice screaming, 'Daddy, Mum's choking!'

Suddenly he is up and shouting Mum's name, sounding scared, scaring me. 'Eth! - Eth!'

I stop scraping - perhaps it's my fault. The dust, you see.

He is holding her.

My dad is holding my mum, trying to give her his breath. I stare.

There is no phone in our house. I run with Linda to the corner shop to call for a doctor.

There are no flashing lights, there is no paramedic intervention, just two children standing on a cobbled street outside a terraced house. The light from the open door makes puppet-show shadows of the people inside. The dark shape of a large van parked outside to my left may be that of the ambulance that came to take our mum away. I don't want to go inside; I know she has gone. Linda is crying. My daddy is crying. He hugs me, tells me Mum has gone. Uncle John arrives, says 'It'll be okay.' I cry a few tears and then stop.

*

Our older brother Michael comes home much later. 'What's going on?'

'Haven't you heard? Mum's died.'

Linda had already slipped into a matter-of-fact coping state; she couldn't have foreseen the effect of her answer.

I shared a bedroom with my brother. He used to throw things into my bed from across the room in the dark, and I'd hear him sniggering under the sheets. Tonight, I hear him sobbing.

I hear him sobbing for many nights. And I hear the same word over and over: 'Why?'

I am scared. Scared because I don't feel anything. I feel sad for my daddy and for my brother. I feel sad for my sister and for my mum. But I don't feel anything for me. I sense anger and injustice, but I don't know how to express those feelings. So, I push them down. *Down, down, deeper, and down.*

I buried a little boy under a weight of incomprehension and left him in that room to cry quietly by himself in the dark.

1.

The Bird Man of Morley Street

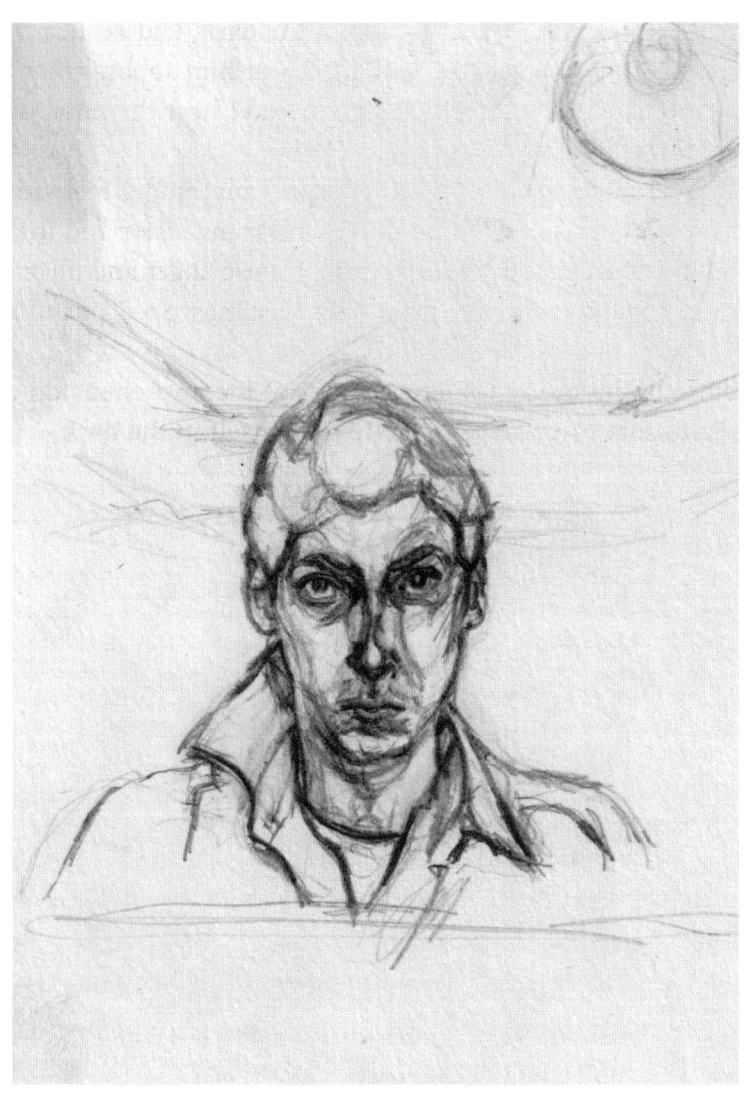

Mum died in our terraced house on Morley Street, high on a hill beneath the tallest chimney stacks in St Helens. If I put my cheek to the stone pavement outside the front door, I was eye-level with the clock face on the tower of Beechams' pill factory in the town below. The insurance man collected our weekly premium against flood, fire and theft. Knowing that water lies level, I concluded that if our house contained an inch of floodwater, the town below would be submerged. We had a working fireplace and a gas cooker, so I suppose fire was plausible, but as far as I could see, there was nothing worth stealing apart from my brother's Raleigh bicycle. Below my cheek and the cobblestones lay deep seams of coal, silica and lime, raw materials for Pilkington's glass factories that employed many of the people in St Helens.

You could taste the smoke from those factory chimneys, and from all the houses, especially on cold, wet evenings when it formed a thick fog, smothering the gas lights that glowed weakly above the shiny cobbles. Before the arrival of harsh, bright electric light, everything felt soft in the street. The stone pavement was a gentle, familiar surface, evenly laid; it made for a perfect hopscotch pitch. If I ran and fell, I might bang my head, but those hand-laid blocks felt like marshmallow cushions. Neighbouring streets were undercut by disused tunnels - deep coal seams eroded by rainwater. The subsidence caused houses to collapse, but ours was solid.

I never thought we had the best house on the street, but our house was different. A glazed brick finish, common to just five houses, gave a shine to them; the others were made of unfinished brick that weathered and crumbled. I could throw a tennis ball against a knee-height ledge and the 45° angle bounced it back perfectly. I spent hours playing throw and catch games, making up rules and routines, trying to find order in the repetition of sound and movement. Like a solo game of ping-pong.

Growing up with black-and-white TV programmes made for children to 'Watch with Mother', my perfect family role models would have been *The Woodentops*. Introduced and narrated by a well-spoken English lady who sounded like Queen Elizabeth II, nothing much disturbed the wooden puppet family's weekly routine. There was 'Mummy Woodentop and the baby – and Daddy Woodentop – and Willy and Jenny the twins – and Mrs Scrubbit who comes to help Mummy Woodentop, and Sam who helps Daddy Woodentop, and last of all, the very biggest spotty dog you ever did see. And they all lived together in a little house in the country.' When the programme ended, the word 'GOODBYE' floated above the Woodentop family's heads, while a melancholic piano refrain filled their unblinking eyes with a look of sadness. A sadness mirrored in my own eyes, never having watched with my mother and knowing that I never would.

I have very little memory of my mum. If I recall an image of her in the kitchen, cooking or doing laundry, it feels like something I've made up. I never saw her in the mornings before I went to school; my dad always put breakfast on the table before he left for work. I realise that this is what I remember after she died, and she may have done everything before then, but I have little or no recollection if she did. On one of the rare occasions my brother Michael talked of Mum, and only when asked, he spoke of a healthy, active young woman who enjoyed playing tennis and golf.

The mum I remember never exerted herself; even a short walk from the hairdressers left her out of breath. On our annual summer holiday to Blackpool, Mum was often ill in bed with a stomach ache. My dad and I would go for a walk along the sea front if it wasn't too windy or raining. But if it was, and it usually was, we would shelter at the Pleasure Beach. Not a sandy beach, but a concrete fairground, filled with the screams from the Wild Mouse and Big Dipper rollercoasters cutting through air thick with the fragrance of caramelised sugar, toffee apples and candy floss.

I loved the amusement arcade, the 'roll-a-penny' and 'ski-slalom' games. But my favourite place was astride the huge galloping horses of the Derby Racer carousel - gliding majestically to the whistle and clang of a barrel-organ waltz. I would collect paper cups to feed to the painted plaster tiger, whose deep booming voice growled, 'Feed me your litter!' My sister Linda and her friend Evelyn used to come with us to Blackpool, but as 1967 hemlines became shorter, and the mascara and lipstick darker, they stopped. Without older people to pester, I was alone and always out of pennies. I would be secretly terrified of the tuxedoed animatronic, laughing and jerking mechanically in a glass case outside the fun house, its head split in two by rows of snapping white teeth. The sound of its crazed cyclic laughing; the fake laughter of a gameshow host, mixed with the ripping cough of a heavy smoker, would haunt me for years.

On the walk back to the guesthouse along the Golden Mile, my dad and I would stop to buy a takeaway of fish and chips. We'd eat sitting on a wooden bench, sea spray on our faces, and the crash of the waves against the sea wall below us; the taste of salted deep-fried fish and potatoes, and the aroma of malted vinegar, soaked up in yesterday's newspaper, all combining to create tomorrow's memories of a rare holiday together. As dark clouds rolled in over the North Sea, the Golden Mile was bathed in the glow of a million coloured light bulbs, hanging in garlands strung lamppost to lamppost. We could feel the slow-moving trams, illuminated and decorated as galleons and spaceships, rolling and rumbling on heavy steel wheels.

Back at our bed and breakfast, Dad would fetch Mum a glass of peppermint cordial from the small bar in the hallway and go upstairs to see how she was. Every day I hoped she would feel better tomorrow. If the sun came out and Mum was well, we would go to the real beach with sand and waves. I would run ahead to set up those tricky-to-assemble deckchairs. I loved to see Mum and Dad relaxing and snoozing the afternoon away. I would make sandcastles, decorated with little flags of other countries, and dream of the bigger world that I knew was out there somewhere.

The rest of Morley Street was home to characters who seemed to belong to another time. They remind me of what it was like to be a child from St Helens, the North West and working-class England in the late 1960s and early 70s. Johnny Kerrigan was Irish and saw himself as a fine gentleman, wearing a bowler hat and his Sunday best to church. He even had a walking cane and white spats. But it was all sadly faded glory, nothing was white, nothing was clean, and his suit was greasy and shiny. He'd whistle as he walked down the street, our own Charlie Chaplin – 'there goes our Johnny'. If Johnny Kerrigan's door was open it usually meant he needed something. I'd shout through into his hallway, 'The usual, John?' A distant, 'Aye, lad,' floated back on the foul odour from inside.

I'd run across to the corner shop. 'Hello, Mrs Clitheroe, can I have half an ounce of thick twist, for Johnny, please.' Mrs Clitheroe, quiet, smiling and, to me, always an *old* lady. She knew it was for Johnny. 'Here you go, Peter, tell John it's on his tab.' The first thing that hit you as you walked through Johnny's front door was the awful, acrid smell: overripe cheese and unwashed skin, floating on a non-specific warm, damp mix of pipe-tobacco, paraffin, grease, mouldy vegetables and cat pee. A constantly changing olfactory assault, unpleasant but familiar, almost welcoming, in small doses.

I never saw beyond the room where he sat, like a dark cave – with no electric light, his round, wire-rimmed, grimy spectacles only reflected the grey gloom. There was a fireplace with a hook to hang a pot on, and a stone for the kettle. If he was eating, Johnny fed the cats too, throwing scraps of raw bacon onto the floor. But the scraps also attracted the mice and the cockroaches, and Mrs Banks, who lived next door, had to sprinkle cockroach powder along the common wall. Johnny Kerrigan played the banjo. And as he strummed, he sang words that only made sense to Johnny in his decaying world.

Go Johnny, go, go, go!

Mr and Mrs Banks, Johnny's next-door neighbours, owned one of only three cars in Morley Street. Theirs was the newest and 'a classic' before it was a classic. An American-styled Ford Zodiac, bright yellow with chrome-trim fins. Mr Banks was obviously doing well, and Mrs Banks was at home most of the day, every day, always needing to borrow an egg or something for their only child David's evening meal. Similar in age to my brother Michael, David played electric bass guitar in a band called Chris and the Autocrats. David practised at home in the front room, and it was from his bass notes that I got my first taste of that window-buzzing, low-end rumble. I was intrigued and subconsciously filed the experience away for future reference.

Mrs Banks liked to play bingo, but Mr Banks never left her enough money to overindulge because if he did, she would still borrow eggs but never be home to make dinner. My mum and Mrs Banks must have been friendly; they'd occasionally go to the bingo together, but I don't think they were best friends. I don't recall my mum meeting with friends or if she even *had* any friends, other than Mrs Banks. Did Mrs Banks harbour ideas of being a well-kept woman? I suppose there was a lot of that, keeping up with the Joneses, or rather keeping up with the perfect housewives of 1960s TV adverts, when women saved the day with gravy powder proclamations - 'Bisto browns, Bisto thickens, Bisto seasons all in one go' - or washing-up liquid - 'Now hands that do dishes can feel soft as your face, with mild green Fairy liquid'.

The sickly sweet melodies of advertising jingles, sung by voices reminiscent of the ubiquitous Mike Sammes Singers, were perhaps my first musical training. I was a good listener, and unfortunately I can still remember them all. The men in TV adverts, meanwhile, were like aliens to me. Beer drinking, cigarette smoking, bristle

shaving, 'Tetley Bitter men – if you can't beat 'em, join 'em'. I preferred 'Tetley make tea bags, make tea'. We even had a Mrs Jones
down the street at number 124, a quintessential Mrs Jones. She was
'Mrs Jones of Morley Street' because you had to keep up with Mrs
Jones and I used to play with her only child, another David. We
rarely saw Mr Jones, who was very quiet, tall, glasses, stern-faced.

Mr Banks, Mr Jones, even my dad, were working men who
were mostly absent. They came home from work, went through
the hall into the living room and you never saw them. If you did,
any words proffered would be curt and cautious. Mrs Banks never
invited us in, but Mrs Jones did. She was always well made-up,
her hair in a beehive twist, full make-up every day, a tightly fitted
pencil skirt, stockings with a seam down the back and high-heeled
shoes, even in the house. I imagine she was dressing to be looked
at. *There she goes – Mrs La-de-da*.

There wasn't much interaction between adults – children
played outside in the street, the parents were presumably indoors,
but rarely seen together. It wasn't a gossipy street. There wasn't
a lot of leaning on the garden fence because there was no garden
fence to lean on. Garden fence gossip is suburbia. David's mum
was not a semi-detached suburban Mrs Jones.

On blue-sky summer days, the sun reached its zenith and
began peeping over next door's roof and chimney stack into our
narrow back yard at about two o'clock. My mum would place a
wooden chair against the back-yard gate, to sit and sunbathe. She
sat fully clothed, with just her face, neck and arms uncovered.
Even in summer the sun's arc was low, and by about four o'clock
it had dropped below the roofline of our house, which then cast
a growing chilly shadow over first the north wall, then the chair,
then my mum and finally over the stone lintel above the back
gate. I was sad that her enjoyment of the sun was so brief. I would
have moved the roof for her, if I could.

I more than liked Mrs Jones; she was the closest we had to a
schoolboy fantasy-pin-up in make-up and red lipstick. I don't

think we knew of other mums like Mrs Jones. David wanted for nothing and whatever he needed, he got, including friends. If we weren't out on the street, we'd be playing at Mrs Jones's house – David's front room – and she would supply us with soft drinks, pop, crisps, sandwiches, enticing us in because she wanted David to have friends. David could buy a game a week and his front room was our hive of activity after school. But he could be quite fickle and some days he didn't want you to come into his house. He'd say, 'I'm playing with Alan.'

'But you never play with Alan!' Until he did.

This was my first brush with a door policy, and it was quite cruel, because if you didn't get into David's front room, there was nowhere else to go. So you'd wander the streets, kick a ball around, try to keep warm – and try to avoid the older lads who lived in the streets down the hill, where the people and the pavements got rougher. There were late-night games under the gas lamps, played from wall to wall across the cobbled street, catching games, invented games and even a pissing game round the backs of the houses where the coal was delivered. Whatever it was, we'd play until it was dark – nobody really bothered shouting for you to come in.

The church provided something to do and seemed to connect everyone. On Sunday mornings, before Mum died, my dad and I would walk to Holy Cross church near Shaw Street railway station. On the way home we'd stop at the newsagent between Pocket Nook and Finger Post; there might be an old *Superman* comic I could look at while Dad was getting cigarettes. On cold winter evenings I'd walk down to Lowe House church hall for choir practice wearing my favourite and only warm coat – brown nylon, three-quarter length, tight and fitted, with those little plaited leather buttons which were probably plastic, but I didn't care. I loved that coat. I'd been going to church since the infants' pre-school days, when we were taught by nuns. They were like holy grandmothers to us, like an extended family.

We were always aware of the church – it was a little daunting, feeling the overshadowing presence of God. You were judged on how good you were as a morally upright little Catholic boy, but it wasn't all hellfire and damnation. Mrs Price, our class teacher, slipped me creamy-tasting butter-mints, and because I was a choirboy, encouraged me to sing harmony in music class. We sang along to a TV programme for schools called *Making Music*. Notes on a music stave lit up as a simple melody passed over them; the single note repetition of 'Old Abraham Brown is dead and gone' has never left me. We were given a chime bar, a triangle, or a tambourine to play. Sometimes they were even played in time with the lights on the TV screen.

I have always had a love of tuned percussion. At the end of every Siouxsie and the Banshees' recording session, just before final mixing, I would run off to raid the dusty depths of a percussion warehouse in London's Wapping Wall, or spend an afternoon in Chinatown's catering stores, fingertip-tapping aluminium cooking pots and salad bowls, listening for notes and resonances with which to create percussive melodies.

The church gave me a little of my musical tuition. It's where I learned about intervals, harmony and structure, even sight-reading. Father Gibbons was one of the older Jesuit priests, a very gentle man, but not a very accomplished pianist. He'd play simple chords and single-note melodies, and we listened and learned how to sing and to memorise. Once we had the music in front of us, we'd be able to equate the memorised melodies to the notes on the stave. All the words were in Latin, so the meaning and emotion had to be found within the cadences of the melodies. Latin was a language that for us only existed in the church, and to sing in such an ancient tongue made us feel like members of a secret society. It created a sense of something exclusive, something closer to wherever God might be, what you might call an 'occasion'. I loved the acapella sung service of the Compline mass. It was singing in its purest form, akin to the lowly sound of reverence I imagined echoing through the cloisters of an ancient monastery. The choir would glide into the church, each boy dressed in a white alb, a full-length white cotton robe, tied at the waist with a rope belt, a face-hiding hood, and a small wooden crucifix hanging on a string necklace. We may have resembled a shifting snowdrift, but that serene image was sadly undermined by the scruffy shoes and tatty hair poking out beneath hemline and hood. It was rough and ready but with a lot of ceremony, and for one night every year, we felt special. It was a performance, and perhaps there was a sense of privilege that accompanied a feeling of being a little closer to the heaven that we Catholic children had been told so much about.

The pinnacle of my choral career was singing at the blessing of Liverpool's new Catholic cathedral, known locally as Paddy's Wigwam. This was a typical Liverpool reference to the many Irish Catholics in Liverpool and to the stained-glass turret topping off the cathedral's tepee shape. A bold concrete construction, greeted with a reaction of either love or hate, its other nickname was 'The Mersey Funnel' – a rhyme with the tunnel under the river upon which the famous ferries cross.

On 14 May 1967, presided over by Archbishop Beck, the cathedral was consecrated. Choirs from many local churches and schools were gathered and assembled as the massed choirs of North West England. After many weeks of rehearsal in our own church halls, the consecration ceremony was the first time we'd heard the result of all our practice. We sang an assortment of classic hymns, ending with a stirring rendition of Handel's 'Hallelujah Chorus'. It was huge, it sounded wonderful, and it was joyful to be a part of local history in the making. Performing on such a grand scale affected me deeply and made a lasting impression. But, sadly, it was the beginning of the end of my relationship with the church.

Dad turned his back on religion and the church on the night Mum died. On another dark night, that same week, a group of lay preachers innocently collecting for the church knocked at the door and rubbed him up the wrong way. It was the worst time to have come calling, as my dad, usually so easy-going, felt that they had shown a lack of respect. They couldn't have known. Dad was angry with God, angry with the church, angry with everything. And that was it. The end of his concern for the church coincided with my own departure from caring about God or Him caring about me. The nurturing feeling the church had given me, and the peace that came from believing that God was always present, abandoned me that night. This was when trying to fill the pain of the absence began. Music would come later. First, there were Budgerigars to attend to.

It probably began with the film *Birdman of Alcatraz* starring Burt Lancaster. I was always a bit of a nature boy, and I was really drawn to the central character of that film. After Mum died, it was a way of bonding with Dad, especially as his way of coping seemed to be by constantly immersing himself in work. My dad was a joiner in the building trade. My dad's boss, Mr Williams-Rigby, kept a collection of delicate, yellow canaries in rows of specially constructed cages housed in a purpose-built shed. Encouraged by my dad, I started a Saturday job.

I would go into work with him on Saturday mornings and earn a bit of money by cleaning out the canary cages. That's when I twigged. I remembered pub entrepreneur of rings and watches, 'Diamond Jim', and 'Shotgun', the steeplejack. Shotgun also trapped greenfinches and sold them to canary breeders to develop a hardier strain of bird, better equipped to survive cold northern winters. I did some research and discovered that Australian budgerigars seemed fine with the British climate. Budgie breeders instead focused on their ideal-looking bird, and through that process they came up with many different colours and types. My friend Tom kept pigeons. They're big, dirty and boring. Pigeon fanciers transport their pigeons by car to some place far away from home, release them and then delight in them returning home. We didn't have a car, and I didn't fancy being a pigeon fancier. I thought I'd like something more exotic - but being as it was cold up north, and exotic was expensive, I opted for budgies.

My dad took great pride in building two large outdoor aviary-type cages called flights, with doors for access and a thick concrete base to keep the cats and rats out. Inside the shed, rows of wooden cages provided a safe space for courtship and nesting boxes for little budgie eggs to hatch.

I was fascinated watching Dad create all of this in our small brick-walled back yard. The cages were beautiful, black gloss outside, clean white on the inside, heated in winter, almost more luxury than we had indoors. I had such admiration for my dad's skill. Together we visited established breeders to buy good birds to breed with. The pride of one breeder's aviary was a Lutino cock, red eyes like an albino, only with yellow pigmentation. He was expensive, so being friendly, the breeder also gave me a skinny little bird of undefined gender that he called a 'Rainbow'. He said, 'You can have that one, it'll help you on your way.' So, we came home with two birds for the price of one expensive variety.

When the cages were ready we released the budgies into them. Unfortunately, the yellow Lutino was a totally self-obsessed male, uninterested in anything but himself. It turned out the undefined little Rainbow was a hen and she was off to the races – she became an egg machine. We bought more birds to join them, including a proud handsome grey cock who took to the rainbow hen and sired many handsome grey chicks, with a hint of their mama's rainbow colouring. I joined the Junior Bird League and the British Budgerigar Society. I began to draw budgies in my school art class, most memorably and mischievously a watercolour of two birds in a 69 position, not a Kama Sutra 69, more a pop art composition of two perfect birds. It wasn't completely terrible, and I did learn how to draw the 'ideal' British budgerigar show bird, with *perfect* plumage, markings, the *preferred* head and beak shape, and the *correct* colouring of the 'cere', denoting gender. Sex education too.

At weekends in the shed I enjoyed preparing the birds' food – a mix of canary seed, millet seed, cod liver oil and yeast. A fortified feed that kept them strong and healthy. Usually, caged birds need supplements like iodine to boost immunity, but the mortar between the bricks in our back wall was high in lime and the birds thrived pecking at it. They got all their nutrients, but the wall began to crumble.

We eventually started selling budgies, advertising 'Baby Budgies for Sale' in the local paper. The going rate for pet budgies was about 25 shillings – just over an old British pound apiece. I'd pack them in little cardboard boxes, just like a professional budgie breeder. Doing the maths, we would have had about twenty breeding pairs, each pair might have two batches of eggs in a season, with an average of three eggs per batch. So, at 25 shillings a bird, that brought in around £120 a season.

It was hard work, but it could be quite lucrative. My dad helped a lot, but half a hundredweight of bird seed wasn't very expensive, and after just a year of breeding budgies, I had money in my pocket so I put some towards the first stereogram for the family and some clothes. Most importantly, though, budgies would later give me my nickname and also help pay for my first proper drum kit: a five-piece Beverley finished in a gold wrap. My dad put down the deposit and I tried to keep up with the instalments. This was the kit I played everything on up to and including the Slits' opening slot for the Clash on their 'Sort It Out' tour, and on their debut LP *Cut* in 1979. I think that warrants a celebration as a jolly good investment. And it all came about because of budgies. Cheers!

Sadly, the budgies would eventually fade into the background, probably because of the long hours I had to sit with all the budgie breeders in meetings held in a tiny upstairs room in the Clarendon Hotel pub, in some godforsaken part of old St Helens. Old blokes in flat caps, drinking pints of beer, smoking ciggies like Pilkington's chimneys. I was the only youngster in the room, but I thought that's what you had to do to become a good budgerigar breeder and to win a rosette at a show.

The next morning I'd wake up with a bad cough and have to go to school with weeping red eyes, looking like a panda with conjunctivitis. Dad had put so much effort into building the cages, encouraging me, taking me on the bus to bird shows in and around the North West. But I lost interest. That's when the drums took over.

2.
The Young Ones

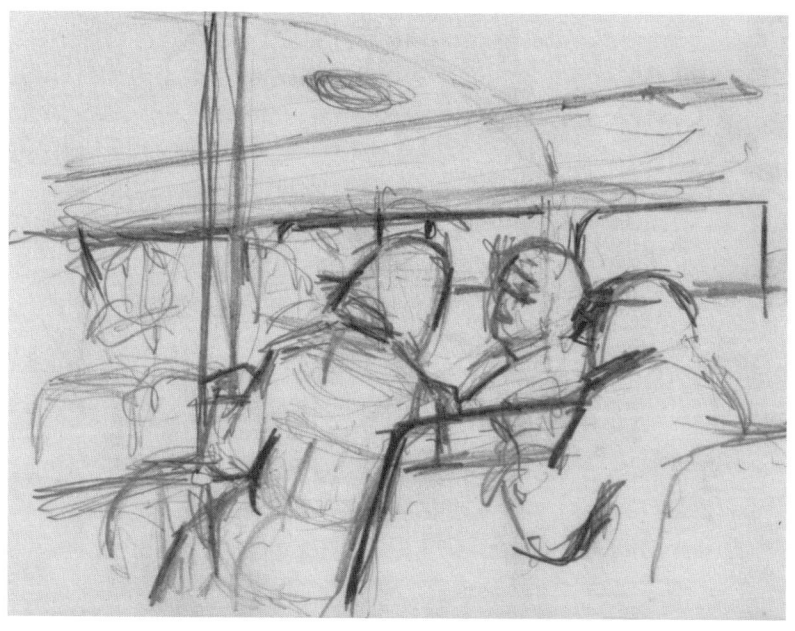

Like the smoke from the factories, music drifted in and around Morley Street. The constant roar and hum of the factories soothed me to sleep, and so did music. Victoria Park was a couple of hundred yards away, and on summer evenings, from the bandstand in the park, I would hear rhythm and blues bands playing the classics of the time: Beatles covers, Cliff Richard and the Shadows. I could never really hear the vocals, but I could hear the drums and bass as they floated intermittently on the summer breeze and in through my open bedroom window. This distant beat music and the constant drone of the factory furnace were the only things that would block out my recurring nightmares.

In one I was constantly running as the ground fell away behind me into a chasm of flame, a fiery inverse of that feeling I had with my cheek to the cobbles of Morley Street, imagining St Helens consumed by water.

In my other regular bad dream everything was too big, my thumbs and fingers grew enormous and clumsy. I was too large to fit into the world and everything smelled of burning and tasted of rubber. I dreaded drifting off to sleep and would lie awake listening to these musical fragments, soothing rhythms and drones floating over the rooftops and chimneys of St Helens. These sounds entered my dreams with their comforting repetition and ignited my desire to play drums.

In the summer of 1970, David Jones's front room providing the setting once again, board games like Mousetrap, Cluedo and Monopoly stopped when Alex Peachey arrived with a record player. David and I were maybe twelve years old, but Alex was a few years older and had left school and got a job at the local glass factory, so he was making good money. It wasn't an auspicious start – the first records we played were borrowed from David's dad. Holst's *The Planets* suite comes to mind. Alex's dad's collection offered up bawdy army songs. Enough said, really. But I had an older brother and sister, so plentiful access to classic hit records from the Walker Brothers, the Beatles and the Rolling Stones. My personal collection started and stopped with Mandy Miller's 'Nellie the Elephant' (still a classic), but Mrs Jones let us play her copy of Simon and Garfunkel's *Bridge Over Troubled Water* and drums came pounding out of the most surprising places.

I'd always loved reggae, and the Upsetters' 'Return of Django' was the first single I bought. I knew the beats, but oddly never thought of playing reggae. I liked the early reggae hits like Desmond Dekker's 'The Israelites', and Jimmy Cliff's 'You Can Get it if You Really Want'. Trojan was *the* label, and later Island, but I didn't particularly like Bob Marley, when reggae became more mainstream. I liked the fun and silliness of the Upsetters and Lee Perry's material, which was considered 'off the cuff' and not to be taken too seriously. It wasn't until the arrival of heavier dub reggae from Jamaica in the early to late seventies, as punk was happening, that the memory of that early music came back to me.

Back in Morley Street, we had developed a structure to our sessions. We'd sit with the record deck, diligently listening to each other's choices. It was both educational and extremely trying, especially when we discovered progressive rock. There were strange records from artists like Amon Düül II, Neu! and Faust, none of which made much sense to us at the time. The album covers were brilliant, but where was the music? What was going on? I always remember hearing Amon Düül's 'Race from Here to Your Ears', from their album *Dance of the Lemmings*, and thinking, *Wow, this is amazing – what is it?* It's apparent now that all these little things would be filed away for future use, to become a common language when I eventually met up with Steven Severin and John McGeoch in the Banshees.

David, Alex and I had the Beatles as a common reference point, but mostly we were buying records because of the artwork and band names, not a particular style or genre of music. We were not led by the charts, which I suppose was the key. It was a trip of mutual discovery and probably one-upmanship. How long can you tolerate *this noise?*!

Like *Doctor Who's* Tardis, David's front room landed us in tomorrow's world. A Marconiphone portable cassette player with a microphone arrived - it was a revelation. At first it was used to tape music from the radio, but then we thought, *okay, it's time we made music of our own.*

We recorded everything first take - how else were you supposed to do it? We had bongos and a guitar, but no lyrics, so nobody sang. Alex landed the job of making noises with his mouth and he was strong, so he also played the bongos, fast and hard. I played one string at a time on a guitar given to me by Brian, my brother-in-law. We were called Leather Dog, Furry Boots - that was my clever title - and we made one cassette and played it to Mrs Jones, who said she liked it. We took photographs for the sleeve and, as I thought my new skinhead haircut with shaved partings was the wrong look for the band, I wore an aluminium dog bowl on my head, which admittedly made me look more like a commando than future new wave legends Devo, but it was all very innocent.

Leather Dog, Furry Boots was heavily influenced by Kevin Godley and Lol Creme from 10cc, who had a side-project (I must have noted that idea for future use) called Hot Legs. They released one song, called 'Neanderthal Man', which consisted of a beat, a bit of a drone, a middle eight played on recorders, and a very repetitive refrain. Maybe they too lived near a factory? T. Rex and Medicine Head were also influences and a bit more rock 'n' roll, but we soon realised that with very simple instruments you can make a lot of good noises. Medicine Head were zipping up the charts but not making it big, and that was cool, cooler than being Sweet. David wanted a haircut like singer Brian Connolly, but we didn't want to copy Sweet - they were Led Zeppelin wannabees, with cute poppy lyrics. Without realising it, we were already prejudiced against popularity and chart acceptability, but we had no ambition to play live or be 'a band'. I don't think we knew what that really meant. Perhaps we were punk before punk?

My spell as a one-string guitarist didn't last beyond Leather Dog, Furry Boots. And although it had been the sound of distant drums and rhythms from the bandstand soothing my nightmares that had made an impression on me, the impetus to start playing the drums began with something more tactile: a love of music stands.

At primary school, I'd been the only one allowed to sing harmonies and the only one allowed to put up the music stands in the class. It was a bit like setting up those tricky deckchairs on Blackpool beach, frustrating and sometimes impossible. If you got it wrong, the music stand would get bent out of shape. Mastering the screws and telescopic pole of the stand made setting up cymbals child's play. As a kid, I loved my brother's Meccano construction kit and Lego bricks. I loved building things. I would simply look at drums in magazines and in the shop window of Novello House, and I used to draw them in the back of exercise books.

At home there was an old banjo with no strings, a circular rosewood body and a stretched calfskin head. I loved the feel of it, my first drum. Some months later, I bought a second-hand bass drum with a mounted tom-tom and a floor tom from The Magpie's Nest second-hand shop on North Road. I just added bits to make up a kit. Inspired by Hawkwind, I got a second bass drum with more toms and put them next to each other. All totally different. For a while, all I did was put drums together and simply look at them.

I started by playing along to chart records. I hate to admit it, but it was probably the Bay City Rollers track 'Keep on Dancing' that got me going. It was like a drum challenge - how do you play that fast? There was also 'Wipe Out' by the Surfaris, which simply made my hands seize up! I had to play quietly so I acquired brushes, thinking that they were made for playing drums quietly, which they are, but obviously for a different style of music using a different technique. I didn't know about either, so I'd just use brushes like sticks - quiet sticks.

There was an old carpet-slipper factory round the corner on Windle Street. The waste bins outside the factory were a good source of offcuts - fake-furry slipper fabric offcuts. The colours were outrageous, strips of pink, blue and a vivid, garish green and yellow. I would fix a piece of furry fabric to the metal hoop of the drum with Sellotape, letting a flap rest loosely on the drumhead - to act as a dampener. When the drum was hit, the furry fabric flipped up, letting the drum ring for a second, then flopped flat again to dampen the sound. This flipping and flopping is ingenuity at work, I thought. My ingenuity followed me through to my first live gig where an older drummer came up to me and said quietly, 'What on earth have you got on your drums?' My kit was also tied together with lengths of coloured rope. I'd noticed that Ringo Starr had two steel anchor points at the front of his Ludwig bass drum, presumably to stop it skidding across the floor when he hit it. My kit didn't have any of those, so I passed a thin rope around the back of my three-legged drum stool and tied it to the two tuning lugs at the bottom of the bass drum. I did the same with the hi-hat cymbal stand. Connected in this way, my weight would hopefully hold them all together, except I wasn't very heavy and so wherever the drums went, I would go too.

Looking back, I now realise that I could play the drums at home only because Linda, Michael and my dad were at work - my mum was absent.

I didn't try to play jazz beats and I didn't try to play any of the music I'd been listening to. Instead, it was a whirr of things like Black Sabbath, Deep Purple and the band Budgie from Wales. Ray Phillips, Budgie's original drummer, certainly had a subliminal influence on me. He used two bass drums in quite a unique way. It was simple, heavy music. Nothing complex, just rock 'n' roll heavied up. Nor was it like Black Sabbath or Led Zeppelin, which had bigger productions. But, for a young self-taught drummer, it was like the key to unlock a mystery - I could visualise what I was hearing. I thought, *I get it, I understand this.*

For all the appeal of Mrs Jones, David's front room wasn't big enough to accommodate the next wave of experimenting. Again, 138 Morley Street being so empty meant that we could get away with so much more, especially as most weekends Dad was away in North Wales, working on a retirement house for his boss Williams-Rigby. Our house originally had the same two down-stairs rooms as all the other houses in the street, a sitting room and a living room. Nobody ever sat in the sitting room, except on special occasions, like a christening or a death. So, Mum and Dad decided to knock down the dividing wall, and our living room doubled in size. It made me think of the Beatles' four terraced houses with one interior in the film *Help!* And of course, it meant we had a bigger space to play in.

Alex had a projector and he'd got hold of an early black-and-white 'blue movie', which he projected onto my bass drum. David was a little embarrassed, I think, but John, a guitarist who wanted to be Jimi Hendrix and had joined our original trio, was a bit more worldly (his dad probably had 'nudie' magazines at home) and was into it.

By this stage we were heavily influenced by Hawkwind, and the idea that they had a naked dancer on stage - it was all a bit of a mystery to us - was exciting; soft porn films were the next best thing. They came in a brown paper bag from under the counter at the local newsagent. The script would usually follow a set-up routine. In the first scene there would be a bowler-hatted gentle-man and a woman in high heels casually walking along a street, and the next thing you know, they're in the front room taking their clothes off. We knew what was going on, but there was a sense that we shouldn't, that our parents wouldn't approve. But, of course, they never knew.

While the cavorting figures flickered on my drums, we'd play space rock jams with John Dutton from Chapel Street playing Black Sabbath riffs. He said he was into the devil and wanted to set his guitar on fire like Hendrix, but he only had one guitar, so he didn't. He *did* kick his amp off the dining table, however, which made a great noise. There'd be attempts at songs from the catalogue in my head, the Shadows' 'Apache' and Fleetwood Mac's 'Albatross'. We were pushing the boundaries of our small world, testing the boundaries of what was deemed 'permissible'.

I was only thirteen the day Chuck Richardson knocked on the front door of 138. That was the day everything changed for me. My sister answered and Chuck let himself in. 'Is Peter in?' he asked. 'We want him to be the drummer in our group.' Chuck must have heard about me from John, who was already in the group. Chuck had blue-black hair, which was certainly and obviously not natural, and a suntan that came from a bottle: a composite of Cliff Richard and Elvis Presley. He had all the moves and affectations and spoke like Cliff Richard with an Elvis drawl. Chuck Richardson, we never knew his real name, was probably in his late twenties but seemed older. My sister really didn't like Chuck because Chuck really liked *her*. Chuck liked all the young ladies.

Chuck had an idea for a cabaret act called Chuck and the Young Ones, inspired by Cliff Richard and the Shadows. We were all extremely young, and in Chuck's mind this was the novelty that would secure us bookings. Colin on rhythm guitar, John on lead, and Salvatore Capostagno, son of the ice-cream man of the Italian family three streets over, playing bass. Salvatore was the same age as me, but had a moustache, and I mean a full one. He couldn't play very well, but his dad sold great ice cream and his mum made a lovely spaghetti Bolognese.

Colin and John had already got the instrumentals down, and

I just had to learn the drumbeats. There was also a structure to a setlist: slow songs first, then mid-pace and finally a rock 'n' roll third set. I might have been listening to Amon Düül and reggae, but Chuck wanted me to play the music that my parents' generation would have been dancing to. The slow songs would be waltzes or ballads from the late fifties and early sixties pop, which for me meant ride cymbal, snare drum, bass drum and fills. They were all very simple. The song 'The Young Ones' was, of course, a big hit for Cliff, and we would open with that as an instrumental, and then Chuck would make his big entrance with Elvis Presley's 'Don't Be Cruel'. We'd play some Shadows tunes, the songs I used to sing myself to sleep with. I realised I knew the drum parts before the drum kit came along. I've always found that very strange.

The plan was to play the local cabaret circuit, the working men's clubs and perhaps the occasional small theatre. Our first gig was an audition, on a Sunday afternoon, in an empty club, to see if they might want us to play the following weekend. I was on the stage setting my drums up with the string to hold them together and the little bits of carpet-slipper material on the heads. I'd just about got everything ready and then I heard the music start, the organ chords boomed and the curtains opened. I was mortified, paralysed with fear, but at the same time thinking, *Ah, here we are, on stage, playing.* Chuck was easy-going but had tried to instil some kind of professionalism into us. I was shy and had my head down, but Chuck knew that it was about projection - he turned to me and said, 'Peter, look to the front and smile.' I had to watch him, that was the key. I looked up and saw him performing and moving, doing all these Tom Jones moves, and it fed into me. I knew instantly that I was responding - responding to him. From that first audition to today, this is how I've always played the drums, in dialogue not with the bass or the conventional idea of the rhythm section, but in connection with the singer.

Back on that first day, I think there was one guy out in this empty club with a pint watching. That was it. We were the entertainment between the bingo and the dancing. The audience would be sat at Formica-topped tables in rows down the side of these long halls lit by fluorescent tubes the whole way down. It was very spartan, all pints of lager and bitter and crisps and pork pies and pickled eggs and bingo cards, and a real routine.

Once the bingo started, it was SILENCE except for the bingo caller: Legs 11, Two Fat Ladies 88, Knock at the Door number 4, and Downing Street number 10. Then somebody'd shout, 'Line!' Ahh . . . mass exhalation. You'd hear someone else squirming, 'I'm sweating on number 9.' Doctor's Orders number 9, 'House!' and there'd be a massive gasp, and everybody would get up and go to the loo or go to the bar. It was mostly the old ladies who just came for the bingo and everybody else joined in later. The clubs made their money selling bingo cards and booze and paid us from that. We did private parties and weddings too – they were terrible. There would always be a punch-up at Liverpool weddings and Christmas parties; there was always trouble, but they paid well.

Chuck would pick our outfits. We had to wear bow ties and a white shirt, black corduroy trousers and blue stack-heeled boots. We each had a different-coloured velvet jacket, and Chuck had a red corduroy suit. We'd go to Liverpool to audition for TV talent shows like *New Faces* or *Opportunity Knocks*. We were never successful in our bid for TV stardom, but we were invited back to play the clubs; we even had promotional photographs to sign and hand out. (Fast forward to 1979 and imagine my surprise when I discovered that bands still had the same glossy promo photographs.)

We were precocious. The other Young Ones' parents were loud and keen – they'd come to cheer us on and get the atmosphere going. We started to get fans, people who would come to the club just because we were playing, but mostly once they'd had a few drinks it didn't matter who was on. We were just giving them what they expected to get. We were not testing the waters.

*

We started with soda pop and music distilled from Mrs Jones's record collection, but Chuck and the Young Ones started my long, three-way relationship with alcohol and music. My grapefruit crushes and dandelion and burdocks became lager with lime cordial, and lemonade-bitter shandies. I'd have a half of lager, but always mixed with something so it didn't taste like a real drink. We were underage so the clubs had to be careful - we were never served spirits - but those half pints of lager and their soft drink disguises were an initiation into the drinking culture. The adults' pint pots used to collect on the end of the table; by the end of the night they were stacked ten-high. When 'last orders' was called, everybody would get up to buy a round of drinks, so there'd be a table full of pints of lager to be consumed within the next five or ten minutes.

It was total alcohol overkill and no wonder people got a bit lairy. Inevitably, while I was packing up my gear there'd be a drunk staggering up to me asking to have a go on my kit. I might have only been fourteen, but I could manage a 'No, bugger off!' There were fights, and some of the families of other members of the Young Ones were fighting families. If somebody was looking at somebody's wife in the wrong way or their daughter had joined them for the first time and somebody was on the dancefloor with her and getting a bit too close, they wouldn't think twice about getting up and 'lamping 'em'. This often happened to Chuck because he was very popular with the women, and once they'd had a few drinks, they didn't hide their affections, despite his wife Maureen being there a lot of the time.

My sexual awakening arrived through Maureen. She was petite, angular and stick-thin. Red and white patent leather coat. Block heels, on plastic knee-high boots, and a go-go dancer's mini-skirt. Her blonde hair was lacquered into a bob - a sort of fallen bee- hive. I suppose it was that 1960s Mary Quant look with a hairband and a curled and back-combed bob. I liked her because she was tough and she stood up for herself. I don't know what background

Chuck came from, but although he was a lot older than his years, in many ways he was very immature.

Maureen got pregnant young, and they had a little boy. It seemed as if they were in the wrong place together. They argued a lot. She was left at home on a rough estate with the boy, and when she was allowed to come out with us, she got really dressed up. The dads of the other Young Ones would nuzzle up to her: 'All right, Maureen, love, you wanna drink?' Their wives would be going, 'Oi, stupid, come here!'

It was often cold on the drive home from the club when they dropped each of us off at our homes. One night, a tipsy, giggly Maureen and I were both under a blanket. It was touchy-feely under the woollen blanket, something that I wasn't really expecting. It was like a game and that's perhaps what the first adventures are - when some girl was chasing me round Morley Street one day I'd been horrified, scared stiff because she looked like she really meant it.

But that was pre-Maureen. Maureen was a woman. She had a child. This was different. In the driver's seat Chuck was clearly getting angry, but Maureen kept saying, 'Peter's such a nice boy.' She was flirting with me, and I wanted it to go further, but I didn't know what I was doing, and she knew she was safe. She was teasing me to get Chuck's attention. She'd probably picked me because I was giving off that invisible sign that says 'need'. I need somebody. I need you because you're going to let me be nice with you. I didn't know how to do what was required, I had no experience. But I was needy, and I thought it was love. I suppose that was my first experience of something secret, and from then on I was always drawn to secrecy, the taboo and power of sex.

'Fuck' is a word that has always been difficult for me to say. It just doesn't seem to flow out with ease as it does for others - fuck. Fuck this, fuck that, fuck you, fuck it. In the Liverpool Scouse dialect, and even more so in that dialect's Irish origins, everything after the 'f' is created deep in the throat, creating a sound like that which precedes a phlegmy spit or gob. 'Gob' in Scouse is also a word for mouth, often appended by the word shite, and used as a term of contempt for someone stupid, as in 'Warra fuckin' gobshite'. There was a lot of this chat in the clubs where we played as the Young Ones, so I knew the word and its practical usage, but to me it was still taboo, an alien word. I was never allowed to say it as a kid, but I always liked it, and as a good Catholic boy I feared it, just as I did other sexual words. Masturbation was another taboo word, which brought terrors to my teenage years.

Because Mum had gone and Dad was so involved in his work, I had no guidance. I was floundering in all areas of relationships: still too shy to meet girls and I suppose very vulnerable to Maureen's advances. I thought she gave me validation by acknowledging my presence as a male, only in fun . . . but perhaps not only in fun. She was well aware of what she was doing. Isn't it strange when inter-band relationships bring it all tumbling down? Oh, the beginnings of a terrible trait.

I started to understand that so much of what I saw around me was a desperate attempt to escape the squalor of it all. I realised that Chuck and the Young Ones and the cabaret club scene were just another level of squalor. There was nothing dignified about them and this was not what I wanted. At the time, I thought it was just because I wanted to be like John Bonham, but I realised that that probably wasn't too dignified either. The underbelly of it was very visible and unattractive, but there was also something exciting about it, like the fairground coming to town. It was a little dark and perhaps a little dangerous, and I knew playing the drums meant that I was one of the few that could be a part of it. Even being in a band like Chuck and the Young Ones made me understand that I was on the other side of the fence, that once you're onstage and playing, you are separate from the people who are in the club night after night after night.

Eventually this seedy, grasping world was too much for Chuck.

He was losing his charm and, I thought, becoming bitter and sadly incongruous. The mums and dads of the rest of the Young Ones were still dominating and had quite an influence on what we did. They'd always find a dodgy van for us to drive around in and my name went on the logbook. I was the official owner of many dodgy, second-hand and probably stolen former ambulances with fan belts that made a huge noise when you arrived home at 2am. The families wanted more of a taste of the bright lights, each of them aspiring for their boy to be the star of the show. But Chuck was in the way and the end was not pleasant. We'd reached the ceiling of our ability and potential, and Chuck just didn't know how to make the thing more successful than it was. The parents were craving more money. There was a big argument, and Chuck was in tears when they destroyed his dream.

I was very aware of the trap he and Maureen were in, the same one as so many of the (admittedly few) people I knew, and I hoped that their little boy was going be okay. Chuck had dreams far bigger than his life was capable of delivering. It had only lasted a year, and my career as an entertainer on the working men's club circuit was over by the time I was fourteen.

I wonder if there's a part of me that was prised open because I was missing my mother. I was never close with other people's parents, apart from Mrs Jones. They were always secretive and cautious, but they had loose reins when it came to their kids - it wasn't like they were in any danger of straying too far. So many of the things we got up to were like a rite of passage, understood between parents and children. I wonder if mine would have been the same? Would *my* mum have let me stay out until two in the morning playing in the Young Ones? Would she have allowed drums in the house? I don't think she would have been able to tolerate it. She wouldn't have wanted me to mix with those families, whom she would have thought of as rough. Chuck would not have made it through the front door. But I can never really know, because Mum's death meant that all the negotiations of what was permissible as a young teenager never took place. I never got to know if there was another side to the mother protector, and there is always that nagging feeling that perhaps my career in music would never have begun.

The true umbilical cord was finally cut when my mum died. Something that perhaps never happens in a lot of people's lives, where the cord remains strong and still holds tight. With the freedom I had came the pain of the cut, and then the process of gathering as many distractions as possible to hide it. Art, music and going to a deep core, inner space. From a young age I imagined that to be an artist you had to be very selfish. Even then I yearned for family and relationships. But I thought maybe I would never have that, because I wanted to be able to follow the muse. I couldn't have a family. It just wouldn't work. Seeing what happened to Chuck and starting to think about how art and music and bands worked, I felt you had to give up some part of yourself to achieve what you were after.

I was aware that most people had an anchor or core of stability that I was missing. Something so sacred that they could never willingly relinquish it. I longed for that security, but I didn't trust it and I felt that a more demanding negotiation was necessary. I was prepared to make a Faustian pact, but I was also indoctrinated with the biblical warning 'What shall a man give in exchange for his soul?' I knew that the core of my identity was up for grabs and I didn't realise how vulnerable I could be.

It was back then, in Morley Street, in St Helens, in those clubs, relaxed by alcohol and touched by warm hands under the blanket in the back of a cold van, that the essence of myself started to drain away. That is, except for what I came to visualise as the last vital drop, held in a delicate glass vial with a tiny cork stopper, the surviving essence of Peter. For years I was afraid that if I so much as checked to see if I was still there, I might just lose myself completely and disappear.

3.
Leaving St Helens

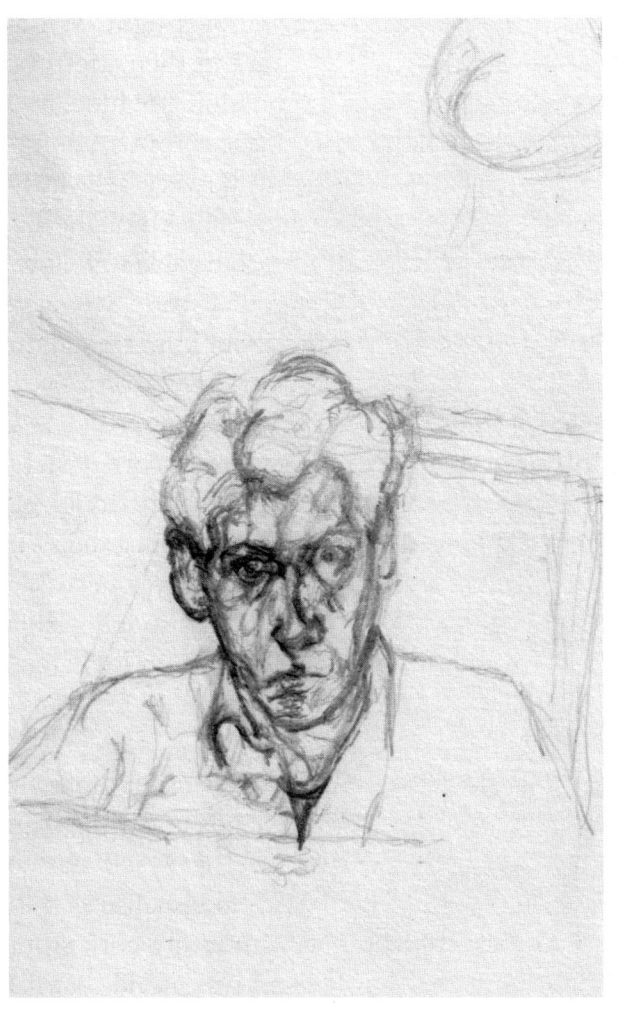

The absence at Morley Street had enabled our mini-happenings with blue films projected onto my drum kit, and after the end of Chuck and the Young Ones my relationship with that knocked-through downstairs room started to get more intense. My dad wasn't a drinker, but he'd be out more at weekends, mixing with old friends, and courting Elsie, whom he would eventually marry. My brother and sister would also be out on Saturday night, so I had the house to myself. I would sit playing records on my own in the dark, getting more than a little high on music and cider: a bottle of Woodpecker, which progressed to a bottle of Strongbow, which became two, but *of course* it was all under control, because it was 'just cider'. I bought it from the off licence, known locally as the 'Outdoor'. A small shopfront with a little latch-key door and two steps up into a small forbidden world of alcohol. With its gravity pump for draught beer, it smelled like a bar. I was secretly drinking cider to get a buzz going, but also just to get out of my head. It became a physical process, an attempt to make an emotional connection to some other side. I thought that I could control alcohol, using it to help me relax, to find the part of me that was necessary to negotiate with the dark side of my mind.

I was desperately trying to commune. I imagined that I could perhaps cross over and make a connection, to see Mum again, or even her ghost. On the wall above my bed was a poster of Curved Air's Sonja Kristina in a tight top, with her long hair flowing over her breasts. I'd listen to Curved Air's album *Phantasmagoria*, to her voice whispering the words 'and you keep looking over your shoulder to see if I'm there'. The extreme stereo panning effect swirled the music around my tipsy mind. I was banging my head against a metaphorical wall, to somehow break this bond with the world without Mum, a world that felt bleak. It was a ritual, carefully prepared, and was perhaps the first ritual of my own. I'd noticed that people had a ritual when they took drugs, smoked pipes or cigarettes. I'd seen it as a kid with Johnny Kerrigan's thick twist. There was ritual everywhere, certainly within the church, and in the living room at Morley Street where I had made my first altar with the sofa and cider in place of wine.

As I listened to music, banging out the beat with my body, the movement was ferocious. I broke chairs and springs in the sofa. When I met Ariane Forster (Ari Up of the Slits) a few years later, it was the first time I'd met somebody else who would be banging into their chair when listening to music, to make the music *more visceral.* I was learning in this violence about beat and rhythm, about the distance between and the weight of the beats, but I was doing it away from the drum kit. I broke so many chairs and damaged the sofa so badly that my dad bought an old rocking chair. He thought that would solve it, but it was a rocking chair with big spindles, so I would crash over backwards. Then he put screws in the bottom, but I ripped holes in the carpet. He got me another with a solid, heavy wooden base with bigger springs, but I broke that one too. The rocking chairs were not helping.

Perhaps breaking chairs was a distraction to avoid talking to my dad about what I was going to do when I left school. Maybe my dad preferred to supply more chairs rather than have that conversation about why.

Saturday night was often another chair-smashing session. Live albums like *Greasy Truckers* and that of the first Glastonbury Festival were recorded at the gigs I could never go to because there was never anything like that near St Helens, so I'd imagine them as my own gigs. Humble Pie's live album *Performance Rockin' the Fillmore* is what really did it for me. I found out later that the drummer Jerry Shirley was only nineteen or twenty, as young as Mitch Mitchell was when he played with Jimi Hendrix. There was something about that album and his playing that I took with me.

I learned so much from it about the ability of music to connect because I could *hear* it; I could hear the audience communing and Steve Marriott guiding it, something so primal in that exchange. It was the key that I was looking for.

It's odd to think of Morley Street now, with all of that happening in my teenage mind, as just an ordinary home. There are so many olfactory memories in every cupboard and in every dark place. The birds and the budgerigars were a way of bringing new life into the old bricks and mortar, but as my interest waned and music took over, we sold everything off and the aviary was dismantled. We were moving on; my dad was getting remarried and leaving, keeping an eye on me from afar, but I don't think I ever really left. Strange how a small mid-terraced house can hold so much, and so many memories.

At the same time as these changes were going on at home, the Young Ones, with Chuck ousted, started playing their own gigs. We'd do the latest chart hits, songs by Status Quo, Sweet, Slade or Free, but there were a lot of other bands doing the same thing, the difference being that they were older than us and they knew how to play, while we were still floundering. We went through terrible name changes, like Taurus and Shadowfax, and played school parties and the local YMCA.

Before it fizzled out, David Jones briefly joined us as the bass player. With his Brian Connolly haircut and Gibson SG copy, David had become better than even David Banks. He introduced me to some of his friends from school who were also proficient at more complicated music. I joined them for a couple of rehearsals, trying to copy Yes drummer Bill Bruford, playing long instrumentals with odd time signatures, but it was still youth-club stuff.

After that I bumped into these guys who were playing Steppenwolf's 'Born to Be Wild' and Canned Heat-style blues. They were older and seemed more serious. I wanted to take over the drummer's throne in that band. Paul Darlington already had a nickname: 'Softy'. I liked Paul, he was good, but a bit too busy for me. He could play the rudiments and had a very light touch, hence

Softy. A guy called Trevor played the flute, though I think he was only in the band because his dad was a farmer and had a barn out in the country where they could rehearse. I'd seen them play live at the working men's clubs, the same places that I'd played with the Young Ones, and I realised that even *they* were just proficient part-timers.

There was a year or so of this, being on the periphery of various musicians, playing with a guitarist who would call me on Morley Street's newly installed telephone. Steven Briers would put the phone receiver in front of his amp and play me the latest riff he'd learned, like Hendrix's 'Foxy Lady' or 'Purple Haze'. It sounded great through the telephone. My first experience of audio compression! Meanwhile, I was in the last year at school, something I remember through the clothes I wore back then.

A cardigan my mum had knitted for me, bottle green with brown-leather-covered buttons. I wore it over my star-patterned, scoop-necked, flared-sleeve shirt throughout my last year at school. Mum loved to knit and was knitting the night she died. That bottle-green cardigan was my last connection to my mum.

Around the same time, under the influence of Marc Bolan, David Bowie and Robert Plant, I was developing a curiosity about women's clothes. Importantly, I had the bedroom to myself. I found and brought home a shop-window mannequin, a plastic female figure like a bendy Barbie, and I put my cardigan on it to dress her. This was when I started to play with ideas of fashion and fantasise about the wonder of a partially clad woman's body. My curiosity about women's clothing came from wondering what went on in those drawers that you're never allowed to go in when you're a kid.

When I was sure I was alone, I would try on stretch tights to see how they worked because I still had a boy's figure. I wouldn't say it was even cross-dressing, just a curiosity to see what it was like to be in the female form. Outside this experimentation, women were a mystery. School was mixed gender and some of the girls were way more advanced physically and knowledge-wise. If I was invited to stay behind at lunchtime because one of 'those' girls was going be in the stockroom, with permission granted to 'investigate', I'd run a mile. Even though there was a blonde girl who looked like a young film star, it was just too far beyond my comfort zone. I didn't feel at ease with what I thought was expected of me with girls.

Ever since then I've wondered if I was hiding. Am I still? As soon as I could, I wanted long hair and I wanted to mess with people's opinions. When I look back on my gender and sexual identity at that time I find it very difficult to figure out. My key female role model had disappeared. Perhaps everyone has periods of playing with their sexuality, but Mum's death flipped a switch which, like a malfunction on an Apollo moon mission, made for a slight change in my trajectory. That change, at first imperceptible, became increasingly exaggerated as I moved further and further away from the source, and the trauma of that night. Nobody else was ever going to realise it, I certainly didn't myself. It affected the choices I made during what would normally be the most important time in a young man's life. The period when we weigh up and consider all options. I could see all around me where the conventional life led.

If I had a bit of money, if my dad had given me a fiver, I'd go down to the Cotham Arms on the town-hall square in St Helens. Edna the barmaid knew my dad from the Parr Hotel pub when I was still a lad. She liked to talk of old times, and I liked to listen. During term time, a gang of us from the Gamble art school on the other side of the square would take over the small back lounge. But at the weekends, I'd sit alone, with a pint, watching the old people, the ladies with their stockings rolled down to their knees, and their legs comfortably apart. Couples who never spoke, always with the same drinks, sitting at the same table with nothing to say to each other. They wouldn't even move to get another drink because when one had finished, Edna fetched another.

I was now alternating between staying in Morley Street and

living at my dad's new house in Vincent Street: my stepmother's moods were unpredictable and I sometimes felt uncomfortable and unwelcome. The Cotham Arms and Edna's stories were far more inviting than sitting alone on the local canal bank, so a pattern for solitary drinking was soon set. As well as the solo drinking in the pubs there were clubs too, and drugs were starting to appear. St Helens is on the crossroads between Liverpool and Manchester, and just like in the movie *Drugstore Cowboy*, there was a disillusioned, Bonnie and Clyde romanticism around breaking and entering pharmacies, stealing and selling barbiturates for recreation, and drugs like Mandrax and Tuinal. They'd be available at places like the Geraldo Club, an old dance hall, and although it wasn't far from the budgie fanciers' pub, the two couldn't have been more different.

DJ Tony Fine would set up his monster sound system at the Geraldo, testing the volume with a showman's trick of holding a cigarette lighter in front of the speakers, letting the air movement from the bass cabs extinguish the flame. Tony took no requests but supplied a connoisseur's selection of heavy rock and progressive music, from Led Zeppelin and Pink Floyd to Focus and Golden Earring. I'd be drinking Newcastle Brown Ale straight from the long-necked clear pint bottle, swinging my long hair, spinning like a dervish, and getting really hammered. The Geraldo soon became a weekly ritual, and waking up for school the next day got more and more difficult. Despite the heavy bass, the dazzling detail of the sound system, and the flashing glare of strobe lights, there was a whole slew of people passed out, asleep. They'd arrive, find a dark corner, pop a pill with a pint, and have a cheap night out. Money was scarce, but there was always a queue to get in, and once in, it was barbiturate blackout time. It made me wonder, *What's the point? What's all that about? Why would you do that?* I never did. I loved the releasing, numbing effect of strong alcohol. I was entranced by the power of the music, the heavy, darker side of it. It was now just the music, and the dream of creating it, that kept me in St Helens. For a while, at least.

I left school as a young sixteen-year-old with a portfolio of high-school artwork and hopefully enough qualifications to secure a place at the local art college. That summer, I took my second trip away from home and began my first and only normal, albeit temporary job, as a hotel kitchen porter on Newquay's Fore Street in Cornwall. It was 'Foxy Lady' telephone guitarist Steve Briers who invited me, and so with his cousin driving and with only one eight-track music cartridge for distraction, we arrived at the Cornish campsite knowing every falsetto note of Uriah Heep's 'Wonderworld'. Falsetto car vocalist Steve was also experienced with girls and was on a mission to meet with his sometime-girlfriend Janet with the tight-fitting Levi's jeans. Janet was a dark-haired, dark-eyed wild child. That night she was being elusive, but Steve didn't hang about. Our first night out in the Sailors Arms pub, he got talking to a blonde-haired girl from New-castle, and romance was restored. His blonde date had a friend. With pale skin and a cascade of dark curls, Christine was more Pre-Raphaelite than any Dante Gabriel Rossetti painting. Christine led me to her campsite tent and welcomed me in. I had my first fumbling failure, which was a crushing experience, especially with Steve and blondie making a lot of passionate noises in the neighbouring tent. Christine was kind and visited me in St Helens later that same summer. Steve and her friend picked up as if still on holiday. For me it was even more difficult in my old bedroom in Morley Street. Christine went on to study design in Stoke-on-Trent and we never saw each other again.

I'd always had an interest in visual art. My first introduction was a portfolio of watercolours and stained-glass window designs by my mum's talented brother Alec, who died young and was never talked about. I suppose post-war discussion didn't dwell on the brief lives of so many young men. I heard that Alec's battle was with his mind, that his death was probably due to mismanagement of his mental condition. Psychiatric or mental hospitals in the 1960s were dark, forbidding buildings, where patients were locked away behind high stone walls. Tales of patients screaming in padded cells, and long dank corridors smelling of incontinence, disinfectant and paralysing serums gave us children bad dreams and only fuelled our ignorance. Like most things that are now unacceptable, we regurgitated all the name-calling and labelling of the asylum and its patients. Rainhill Hospital was the 'loony bin', and frightened children can be very cruel.

With my dad remarried and my sister preparing to start a family, I left Morley Street and moved into Vincent Street with my dad and his new wife, Elsie. Elsie had a small collection of art books with colour plates of paintings by the Old Masters through to the French Impressionists. I started to look at art in a more analytical way, to gain a deeper understanding and find something that spoke to me on a more personal level. I liked the challenge of Francis Bacon's early work, the panache and finish of early Lucian Freud and David Hockney's inventive playfulness. I was torn between Bacon, Hockney and Freud - each of them an inspiration. They changed my world, and my thinking. No one I knew was drawn to those painters and they became a private thing for me that existed in parallel with music. I could play drums now, but I really wanted to paint, or at least I really wanted to try, even if doing both seemed utterly unobtainable, so I enrolled on an arts foundation course.

The School of Art and Crafts occupied the basement and top floor of the Gamble Institute, an imposing Victorian building on the east side of the town-hall square. Another façade of red-glazed brick, the whole ground floor was home to the town library, which I'd been a member of since I was at junior school. Across the street from the college was the Greenall Whitley Brewery, which supplied St Helens with beer and flooded the surrounding area with the constantly changing smell of the brewing process: the warm aroma of malted barley infused with the smell of yeast or hops, depending on the day of the week. These airborne flavours always made me hungry. The same can't be said for the earth and cowpat smell of wet clay in the college basement. The ceramic department was not the place for a delicate nose or stomach. When a new batch of clay was being opened for wedging, it smelled like an open sewer.

Like the mould under the stairs at Morley Street, smell was a big part of college life. It was a wonderful, creative atmosphere. I would discuss art and music with my first real friend Paul Simkin. A gifted draughtsman in the style of Aubrey Beardsley, Paul had a dream to play a Gibson Les Paul, but LOUD! That's what he always wanted to do, play a big, fat E chord at full volume through a 100W Marshall stack. One day, Paul, one day.

Alongside those of us studying art were trainee hairdressers and painters and decorators learning their trades using huge pull-out screens covered in wallpaper. We all took a morning break in the same refectory. The young female hairdressers with their painted nails, new hairdos and tight, figure-hugging clothes. The salt-of-the-earth P&D guys, who wore tight T-shirts under their white-paint-stained bib and braces. Then us, the loud, foppish, art-student wannabes. There was a real difference of mentality, a kind of tension, but not friction, between the groups. We all had something in common. There were very few employment options for young people in St Helens and we were all trying to escape the glass factory. This little community in which each of us were studying a different technique and finding our own way was a release from the mundanity of where we were. Whether as a painter of window frames or of framed canvases, we had no idea if our time at college was going to be a way out.

My dad asked, 'What do you get at the end of it?'

I said, 'I'm not sure. A diploma?'

He replied, 'Well, as long as you're happy. That's what matters most.'

I was about to get very lost.

4.

Out Cold in Liverpool

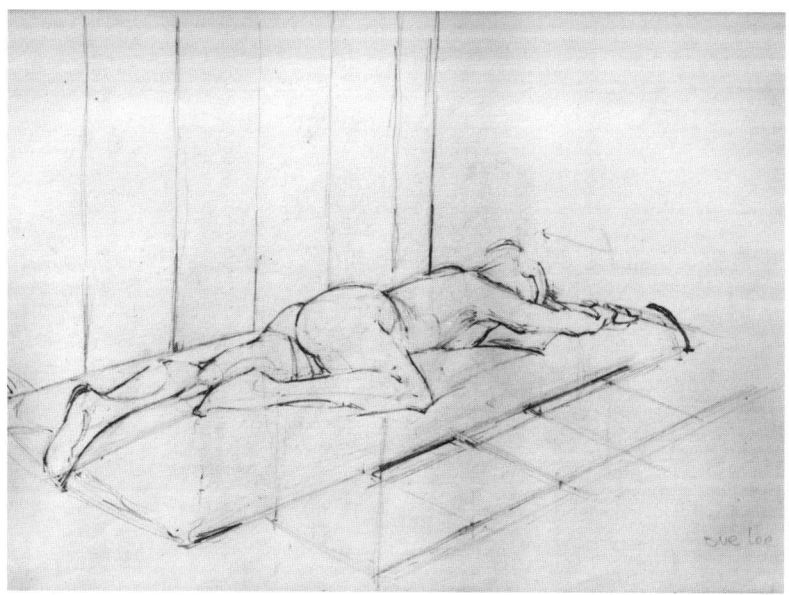

At the School of Art and Crafts, I had been able to do anything I wanted. I was dreaming with no need to define it. Fine Art was the degree course I wanted to take and my foundation course tutor, Selwyn Jones-Hughes, said that Liverpool Polytechnic had by far the best painting department in the country. I'd been down to the south coast of England to visit the art department at Portsmouth Polytechnic, up north to Newcastle and just along the East Lancs Road to Manchester. I felt really torn because my friends were leaving for distant parts of the country. Liverpool was just down the road, so it didn't really feel like an adventure. But I had a plan B for music. If I stayed close to St Helens, with Steve Briers and his guitarist friend David Wardlaw, a gifted blues player in the style of Canned Heat's Henry Vestine, we could make something happen. As it turned out, Steve and Wardy only came to Liverpool once, didn't like it, and never came back.

I already felt like a lodger at my stepmother Elsie's house. Once I moved to Liverpool I rarely went back; home became more and more distant, and I became less and less attached. These were the first signs of Budgie stretching his wings. *But first, I had a haircut.*

Up until I turned eighteen years old, my hair had been growing long below my shoulders. Using my sister's salon-model hairdryer set pointing upwards from the floor, I could dangle my hair in the hot updraught and almost create an approximation of Marc Bolan's corkscrew tendrils. With a dash of patchouli oil, it was a look guaranteed to beget a beating from any self-respecting group of skinheads.

I arrived in Liverpool in 1975 when Roxy Music and Bryan

Ferry's military chic was still the thing, and the Roxy style was embraced by the college band Deaf School. Nearly everyone had short hair. There was a group of young undergraduate ladies in their final year, all sporting jet-black bobbed haircuts, dark eyeshadow and blood-red lipstick. They were all 'achingly' cool. Sandra was a Deaf School vocalist, the others camp followers the Deaf Aids. I thought if *they* told me to cut my hair, I'd do it, and they did. I didn't have the cheekbones of Brian Eno, so that was that – the hair had to come off. I found the straightest old-style barber shop and asked for a short, back and sides. I was instantly transported back in time to Mickey Mee's, the barber shop on North Road, my dad sitting in the chair next to me. Too small for the other big chair, I was perched on a wooden plank placed across the chair-arms. The sound of the electric clippers approaching my neck would seem to dissolve my spine, and I'd slide off the chair like liquid jelly.

After the shearing of the locks, I headed for Liverpool Lime Street station to find a photo booth. Dressed in my camel-coloured duffle coat, a pack of untipped Senior Service cigarettes in my pocket – another dubious Bryan Ferry influence – and a new haircut, I took a series of Bacon-inspired photo-strips. I liked the way Bacon looked askance and away from the camera in those early selfies. So, I posed with my best look of indifference. I couldn't hold it for long.

During most of my time in Liverpool, I didn't have much money and the larder wasn't very well stocked. There's a photo of me with dyed black hair and what I thought were fantastic cheekbones, but when my sister saw it she was very worried. I was so gaunt. My first bedsit was in a terrace in Edge Hill, opposite the old Littlewoods pools company building, a modernist structure like an upside-down T with a clock-tower in the middle of it. I'd moved in with three third-year students, Mick, Keith and Ninian, who were about to graduate – if they were lucky. Ninian had long curly hair and spoke very correctly. A larger-than-life character from Berkhamsted in Buckinghamshire, and a member of the

Sealed Knot – a historical re-enactment society – his room was full of wooden pikes, replica muskets and old Civil War uniforms. He was always trying to enlist me into the Cavaliers' cause. Mick and Keith hailed from St Albans and had quilts, eiderdowns and cosy home comforts like books, pipe tobacco, paint, easels and little wooden mannequins.

Regardless of the time of day, my room was brown and dark with only a white metal bedstead and a thin striped mattress. I tried to make it a little less spartan with a cheese plant, aspiring to a look like Lucian Freud's *Interior at Paddington,* but with no view and the wrong plant, it remained a spartan interior at Edge Hill. The kitchen was horrendous, a harbinger of *The Young Ones* (the TV series this time), with a constantly elevating pile of boxes and cartons in the corner, ruled over by the mice. If you ever hear a mouse inside a box of cornflakes, it sounds like something huge moving and eating in slow motion. The bathroom was even more depressing, and nobody used it. Hot water was heated via a coin-operated meter, and it would cost the equivalent of a good night at the pub to heat enough water for a decent soak. And even if you did treat yourself, the bathroom was always cold and the cast-iron bathtub quickly absorbed all the heat from the water. Too cold for a bath and too cold to stay in the brown room, I'd put on my duffle coat and become a smelly student in the pub. The pubs were fun until they were fun no more, and one night I was followed home by somebody who was up to no good . . .

I suppose I must have looked like a soft target, somebody they might have their way with. I was a newly shorn eighteen-year-old with a fourteen-year-old's complexion, tight skin and blue eyes. I was skint and would always say yes to the offer of a pint. It wasn't unusual to meet somebody and then the next minute this moustachioed bloke would be leaning into you going, 'Give us a kiss!' And then worse.

On this dark night I was staggering back to my freezing brown room and the cold comfort of my cheese plant, the Liverpool rain soaking through my duffel coat. A car pulled up alongside me and the window came down, the offer of a lift coming with the warm air inside. I thought this was a total lifesaver, but there was a price to pay, and I had been terribly naïve. He parked the car up and flicked the lights off and said, 'I wouldn't mind if you would just take a look down here.' I felt like I had no choice. I was scared. I thought, *okay, just get this over with.* I was drunk. You start to sober up quickly, but you're still drunk and you know that this is not what you expected. I suppose this is a rare story from a male point of view, but of course it happens. I know because it happened to me.

For years I told myself it was nothing too bad, and I suspect that I've blanked out the worst of it, but I do remember it shaking me. The next morning, I went to Keith's room and broke down in tears and said, 'It was so horrible last night. I thought I was going to get murdered. This bloke picked me up and it was raining . . .' He was shocked, and I realised that he'd never heard a story like this before.

The same need that Maureen and Chuck had spotted in me had enabled a far darker consequence. The other students seemed to be safer because they'd established a way of being together that I wasn't a part of. They say you can be lonely even when part of a crowd, and I suppose I didn't feel like I belonged. Perhaps trauma creates a chink in the armour that's supposed to form earlier on in life.

138 Morley Street was only ten miles down the road but it, Peter and Mum all felt so far away. For a while back at home, art had helped me to cope with everything, but now at Liverpool Poly even that was failing. Midway through the first year I did what had been deemed to be the wrong painting and the Abstract Inquisition came down from the tutors.

I was attempting an Allen Jones-inspired painting of a reclining nude woman with a strawberry-shaped mouth and cherry-red nipples. The tutors mocked it, saying, 'If you want to do life drawing, go to the Life Room down the corridor.' And that was it, I was cast out to the darkest depths of the dimmest room in the building, where the inmates worked by daylight and didn't switch on the overhead fluorescents until the evening light had completely died. I spent months drawing and painting from the model Su-Li, who in the 1960s had been a model to many famous painters in and around London's Slade School, where our tutor Mike Knowles studied with one of David Bomberg's former students, Frank Auerbach.

Mike had a big beard, smoked a pipe and was a safe person to be around at lunchtime in the pub. If we went to the local pub, Ye Cracke, we very rarely got back before three o'clock. I knew by then that if I drank at lunchtime, I was gone, so I had to hold off until everybody had gone home in the evening before I started. Mike and others in the class would work all day on the same drawing or painting, and even when the light went down you could still hear the pencils going. It seemed like they were on to something, this need to be serious about art. It was as if they felt it had to be hard, gruelling stuff, whereas on the other side for me were the Royal College of Art Modernists, David Hockney, Ron Kitaj and Allen Jones. Theirs was a serious art, but not so serious that they felt every painting should be wrought from blood, sweat and tears. I was floundering and didn't know what I wanted to do. Mike did his best. I had three paintings on the go that had the potential to get into an exhibition, with the prize being some much-needed cash. Mike came out on a cold black night to have a look at them in my new Ampthill Road bedsit. With the best will in the world, I couldn't get one painting together, never mind finish three. He said, 'These are great starts, but they're not going to be ready in time.' Thankfully, music was once again starting to come back into my life, perhaps to my rescue.

It was in the Aigburth student house where I had met up with some new friends. There was graduate Jerry and his girlfriend Lynn, who shagged every weekend to Stevie Wonder's *Songs in the Key of Life,* which was very frustrating because I had a bad crush on Lynn. There was also Henry Priestman, John Campbell and Martin Watson, who had formed a band with the unlikely name of Albert Dock, who were about to replace Deaf School as the new college band.

As we moved from 1976 into 1977 there was a shift in music happening and the jukebox in the college refectory confirmed what we all instinctively knew: the arrival of punk. There was the first punk rock single, 'New Rose' by the Damned; 'Go Buddy Go' and 'Peaches' by the Stranglers, and, of course, 'Anarchy in the UK', the debut single by the Sex Pistols. The jukebox was probably stocked by contacts at Probe Records on Mathew Street, where people had links to Stiff and Radar Records. Deaf School were still signed to Warner Bros and looked to be on their way, but for them and other bands like Manchester's Sad Café, punk came along and stopped them in their tracks. Albert Dock renamed themselves 'Yachts' and signed to Radar Records. Things were changing, and they were changing fast.

I was liking what I heard from the Clash and some of the Damned, but because I had no money to buy albums I only knew the single cuts, from the jukebox, and what we saw live. It wasn't quite yet Eric's, the club that would become the centre of the new Liverpool music scene. It was Eric's without a home, a strip club, somewhere on Mathew Street. We would have a drink downstairs after we'd finished work in the college studios, play music, then head down to Mathew Street if there was a club night on. At first it would be the tabloid-appointed, shocking and sensational gigs from bands like the Runaways with a very young Joan Jett. That night, Mathew Street was closed off by the police because of the almost riot-sized crowds desperate to see this female band in studs and underwear direct from the front pages of the *Daily Mirror* and the *Sun*. Then Talking Heads, Blondie and the Ramones all came through town together, like the dream package tour. Eric's club founder Roger Eagle sported a moustache but had his knowledgeable ear to the ground and had booked the Americans before anybody else, before they'd hit the tabloids – he had also secured one of the first Sex Pistols shows outside London, before controversy made it too dangerous for them to play anywhere. Slowly, I was becoming immersed, finding some clues. Some could play, some couldn't. Some had technical expertise, others were self-taught innovators. With scant knowledge, any stage was now up for grabs.

Even though music was starting to come back into my life again, I was still focused on art, especially late-night self-portraits. I also tried landscape drawing outside, but Liverpool was bitterly cold. Not that indoors in the bedsit was much warmer. I was taking my drawing seriously and felt the need to sit down with music and draw by candlelight. I didn't think about it. I just did it.

I would draw for the duration of one side of *Evening Star* by Fripp and Eno. I'd flip it over and when it ended that would be it. I liked the meditative aspect, using the music to help me achieve a state of otherness. If I look back at my sketchbook, with these studies I seem so serious. My persona (my mask) has always been happy-go-lucky. I don't have a poker face. For the first time, doing those self-portraits, I saw a Peter that I wasn't seeing in the mirror. College hadn't taught me to draw or paint. It hadn't even taught me to look, but it had shown me how to see, to relate, analyse and make connections. I had always liked self-portraiture and that's what I was drawn to: Bacon, Freud, Gwen John, James McNeill Whistler. But as much as I enjoyed painting, I was finding it too solitary. I knew there was a world out there that I was missing out on. I could hear the one door slamming and another door opening. I felt like I needed to be out there, where it was all changing.

Just as Chuck had turned up at Morley Street when I was thirteen, some guys from St Helens knocked on my door out in Aigburth and said, 'You play drums, don't you?!' It was an accusation.

'No, I don't. I'm a painter,' I responded.

As they came from St Helens, it seemed that my idea to stay

close to home had borne fruit after all. They told me they had a support slot at Eric's club, opening for a band called Siouxsie and the Banshees.

'Have you heard of Siouxsie and the Banshees?'

'Yeah.'

'You like the Clash?'

'Yeah.'

'And the Pistols?'

'Sure.'

'Well, we're going to open tomorrow night at Eric's. Are you in?'

I feigned a moment to think, and then said, 'Okay.'

We didn't get down to Eric's in time to support the Banshees - in those days, you had to get in, set a drum kit up side-stage, punch somebody out who was trying to get their kit on at the same time, and whoever won got the gig. You'd sometimes see drum kits come flying out the side door. We were not organised enough to manage it, or perhaps it had just been a trick and they'd used the allure of the Banshees to get me to join.

It was probably the first time the Banshees had played at Eric's, and it was chaos, with a lot of broken glass around the stage. Holly Johnson was down at the front, his head shaved and tinted a pale green. He wore a string lasso around his neck with a loop on the end that he was tugging at as if to say, or threaten, 'I would die for you.' Jayne Casey and Paul Rutherford always danced together. They had a skipping dance: hop, skip, hop, kick, not pogoing. Pogoing was what the nonces did. Pogoing was not allowed because pogoing was just passé. It was the surest sign that you'd read and believed the wrong thing, that you were already out of date. Of course, pogoing continued and was followed by spitting, both of which were a big No! The Banshees were a little outside that standard punk audience, sharing a space and aesthetic with X-Ray Spex and Adam and the Ants. But, unlike Poly Styrene and Adam, they hadn't been signed and had no recordings available other than their John Peel radio sessions.

What I took away from that gig was how chaotic they were on stage, how every song seemed to just disintegrate, with no ending. The drums were pounding yet musical, and the guitarist was annoying. His bright orange hair matched his guitar's bright orange lead, which was long enough to reach to the back wall of the club. He kept running off stage and banging into people, including me, knocking my drink flying. I had nothing against him - I just didn't like him.

It was Siouxsie who really stuck in my mind: resplendent in these little silk running shorts, black tights, black patent leather pointed boots, a shock of black hair and a sheer black negligée top, but not a sexualised look in any way. I recognised that she had something uniquely powerful; watching her felt more like witnessing performance art than a pop star. I saw her as a model. I saw her body, her stature, as a statement, not even a musical statement. It was a stance of defiance. It hit me so intensely that when I got home, I had to *do* something.

Mike the sculptor from my first bedsit had given me some red wax strips that dentists use to make impressions of teeth, and thin copper wire that was used as a kind of armature. He used this copper and wax instead of clay to make little sculptures. I'd never attempted anything like this before, but after seeing Siouxsie, I returned home and got the wire-snips out and started putting a little armature together. The first thing I made was a microphone stand: three legs at the bottom, one central stem, a little blob of red wax on the end for the microphone. And then I started making Siouxsie, with her elbows up above her head, pointed like wings with hands clasped behind her neck. I made an image of this woman I had never seen before, placed it on my desk and that was it. I didn't think anything else of it. I'd never made a wax portrait of anyone else, and I never have since. There was just something about that whole evening, that night, and I had the tools and half the mindset that it didn't seem such a strange thing to do. I thought for a while that it might be a new line of artistic work I should be doing. It had worked so well I was obsessed by it, but I couldn't do another one. When Siouxsie wrote about a little 'Voodoo Dolly' for the album *Juju*, I immediately thought of that odd night in Liverpool and the wax effigy that I made. *And that I never even pushed any pins into it.*

5.

Spitfire Boy

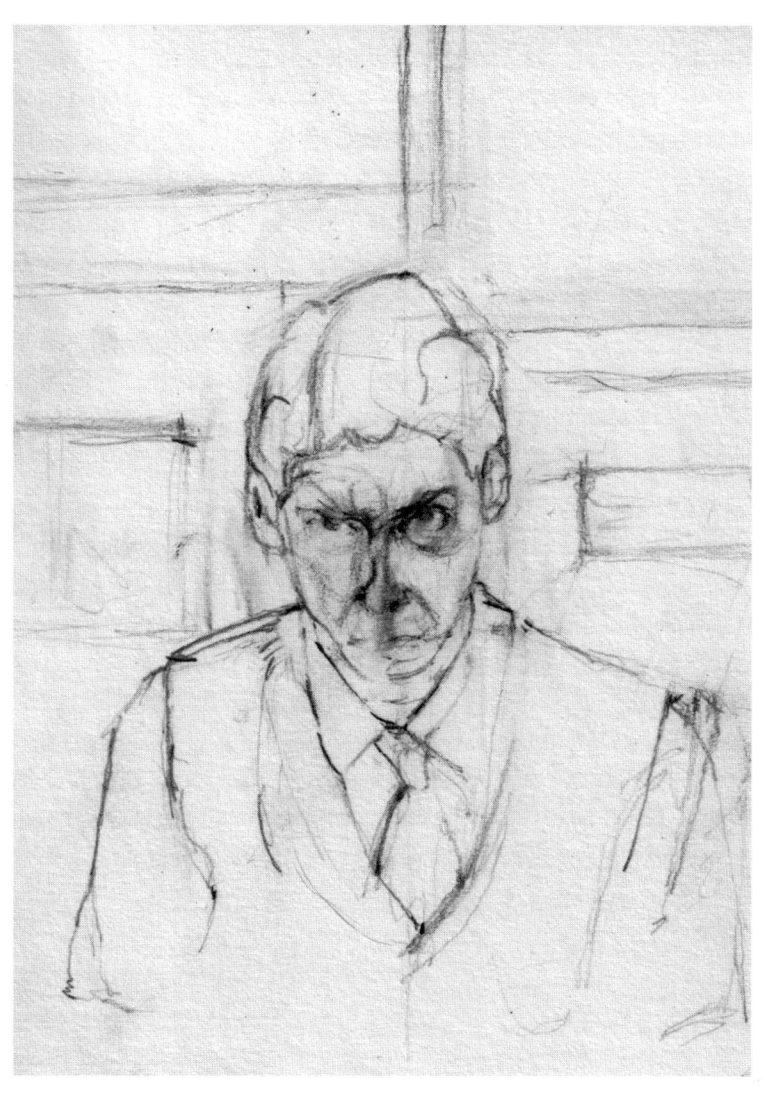

That Banshees support slot might have been a bit of a ruse to lure me in, but it had worked, and here I was in a band again. We rehearsed in an old police station, a space run by a real oddity named Charles Alexander. Charlie rode a Harley Davidson Electra Glide motorcycle; it was the biggest two-wheeled machine I'd ever seen. He had wavy, shoulder-length hair and wore cowboy boots beneath regular trousers. He was not a punk and he must have had money; with his plummy accent he was certainly not working class. Charlie was always charming and seemed to want to champion us. 'If you need a place to rehearse, bring your gear here,' he said.

The police station had been renamed Bridewell Studios, and we set up our stuff in one of the old cells. Bridewell Studios didn't seem to be a going financial concern, but back then nothing was. We were the only ones there over the course of three nights, but we managed to put a set together. Pete Griffiths was on bass and David Littler on guitar. They hadn't rehearsed much before, but I had, so I knew how to routine songs. I thought they had written their own songs, but we were doing cover versions. Dave had learned a lot of Ramones songs and had roped Pete into playing bass, which he played economically, one string, one note at a time.

I played with a lot of variation but never too complex. I'd heard those first albums by the Clash and the Damned and I started to hear connections between, say, Rat Scabies' drumming and what had come before it, drummers like Keith Moon and Mitch Mitchell. Then there were complete wildcard tracks like 'Son of Sam' by the Chain Gang. I could hear drums that were really pushing for something that hadn't been allowed before - untutored freedom. I thought I could do something new in this space.

A lot of bands at the time had members who had no previous experience and they needed someone who could play to some degree. There's always talk of punk being Year Zero, and perhaps at this point John Lydon hid his love of Amon Düül, Can and Faust. I was always borrowing from Black Sabbath and Jimi Hendrix, because I grew up on that stuff. What every band seemed to have in common was a frontman who had enough nerve and guts to get up there and scream and shout, in a pretty unpleasant way, in a caricature of a working-class English accent. That was the thrash punk rock caricature, a three-chord riff, kicked off by a 1-2-3-4 count that indicated FAST! We used to hear pub bands in Liverpool on a Saturday night and go, 'Is that all they can do? Play cover versions?' But that's how we started, by doing cover versions of the Ramones, the original cartoon punk band from New York City.

It was all well timed. The Sex Pistols landed at just the right moment to give a voice to disenfranchised youth. But in reality, 'Anarchy in the UK' is a song not too far removed in feel from the swagger of the Faces. It isn't *that* outrageous: it swings along, with a slow Iggy and the Stooges tempo. The big difference was that the Pistols had Johnny Rotten instead of Rod Stewart. Rotten ripped the skin off everything pretentious in a voice that snarled with complete disdain for the music business. The music industry was haemorrhaging money at the time, in thrall to bands like Yes who would take two years to make hugely expensive records. Suddenly every label wanted to sign a Pistols soundalike band for little or no money. If it hadn't worked after two songs, then out you went. Nurturing wasn't big on their agenda.

After a few days of rehearsals in the police station we decided we needed someone to front the band. We eventually press-ganged Paul Rutherford into being our vocalist. He was always dancing at Eric's so we thought he would be the perfect frontman. He had never been in a band before, but he could sing all the songs on the *Horses* album by Patti Smith, in a sort of New York accent, which was pretty impressive for somebody from Liverpool. He had all the nuances down, even singing words that no one understood, because that's the way Patti Smith sang them. He had mastered all her little vocal inflections. With the help of Jayne Casey and Holly Johnson pushing him in the right direction, we got him up on stage that first night at Eric's. Paul wore Vivienne Westwood trousers from Seditionaries, and a ripped T shirt featuring Tom French's semi-naked cowboys, with their cocks almost touching. With a bent table-fork as jewellery and his hair backcombed into a tangled mess, he was ready. Guitarist Dave wore a mohair jumper with ultra long sleeves, Pete sported a 'flasher' mac and had shaved off his eyebrows. I'd cut the sleeves of a regular army shirt and had bleached the colour out of my hair.

The name Spitfire Boys was coined by Wayne, later Jayne County, who flicked a nail behind their teeth and said, 'You should call yourself "Spitfire Boys".'

As we were leaving, Wayne handed me a signed copy of their single, '(If You Don't Wanna Fuck Me Baby) Fuck Off!', signed, 'To Petra, with LOVE.' I thought, *How nice, they personalised it for me.* Wishful thinking. Only now do I realise that Petra probably wasn't a misspelling of Peter, it was probably never even meant for me. Still, I will always cherish it.

All the people at our first Eric's gig were there for Paul because everyone knew him and the rest of us were the 'woolly-backs' (anyone who isn't a scouser) from St Helens. Paul was young, scared and full of adrenaline on stage; he dealt with it by shouting and telling people to fuck off.

'If you don't like it, fuck off!'

That was all the excuse they needed.

'Oi! He just shouted fuck off at us! Bloody punks. Who do they think they are?'

Most of the gigs seemed to end up with us running for cover. We went to London to record our debut single, a track called

'British Refugee', which had the word 'fart' in it. It's a silly lyric and I think Pete, who wrote it, would agree. On the B-side was 'Mein Kampf', which the lyric described as 'a load of shit' so the label censored it with the word shit 'muted'. The song was pressed with a blank space where the 'shit' should have been. It summed up our whole London music business experience. We had never been in a professional studio before and the people running it had never recorded anybody like us before, non-musicians, with no experience, who didn't know what they were doing. It didn't sound bad, except for the playing and those lyrics, and we were just pleased to have done it. Sadly, it didn't get the picture sleeve we wanted, and neither did it come out on our own label. For our services we received as payment one crate of Pils lager, which meant we probably had to beg, steal and borrow to cover the cost of petrol for the drive from Liverpool to London and back. When a box of vinyl 45s arrived, nobody wanted to stock it and nobody wanted to buy it. We couldn't give the records away, so when we played the next gig, we just threw them out into the audience. Some of them survived. I do still have one.

We did eventually manage to play some gigs beyond Liverpool, but sadly in all the wrong places. There was a rain of broken glass at a rough wedding in Croydon - well, it wasn't broken when it was raining down on us, but it was by the time it hit my drum kit. We made it down to central London to play Covent Garden Rock Garden. The Slits were our only audience. This was because nobody else knew who we were, or why we were even there on a Wednesday night. But we didn't care. How could you when you have the Slits as your audience? There was one last trip to London as the Spitfire Boys in late October 1977, which was full of mischief. We were wandering around Euston Road, looking for Quentin Crisp's flat, as you do, just as years later I would be looking for Francis Bacon's studio. We never found Mr Crisp, but we *did* stay in a Euston Road squat, listening to Lou Reed's 'Street Hassle', before heading down to Wardour Street for a gig at the Vortex promoted by *Sniffin' Glue*, with the Killjoys topping the bill.

The gig was hot, sweaty, claustrophobic and chaotic. Kevin Rowland in the Killjoys looked like a car salesman up on stage. There's nothing wrong with that, of course, but I thought he must be hot in that sheepskin coat. We didn't know the rest of the band, but we automatically hated them all, simply because they were headlining and we were not. If you missed your slot or the earlier band went overtime or a fight broke out, you could miss the whole reason you'd travelled all the way from Liverpool to London.

We did our little gig and then we met writer for US punk magazine *Search and Destroy*, Vermilion Sands. Vermilion had red hair, cut like Suzi Quatro, and was dressed in skin-tight leather jeans and jacket. I'd never met an American before. She was tough and pushy and pretty much abducted me, saying, 'You're going to play drums for me.' Her band was called Dick Envy. I arrived at their basement room still handcuffed to Vermilion. She thought it would be fun. It was, for one rehearsal. Afterwards we just went to the pub in Covent Garden where standing at the bar was Steve Priest, the bass player from the band Sweet. We then did the thing you should never do and shouted, 'We just haven't got a clue what to do!' He was built like a brick shithouse, and I could sense the rage building within him, knowing what might be coming next: 'If one more person says that to me, I'm going to pull them to pieces limb by limb.' But he smiled gamely and went back to his pint. It was a strange moment that was at once amazing and deflating. This was somebody I'd only ever seen as an enigma on *Top of the Pops*, with the make-up and the high voice, standing at the bar, with a pint. That sort of thing happened a lot around London. You'd always bump into the likes of Phil Lynott or Lemmy if you went to the right bar.

We still needed somewhere to crash and found it with Barbara, a friend of the Slits and driver for the Sex Pistols, who had a place in Alperton, near Wembley. It was an intimidating arrival: Barbara's friend Linda was sitting at a desk in the front room, rolling something with Rizla papers that was bigger than any roll-up I'd ever made. She looked up at me through glasses with tinted blue lenses, giving me a look which said, 'I'll eat you later.' These ladies were a little older and wiser to the world than I was. Barbara made me feel safe, but not so her friend Linda. Linda never ate me, but as the partner of Banshees' guitarist John McKay, she may have influenced his future and also mine.

We were dreaming of getting our big break in the capital and thought we might have got it when we got a message from the legendary (although at the time we didn't know who he was) Leee Black Childers. He was looking after the Heartbreakers and needed to transport a stage prop for the *L.A.M.F.* album across London to the Rainbow Theatre. It was a mock-up of a broken glass window with *L.A.M.F.* graffitied in pink letters across it – we thought it was very cool, but more than that, we saw it as an opportunity, thinking that we'd just hang out all day and get a support slot.

We arrived at the stage door and wheeled this thing onto the stage, where Jerry Nolan's pink drum kit was set up. It was so exciting, looking at the pink drum kit in the middle of that backline of amps, on the huge stage. But then we were ushered straight out the back door 'from whence we had come'. That was our almost big break: nearly supporting the Heartbreakers at the Rainbow Theatre.

This was the beginning of the end for the Spitfire Boys. There was a big falling-out between Paul and Dave. Dave, God bless him, wanted to be more professional, but Paul didn't want to do anything that was professional; for Paul it was all about fun and clothes from the King's Road.

I felt less lonely in the Spitfire Boys. They were my first gang: two guys from my hometown, speaking the same language, with the same dialect, similar IQs and interests. We'd come together out of a love of Lou Reed and David Bowie, with a desire to re-create the bits that we liked. We were all naïve, silly and reckless, yet driven to do something. Paul coming on board linked us to the fast-changing Liverpool scene. Jayne Casey was already an established figure, so she was the obvious singer of choice for guitarist Bill Drummond, drummer Phil Allen and bassist Kevin Ward. They were just another group until they pulled Jayne in. When Kevin and Phil left, I was already an ex-Spitfire Boy. I was up for grabs, and I was grabbed big time by Jayne Casey for Big in Japan.

6.
Big in Japan

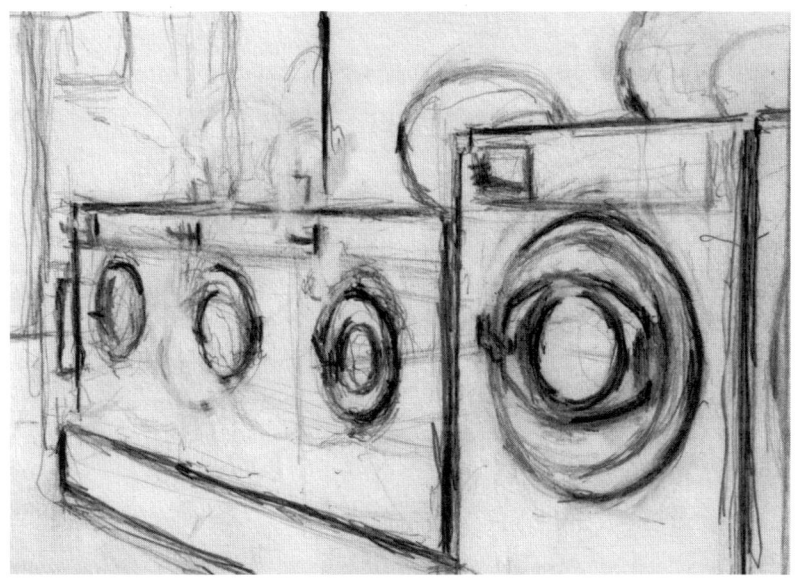

My sex life during those early years in Liverpool remained fraught. I did my best to blossom, and an early crush was Shirley, one of the Deaf School assistants. Her mum was a hairdresser and she always had immaculate black bobbed hair and red lipstick. I knew that she went out in Manchester, so one random night, I took the train from Liverpool Lime Street on a pilgrimage to a nightclub called Pips, wearing white plastic sandals and cricket whites. I only went once but it felt like a lifetime, wandering drunk around this multi-themed disco with a Roxy Room, a Bowie Room and a Glam Room. Everything was a show, everyone there seemed to be taking part in a performance. For me you really had to inhabit and be the character - this was just weekend sequins. It really didn't sit well with me.

There wasn't a gay scene as such in the North West back then. The early punk gigs were open-minded, and beyond that there were men, still called the old dears, the old queens from the sixties era, who hung around the Beatles and all those young boys - Brian Epstein being the most well known, I suppose. The need to keep things under lock and key, guarded about feelings, had relaxed once I got to Liverpool, but I still wasn't sure where I sat. Whose club was I in? I didn't feel connected. I didn't fit. I didn't feel intellectual or crazy enough.

If I was attracted to somebody, it was almost always towards somebody who was unavailable, someone who felt exciting, unusual or different, whether because of the colour of their skin, the way they'd done their hair or the way they were dressing. I was attracted to those characteristics and never much more than that in terms of depth of character or who they were as a person.

Of course, I knew people who *did* meet up with future spouses at that age and were already settling into domestic relationships, but that was anathema to me. Mum's death meant that any idea of having a relationship was difficult, setting myself up for loss and grief. My situation hardly helped. Everybody I chose to be with was horrified at the idea that you would want to stick around after one night – if you even made it that far. Quite often I didn't. We'd get through the door to my bedsit, and they'd go, 'No! I'm not staying here!' Instead, I used to farm it out for other people.

When Paul finally came out to himself, he wanted to cruise and pick up a man. They had nowhere to go, so I said, 'Here's the keys to the bedsit, Paul. We'll be around in case everything goes wrong.' I didn't see him afterwards, but it didn't go very well. They couldn't find the light switch or perhaps the electricity meter had run out of credit. They ended up lighting rolled up pieces of paper and trying to find a candle, which would hardly have made for an enjoyable erotic experience. When I returned later, the flat smelled bad – burnt paper everywhere. In my naïvety, I thought, *Uh-oh, some kind of strange initiation ceremony.*

Worse happened there too. There was a drunken night when a friend and I, two late-teens with bleached-blond hair, were invited to a nightclub and bought drinks by an older guy that we knew from a distance. He was an old-school figure on the Liverpool music scene whose line of work meant he had a reputation for dealing out violence as and when he felt necessary. He was one of the doormen at Eric's. My friend and I went to the nightclub to dance crazily into the early hours. All was well until I said, 'Well, I'd best be getting home now.' He said, 'No, no, no. What d'you think all these drinks were for? No, no. Where d'you live?' Unlike the girls, he was quite happy to come to my bedsit. He said he just wanted to bed down for the night. I passed out. I don't recall details or maybe I just blocked them out. I woke up covered in a bad smell of stale aftershave with bruises and bites all over me. I've always felt that it could have been a lot worse, telling myself that I didn't think I was raped. But perhaps that's just semantics - what goes in where - because it was a rape of innocence and trust. I realised I was in danger, that if I hadn't gone through with what he wanted, I might have come round with more than just a few bruises and bites, something much worse. I know he had tried it on with Pete Burns but didn't get very far. Pete was a fighter, his look was shocking and out-rageous, and he had a mouth to match. Pete could call anybody out and he could handle himself - so could his girlfriend at the time, Lynne. They were an invincible duo, but I didn't possess that superpower. I wasn't violent. I'd never learned how to defend myself.

On the flip side, this insecurity meant that if there was a sexual situation that I looked for, and found, I'd go from the fear of a relationship to 'Oh, can we just get married now?' It had been a disaster with the girls at college, who either still lived at home or were spoken for, not interested or, like me, too shy. It all changed when I left college and started hanging out at Eric's and playing in the Spitfire Boys. Then I met women who were already carving out a role for themselves, intriguing and challenging, like Jayne Casey. Nobody else looked like Jayne. She had a shaved head, black panda eyes and black lips with white make-up. Jayne scared most people. I was intrigued.

I'd seen her in the Saturday-morning shop she ran at the top end of Bold Street, near the bombed-out church. Paul Ruther-ford and Holly Johnson would hang out there, along with other people who became key players in the music scene. Jayne knew people like the older queens because they were the people who accepted her the way she was. I had never seen anybody like Jayne before, someone who could dress themselves and make themselves look outrageous enough to have people shout at them in the street. She would just laugh. I don't think I even wanted to have a relationship with Jayne, I just really enjoyed being around her. She wasn't interested at first, which is more appealing in many ways.

The Absence

When I was still at art school I didn't know that Jayne's world existed. She was dressing outrageously and shaving her head, well before punk. She was ahead of the shock of punk, so when it happened, she was the *de facto* figurehead for Liverpool. This meant she was the first taste-setter for Eric's, adopted by Pete Fulwell and Roger Eagle to decide who should come in and who shouldn't.

I now think that the front Jayne presented to the world might have been about protecting herself, perhaps at the root source of which was incredible damage. The pain always reveals itself, though, like a light flickering on, announcing, 'Here I am!' And it can connect with others who've experienced the same, so even if you've not discussed what lies beneath, there's a strange bond there.

Jayne and I had a romantic entanglement for an intense two weeks at the end of the Spitfire Boys. I remember one lovely day we went out to the Wirral Peninsula, crossing the River Mersey on the ferry. For once it wasn't raining, and we looked back over towards the sun shining on Liverpool and I said to Jayne, 'Some-day all this will be ours.' It was a very John Wayne moment. And it was Jayne's 'joie de vivre' that created it. Everything was fun with little seriousness, and there was clearly no longevity in it. I knew that and that's why it was a joke: one day all this will be ours. It was Jayne who dumped me, and I felt terrible about it, but Jayne didn't need me, or anyone, in that way. Holly was her foil, and you couldn't get near any seriousness with Holly and Paul around. If anything outrageous was going to happen, it would be Jayne winding Paul and Holly up into voicing it, bad-mouthing people or being obnoxious, inappropriate, hurting people prob-ably, albeit mostly in jest, of course. They could be merciless with me, but we had a genuine affection and care for each other. There was always bad bitchiness between the Pete Burns camp and the Jayne Casey camp, even though each probably admired the other, ultimately.

Jayne had pushed Paul Rutherford into that gig with us as the

Spitfire Boys. Paul then pushed Jayne into being in Big in Japan, and that meant Holly came in too, on bass. There had already been quite a few line-up changes. Bill Drummond was the leading force, singing 'Big in Japan'. One song, three chords and two three notes over and over again, but it was a strong three chords and Bill was big. Jayne Casey decided who got into Eric's and I think it was Jayne who decided I should be in Big in Japan when they needed a drummer, or it might have been Ian Broudie who had joined and decided things needed to be more professional. I don't recall how I was invited. I may have just fallen in, purely because I was always at Eric's.

The ceiling in Eric's was so low it was claustrophobic. You had to do a hard right to get behind the PA stack and to the side of the stage. There was nowhere to wait, you just went on. For our Big in Japan afternoon rehearsals, we would enter through the kitchen door. We kind of lived there. In many ways, it was our equivalent of Warhol's Factory. We would be there as much as possible, working on songs as a band, depending on who had turned up. Jayne would pop in for five minutes, Bill would have an argument with her and then she would storm off and leave the band. That happened quite frequently. I don't think Bill ever actually wore a kilt onstage, but in my memory it feels like he did. He was six feet something, and everything he did was earnest and passionate: 'Aye, do this! You've got to stop, Holly! You can't do that!'

Every now and then, there would be a calm side to Bill. We'd go to the Kardoma café and share a baked potato between four. We might have enough for a cup of tea between two, sometimes even a cup each. There was a lot of philosophical chat going on, and Bill was the dad of the group. Paul and Holly were like kids. Jayne was just unpindownable. Ian was always level. He knew what he was on to and what his role was, using his Fender Telecaster to write clever, smart pop songs. Bill was always trying to do something that was going to blow the world apart; his attitude was more Warholian.

On the afternoons when we had big arguments, everyone would storm off, leaving Ian and me to hammer out riffs and beats. I'd never sat down to write with another musician before, but Ian invited me round to his parents' house where we sat up in the bedroom working through ideas. I could see Ian knew what he was doing and just needed somebody to bounce ideas off, but even if I was just nodding my head, it was the first time I felt I was working with another musician on the same wavelength. He often had the song already written when he came down into rehearsals: 'I've got this chord, two or three more chords, and then there's these words.' Even if it was just harmonics and a couple of notes, Ian always had something. Bill would then work hard at trying to create an alternative something that was loud, unmusical, and abrasive against what Ian was doing.

That was how we honed our songwriting skills and image, because Jayne was all about image. It never occurred to us that she wasn't a singer, even though she was fronting the band. It was a job no one else wanted. What Jayne wanted to do was write lyrics with Holly. Together they wrote 'Nothing Special' and 'Suicide a Go Go' - great titles with risqué lyrics that you wouldn't hear these days. It's a bit like Siouxsie wearing the swastika, something that put a whole nation's nose out of joint. It was misguided, but that's youth and naïvety. In Big in Japan we were our own worst enemy because we had the loudest, most outspoken, devil-may-care person as the focal point.

We made recordings and sent them off to Jet Records, the company that made ELO huge. We pooled together what we had in terms of money, talent and ideas and were surrounded and supported by the irascible Roger Eagle and placid Pete Fulwell. They allowed us to come into Eric's every day and use all the facilities for free, the PA system and so on. Fortunately, we landed in the hands of people who cared and, despite the outward abrasiveness and the finger up to everybody, really we were looking for a way out.

*

People say it was Julian Cope (jealous because his most recent group the Nova Mob had failed), but I've always wondered if it was Bill . . . it would be very Bill Drummond to make a petition saying that if you can get a thousand signatures, Big in Japan will stop, knowing full well it would create a myth and a legend around the band. Everyone hated Big in Japan because we got the gigs and we were doing exactly what they wanted to do. Then other bands came along and we were usurped, because at that time things changed so quickly. We wrote some interesting songs and got a bit of a following around the North West, over in Manchester at the Hole in the Wall and Electric Circus, but it never really grew beyond that. We'd already had our Warholian fifteen minutes of fame by the time we put the *From Y to Z and Never Again* EP together because we knew that we were never going to get a deal - and slogging around in a bus was *not* the life for Jayne and Holly. We played our last show, an open-air gig on Mathew Street, and it was documented in the form of at least one photograph. I left Liverpool shortly afterwards.

Big in Japan was a crazy mix of people. We all went on to do brilliant and different things: Bill formed KLF, Ian the Lightning Seeds; Holly and Paul with Frankie Goes to Hollywood. Jayne had Pink Military, before curating Cream - one of the major dance clubs of the nineties - and the Bluecoat gallery, which is a well-established space in Liverpool, just around the corner from Mathew Street and not far from the shop where I first saw her. It's funny to think of Jayne looking after the Bluecoat; that was somewhere we'd probably have wanted to tear down because they wouldn't let us in. It might have been a fractious band, but we gave each other everything we had. Bill knew how to get a theatre project together and brought those skills to the table. He was always good at talking with people and arranging meetings. That was always going be his angle and hence his success would come with the management and the notoriety of schemes like the KLF - what can we get away with that's really going to mess with people's minds?

It was while in Big in Japan that I finally and formally became Budgie. I was Pete throughout most of my time with the Spitfire Boys then briefly 'Blister' for the single-writing credits. This, to avoid being name-checked by the dole office, in tribute to the blisters on my fingers from drumming and to avoid confusion with the many Petes in and around Eric's club. We had Pete Griffiths (Spitfire Boys), Pete Wylie (The Mighty Wah!), Pete Burns (Dead or Alive), Pete Hart (Those Naughty Lumps), Pete Best (the first Beatles drummer) and me. Then in Manchester there was Pete Shelley (Buzzcocks) and Peter Hook (New Order). It was getting mighty crowded for Petes.

I was waiting tables at the pizza restaurant on Hardman Street – I got paid, made tips and had plenty to eat. It was a better deal than selling off my dwindling collection of 1970s vinyl at Probe Records. At the end of my shift, the kitchen's oven still hot, I'd make pizzas for the Gambier Terrace bedsit boys, the Crucial Three, the Nova Mob or whatever 'Griff' was calling his latest imaginary group. On this night it was basically the Spitfire Boys, Paul Rutherford, Peter 'Griff' Griffiths, Holly Johnson and me.

The two future stars of Frankie Goes to Hollywood lay together with Griff on the huge bed, the perfect place for sharing Jean Genet and Andy Warhol anecdotes, while discovering the erotic possibilities of pineapple rings. I disturbed the banter, which was a little too crude for Genet, but Capote would have been splitting his sides laughing.

'Oh, fuck off, Paul!'

'Oh, fuck off, Holly!'

'No, YOU fuck off! It's always me, me, me!'

'No, YOU fuck off! It's always, you, you, you, egomania, egomaniaaah!'

In the midst of this ping-pong affair sat Griff, his louche Lancashire demeanour lacking only suitable pyjamas to complete the Oscar Wildeness of it all.

I close the door. 'Okay, who wants pizza?'

Paul giggled deeply. 'Ooooh, me, me, me!'

Holly teased to the tune of 'Telegram Sam': 'Pizza-faced Pete, pizza-faced Pete, he's always gorra treat - that's pizza-faced Pete.'

'Sounds like a new song, Holly,' said Griff.

'Yer I know - another classic in the making.'

I mock sighed, the back of my hand on my forehead: 'Aw, c'mon, I've been slaving away for hours to put food on the table.'

'Ooooooh, who rattled your cage, little birdie?' said Paul.

'Aw, stop it, Paul. The little budgie's tired.'

'Arr-ay, yer right - poor little budgie.'

'Poor little budgie, budgie, budgie.'

Then Paul and Holly in unison to the tune of 'Ring a Ring o' Roses': 'Oh Budgie, budgie, budgie - budgie, budgie, budgie!'

The teasing escalated as Paul and Holly lost themselves in a quilt of spilt pineapple juice.

'Budgie,' says Griff. 'I like that.'

From the next day I was Budgie. It was only supposed to be a nickname, but when I went to London I had to decide: was I Pete or Budgie? I stuck with Budgie for cynical reasons because I figured it'd be better for people to remember me by. As it transpired, I was right. Here we are. Budgie-san. Who am I? There was a coda to my time in Liverpool that perhaps says something about how Peter was fading and Budgie, as he was to become, was taking over.

I wasn't attached at Eric's, lost in my own world of Big in Japan as I was, but then I met Jeanette. She worked in Liverpool in a bar that was notorious and she was at a dance college. We ended up meeting at Eric's. I didn't really know how to be in a relationship. Jayne had been a fling - as in literally flinging each other around - on borrowed time from day one, trying other people's patience, their bathrooms and bedrooms. My life quickly started to oscillate around the local railway pub out in Kirkby and Jeanette's parents' house. I was the outsider in that little scenario. Though Jeanette gave me an attachment I'd never had: a relationship within a family. Just as my early plastic-sandal foray across to the disco at

Pips in Manchester felt so at odds with my St Helens working-class upbringing, there was a split between my world over in Liverpool as Budgie and the pub and the house and the family with Jeanette in Kirby.

We'd not been going out long when Jeanette's mum Bette was diagnosed with cancer, and the illness took her. Her family were devastated, and I was taken straight back to Morley Street and that terrible night when Mum died.

My mum had gone so fast, without warning, but for Bette it was an agonisingly drawn-out affair. I spent many nights visiting at the hospital, watching in disbelief as the treatment turned her skin yellow, tight and thin like aging parchment, her body just wasting away. There was no talking, no conversation, just a look in her eyes that I perceived as 'please, let me go'. But there was too much love in the room for Jeanette's dad Jim to allow that to happen. They were very tight as a family, very loving, very Liverpool.

I stuck close with Jim and the family. They brought Bette's body home from the hospital and laid her out in the front room with the casket open. I never saw my mum lying in the funeral parlour - I wouldn't go in. I went with them, but I wouldn't go in. I was probably too scared, so Bette was the first person I'd seen laid out. I put my arm round Jim and stood with him, just as I had when Bette was still in hospital, shielding his shaking. He didn't want to cry in front of his daughters. He was devastated and I don't think he knew how everything was meant to happen. Of course, you don't.

I don't know if the family survived it well afterwards. It might seem selfish to me now, but I saw it as a further booster rocket to get the hell out. I wanted to end the relationship, but I didn't know how because I didn't really know how to start them either: failing at both the start and the end. I couldn't go through the grieving process with Jeanette's family. I hadn't even been able to for my own mum. I'm not sure I was of any help to Jeanette, and I don't recall being at the funeral. I just had to leave.

Like the fairground and the circus, always pulling up the tent pegs and packing everything away, I put my drum kit, my bicycle and my cheese plant in the back of a van and headed to London, leaving Peter and Pete behind for good.

7.
Liverpool, London, Milan, Blackout

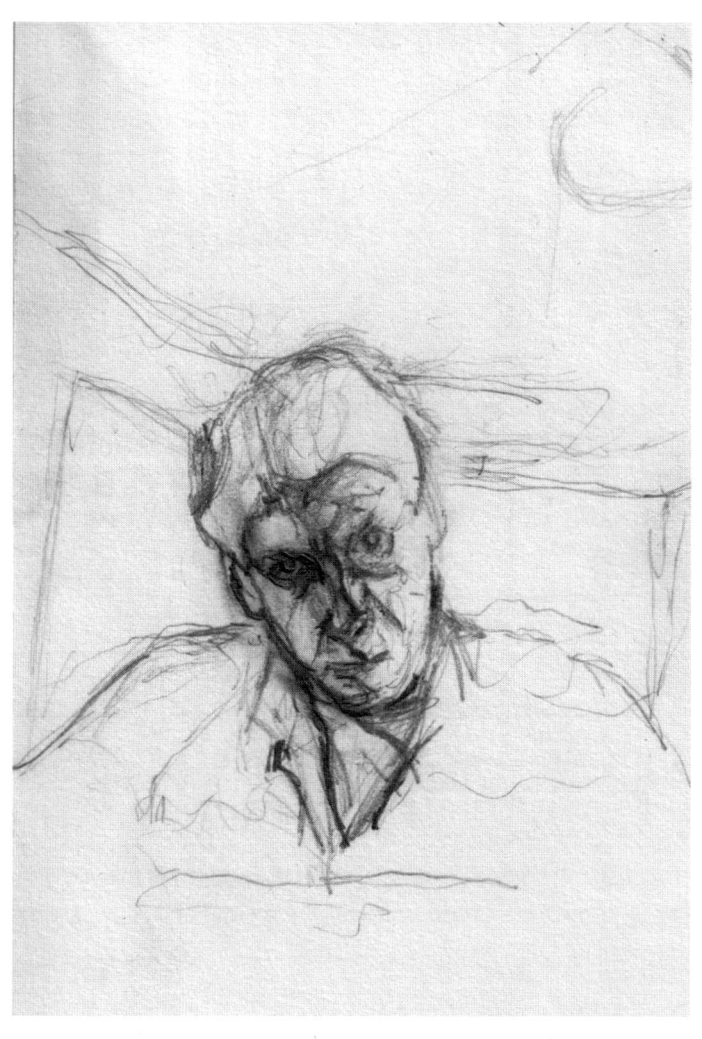

It took a while to get sorted in London. I was squatting, dossing and eventually living on a mattress on the floor of the Swanky Modes shop, on the corner of Camden Road and Royal College Street. Deaf School guitarist and Madness producer Clive Langer introduced me to fashion designers Mel and Esme. Their Day-Glo, skin-tight latex creations lit up the Georgian corner-shop window, which looked like a SEX shop, in what was still a grimy working-class neighbourhood of pubs and greasy-spoon cafés. Through Clive I'd met Sex Pistols original bassist Glen Matlock and joined him at his music publisher's studio in Berners Street, to help record some new songs he was working on after Rich Kids had disbanded. I also played drums for a one-off session at TW Studios with Clive's band the Boxes and finally got to play with the key players of Deaf School. Things were looking up for Budgie.

Eventually, I graduated from the floor of Swanky Modes and took a room on the top floor of 185e Cromwell Road, SW5. Sara, a promoter's assistant who worked Saturdays at the shop, had split with her boyfriend so there was a room to let. The flat was opposite the newly built Cromwell Hospital off Marloes Road, alongside an alleyway that ran through past the Australian pub to Earl's Court station. I had landed right in the heart of Kensington.

London felt so huge compared to Liverpool, and for a while, or until I pieced it all together, it felt like living on the Monopoly board. Every day, every rehearsal room, no matter how stinky or sticky, was another trip in the dream.

Although I was single throughout this transition into metro-politan life, Jeanette and I had stayed in touch. She had made connections with some dancers working for a newly formed *Top of the Pops* dance troupe, and she came down to London for an audition, which became a compromising situation in the flat. I'd built up an easy-going brother-and-sisterly friendship with Sara, advising her on potential boyfriends, but growing tensions between Sara and Jeanette meant that my room at the top of Cromwell Road was never going to last.

Thankfully, during my time with Clive, Steve and Anne from Deaf School, I got to know their manager, Frank Silver. Frank offered to pay my rent and take me under his management wing while I did session work. So I moved out of Sara's and found a new place, on the other side of the Earl's Court Road. But with Jeanette and her new dance-troupe friends dropping in, soon there wasn't enough space. Our relationship was waning and once again I didn't have any experience or understanding to help me navigate my way through and out of it in a dignified way. Instead, we just came undone. Jeanette got a job dancing at a club in Milan, one of those dodgy gigs that dancers and actors must do to qualify for an Equity union card. No Equity card, no job. I said I was concerned for her safety, but really I was jealous and possessive, so I decided to go and visit her.

I booked a ticket on the Trans-Alpino Express and unwisely bought a bottle of vodka before boarding at Victoria Station. I remember very little of the journey, just waking up at Milan's Central station in a carriage full of mothers and schoolchildren. There was an empty bottle of vodka rolling left to right between my feet. I found my notebook, replete with illegible scrawls like 'Proust!', 'Cheers!' and 'Ciao!' There were addresses, phone numbers and all the multilingual international nonsense that a travelling drunk collects while passing around his bottle of booze. That train journey was my first blackout. In retrospect, it was also my first international trip alone, a solo voyage into the unknown. So, all bets were off, and I became the drunk. In a way, being in a band saved me. I had to turn up and be on it, especially as the drummer, because if and when everybody else is falling apart, you've got to hold it together. In Liverpool, we just didn't have enough money to go crazy pre-gig. In Italy, with no responsibility, it was very different.

The appalling hangover was a terrible start to a week spent just outside Milan with Jeanette and the other dancers. The legitimacy of this 'club work' for experience and an Equity card soon began to look shady. It became obvious that the whole set-up was a routine between the police and the local boss involving booze and other substances. The girls were wheeled in and had to look after themselves, although a local gang of young guys befriended them as bodyguards. The Carabinieri would come in swinging their Beretta machine-guns and then place them menacingly on the bar. I always thought they looked like handbags, but I kept that thought to myself. The men would watch the girls dance choreographed routines to 'Funkytown' by Lipps Inc. and Pink Floyd's 'Another Brick in the Wall'. The club was empty most nights and I was just hanging out and hanging on. I was incensed that my girlfriend was there. Jeanette was just embarrassed. A regular boyfriend would have visited to make sure everything was okay, that Jeanette wasn't in any trouble and, duty done, leave. But I hung around, being a pain in the arse, drinking in local bars and cafés, thinking I was in a movie, playing chess with the locals.

Eventually, Jeanette must have given me the money to get out of there. I had to return via Malpensa, the airport north of Milan. I'd never been on a plane before. When I arrived with my little suitcase the chap said, 'Okay. Just leave that with us.'

'No, no, I need to take it with me.'

'We'll check it in for you, sir. It'll be there when you arrive.'

I had no idea what was going on.

That Italian trip was the unravelling of my future, showing me how my drinking could run unabated with no limit, no matter what was in my pocket to pay for it. I'd known a lot of heavy drinkers through my childhood and adolescence, but I had a penchant for jumping into strange cars and onto trains, making sure I had enough vodka. Sometimes it felt as if that instinct had always been there, because I remember the pop truck that delivered cherryade and dandelion and burdock at the weekends, and how they came in these earthenware containers with a cork or a screw top with two rings on the neck to put your little finger through and rest the whole weight of the bottle in the crook of your arm and then just tip it. What a civilised way to drink! It began with cherryade, being able to lift the whole weight of this bottle and not spill a drop. But there was cider on that pop truck and then on the train to Milan, those hundreds of miles of lost memories; aside from the scrawls in my notebook, I must have been going for the same effect with the vodka bottle, don't spill a drop, pass it around, even though I couldn't really stomach neat vodka, and then pass out. Yet I thought I was living the dream. This was the way I'd like to be, living with no responsibility. This was the slippery slope to the bottom I was aiming for, but I was also getting good at avoiding it.

8.
The Only Boy in the Slits

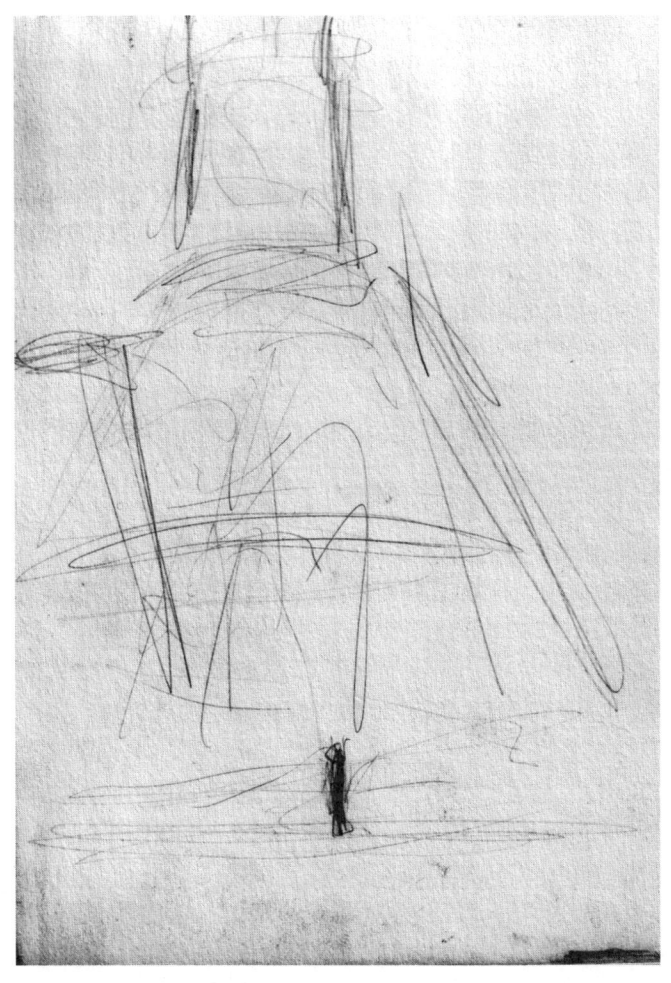

I spent some time as the drummer for former Deaf School bassist Steve Lindsey in his new band the Planets, working at Tony Visconti's studio on Dean Street, in Soho. We lived off the new novelty food, McDonald's, which had just opened its first West End restaurant on Shaftesbury Avenue - I liked the bread but not the dill pickle.

Then there was Louise, a sweet, petite daily visitor who'd pop in at around five o'clock with an assortment of little pepper-uppers. It was another eye-opening moment, someone turning up each day to keep things swinging. Steve was a singing bass player, a songwriter in the Paul McCartney mould, some rock, some reggae - a real mix-up of styles. What was interesting to me was seeing the daily routine of a studio. When I walked in there was a guy with overalls on, painting the walls. I said, 'Nice job, mate.' He politely acknowledged the compliment and turned out to be the legendary producer behind T. Rex and David Bowie - Tony Visconti himself. The engineers thought I knew what I was doing when it came to positioning microphones on the drums. I was the expert brought in to do the session - the one who should know how to achieve Bowie's *Low* snare drum sound. I was acting, with bravado: 'Yeah, yeah. Just put that mic a little lower. That's fine. That's good. Can we spread the overheads please? Okay, that looks better. Fine. I think we're ready.' And if I didn't do anything myself, I got away with it. I could play, but I really had no idea what should be going on with the microphones. Thankfully nobody rumbled me.

Someone had the bright idea to have photos taken outside Madame Tussauds planetarium on the Marylebone Road. I suppose

Jodrell Bank was too far away. Taking a tenuous space theme rather literally, we were dressed in American Air Force jet-pilot cooling suits from Laurence Corner, the army surplus shop on the Euston Road. They were made of a white mesh fabric with plastic tubing following the body's contours. I've still got my copy of the album, called *Goon Hilly Down* after the first parabolic deep space radio telescope, but thankfully none of the pictures have surfaced, because we looked a little bit naff. My lasting memory of these sessions was getting Danny Kustow of Tom Robinson's Band in to play guitar. I loved Danny, we stole marzipan together from a shop on the Earl's Court Road.

> *'Babylonian won't lose much, and we'll have dinner tonight'*
> 'Shoplifting', The Slits

It was a busy couple of years for me, 1978 into 1979. I'd worked with Clive Langer as one of the Boxes on his *I Want the Whole World* EP. The credits list me as Budgie, Drums and Average Bass; the bassist was actually Mr Average, aka Steve Lindsey. There's a song called 'Those Days', which I believe was written as an unrequited love song to Viv Albertine, guitarist in the Slits. Its chorus lyric ('Coz 'oldin' 'ands, I couldn't 'andle, two touching parts, in a tangle') probably meant that Clive was never going to produce the Slits' debut album; a failed romance would be a bit of damp squib.

Slits founder member and one of my favourite drummers Palmolive had left the band and they needed someone. Frank Silver suggested me, and it was decided that the best thing to do would be to go along and meet Ari at her mum's place, to see if it worked out. I went to an address just behind the King's Road in Chelsea, a white stucco-fronted townhouse with iron railings and steps up to the front door. It was probably Ariane's mum Nora who opened the door. When Ari appeared she was wearing just a cropped T-shirt and a pair of knickers, with her matted hair in a headscarf. Ari said, 'We should sit in this room.' It was a huge front room with a big sofa, underfloor heating and a deep-pile carpet, which was very luxurious from my point of view. We didn't talk much, Ari just played me her favourite music. I was suddenly back in that little room with my friends in Morley Street - this was what we did, bonding over sharing music. But this felt different, more intense. I saw Ari react to music in the same way that I did when I used to listen to records at night alone in the living room where Mum had died.

Ari seemed to have that same tic of putting the furniture at risk as she rocked on the beat. She wasn't just *listening* to the song; she was *feeling* it. Ari had the electricity of movement coursing through her, always such a ball of energy. She played me the *Saturday Night Fever* and *Grease* soundtracks. You have to remember that Ari was still only sixteen, and this was the chart music she loved. It wasn't deep, heavy dub like Lee 'Scratch' Perry, U-Roy or Dillinger. She wasn't clued into the heavy reggae scene so much as she was into Tamla Motown and the music and basslines of pop and dance music classics. I was just a few years older, but that meant I was coming from a whole different place, and I'd grown up with reggae because it was all over the charts in Britain in the early seventies. A lot of it was instrumental with that infectious Jamaican dance feel, and this was where we connected. That evening on the sofa in West London was like meeting a kindred spirit.

Palmolive and I hadn't really spoken much, and although I would soon replace her, I felt closer to her because she was a little older and a natural drummer. I knew the beats to the Slits' songs, and I thought that was what I'd be required to do. But this was going to be hard because nobody played the drums like Palmolive played the drums. Nobody. But the Slits didn't want Palmolive to play like Palmolive played, they wanted a more consistent dance beat. Palmolive didn't play that way; she believed drums should be augmenting and phrasing, adding energy, power and feel to the lyrics. These other elements are everything the drums *should* be doing, but that steady dance groove is crucial. I don't recall meeting Viv or Tessa Pollitt, the bass player, to discuss it all.

Perhaps Ari made the decision herself, or perhaps they all said, 'Yeah, Budgie can do it.' And I was in.

My first job was to go into a rehearsal studio with them all to rework their songs for the support slot on the Clash's 'Sort It Out' tour at the end of 1978. Tessa and I hit it off immediately, musically. She was so laid-back. Viv was very highly strung and always had a cough, even though she wasn't smoking. She was slightly older, more worldly and definitely the driving force of the band. Viv was eager to get on and get things done. I was trying to maintain the link between the three of them while also providing something that they hadn't had up until that point, a constant steady beat. My second job was on the tour itself, sitting in the front of the van skinning up spliffs to keep Bob the driver happy - a monster of a man from Liverpool. When I wasn't skinning up for Bob, I was giving him coffee to stay awake. I would always sit with the driver on night drives. Call it personal insurance.

The Clash had a proper tour bus and hotels, but we had all our gear in the van with everybody piled in on top. If we were lucky, we'd check into one room of a B&B and huddle up together to escape the cold. I got used to the predictable comments from guys outside the venues, and journalists looking for a tabloid story.

'So, Budgie, which of the Slits are you sleeping with?'

'Must be a lot of fun being the only guy in the band?'

Innuendo as cheap as a Blackpool postcard. If only they knew . . . whether women together experience a physical synchrony or not, I felt an unspoken allegiance, a bond of love deeper than a mere sexual relationship. I became aware of a woman's ability to embody and express that beautiful balance of vulnerability and power simultaneously. It's a seductive and addictive concoction, which can be entirely misleading, and ultimately ephemeral.

That tour was a major learning curve for me. The girls weren't interested in watching the Clash - just boys doing boys' stuff, throwing guitars around when they weren't throwing shapes, and probably thought the drummer, Topper Headon, was a bit workmanlike. But I'd finish our gig, pack my gear away and watch Topper from the side of the stage every night. I recognised a maestro behind the kit, and it was Topper who showed me how to be a drummer. The way he played was so fluid yet solid, and he hardly seemed to expend any energy. He was so cool, wearing a yellow kung-fu outfit like Uma Thurman's years later in Quentin Tarantino's film *Kill Bill*.

Topper was clearly way ahead of his time. He came as a double act with Baker, a Rottweiler of a drum tech who guarded the kit. Made by Pearl in a shiny aluminium finish, it picked up all the lights and shone like a mirror ball up high, in the centre of the stage. There was always beer and water flying around, and of course a lot of gobbing going on, so Baker would clean the kit every night till it shone like it had just left the factory. Nobody got near that kit except Topper, but I was invited to sit at it one time only. It was the strangest feeling because the seat was high. Topper isn't a tall guy, so consequently the pedal was light and the kit was very narrow. There was no room for movement left to right, just forward and back, and I realised that this was because he played with a physical economy like that of a jazz player.

The first time we met, Topper looked at my gear and said, 'What's going on with the toms?' I said, 'Well, I've taken the bottom heads off, so you can get the mic in, and I've sprayed them silver. It would've been gold because the kit's gold, but I didn't have enough for gold.' Topper told me to take all the heads off, showed me how to tension and tune them, and then paid for the whole kit to be refurbished. He gave me his time. Following Topper's lead, if we had a support band with a kit that was falling to pieces, I'd lend a hand, offer them a decent cymbal. I'll never forget that Topper took the time to look after me, when I was still a novice. Years later he said in an interview, 'I was watching Budgie because he was getting better and better every night and I knew I had to keep my game up.' I didn't feel this at the time, of course. I was just in awe, thinking, *This guy knows how to play!*

When he broke a drumstick, he'd throw it out to the crowd, pick up a replacement, bring back his hand and not even miss a beat. He had his own sticks called 'Topper's Boppers', which were a lengthened version of a Premier H stick, more like a marching band stick with a round acorn and thin shoulder. I copied that stick and called it 'Budgie's Basher'. It couldn't be 'Budgie's Bopper' because Topper had his boppers. I added an extra inch thinking that, in my pre-glove days, it'd give me another second before the stick slipped out my hand and vanished. The light tip with the weight in the handle gave a sweet sound to the cymbals and allowed me to really swing at the drum with a bigger arc.

All these little things help with developing what becomes your mannerism, style or technique, and that's one of the many things I learned from Topper. I was so enamoured with him and the way he conducted himself on stage. I remember one night in a south coast hotel when he'd gone out for a skinny dip with his girlfriend and the crew thought it would be funny to nick their clothes from the beach. The whole tour entourage were sitting in reception waiting for the return of the unhappy couple when bizarrely, TV legend Bruce Forsyth walked in. We all shouted his catchphrase in unison, 'Bruce! Nice to see you . . .' and Bruce replied bang on cue, 'To see you, nice!'

Topper and his girlfriend must have slipped in through a side-entrance, but in my mind's eye I see them being carried by bell boys through the hotel reception, like prizes on Bruce's Generation Game show - Topper, swearing, 'I'll get you back, you bastards!' followed by a dinner service, a Teasmade and a cuddly toy!

The Slits on that tour were part of the fabric of the Clash and the audiences loved us. The music was very different to what they'd heard before from the Slits, with me as their new drummer, trying hard to get into the groove, dig into reggae and keep it danceable and consistent. Ari started to enjoy having more support from a consistent beat, becoming much more focused on the music, her movement and simply having fun. I was new and it had to come together quickly. We had to play new arrangements of old songs that they'd done on their Peel Sessions as well as new tracks like 'Typical Girls'.

I was so focused on the music and this incredible education that I don't remember what we did during the day; we travelled, we stopped, we did a soundcheck if we were lucky. If Joe Strummer had a hotel room, the door would be open to anybody, and if fans were following the tour they could crash in his room. He'd hold court and he loved talking to everybody. There was no 'us and them'.

Mick Jones seemed more rock 'n' roll, leaning towards a Keith Richards role. Paul Simonon was the James Dean of the bass – from any angle, he always looked amazing. There was so much energy, the crowd roaring like fans at a football match, the band playing loud like a more melodic Motörhead. The whole thing was like a big, bad family outing.

There was trouble between Viv and Mick, who were on and off, off and on, totally mad for each other, yet totally unable to make room for each other in this heady place that the Clash had been elevated to. For me, it was a huge step up. I'd gone from working men's clubs, sparsely populated Spitfire Boys gigs, to being the toast of the town in Liverpool with Big in Japan; but even then, we were just heroes in our own lunchtime and there was nowhere else to go. These gigs were another level. There was always damage to the front-row seats in the old theatres because the crowd would smash them up. Venues would hastily repair the seats, which were then immediately trashed, and the bands paid the bill.

At one gig in a city hall, knowing that the pogo was going to happen and that the old dancehall floor was sprung, scaffolding pole supports were installed to reduce the springiness. I went down to see what was happening when the Clash launched into their early mosh-pit anthem 'White Riot'. Down below, those steel poles were bending like flimsy mineshaft props, the whole place bouncing to the beat. It was frightening, amazing and mesmerising all at the same time; the power of the band and a heaving crowd to wreak havoc on a hall that had been standing for 150 years.

The whole experience of being on tour was so different from anything else I'd known. You'd run into bands like the Fabulous Poodles - what a terrible name. 'Hope we don't meet the Fab Poos at one in the morning at Woolley Edge services.'

You always met the bands you didn't want to meet at one in the morning at Woolley Edge services, not that I really knew where Woolley Edge was . . . somewhere between Leeds, Manchester and Sheffield, allegedly. There were all sorts of odd meeting places like that, most prominent among them the ubiquitous hotel reception bar that had closed. The night porter would be summoned, usually an old bloke who had some warm beer stashed away in a back room.

'I'll let you have one of those. Cost you, though.'

We'd bump into old hands like singer-songwriters Nick Lowe and Dave Edmunds, and members of 'Pub Rock' bands that we chose not to remember. I suppose as time progressed, we all became part of the same music industry, but back then it was all very disparate, more of a gang mentality. And here I confess: I still have my copy of Dave Edmund's reworking of Khachaturian's 'Sabre Dance' by his band Love Sculpture. This was perhaps my first single, pushing Lee Perry's Upsetters' 'Return of Django' into second place.

The last gig of the 'Sort It Out' tour was at the Lyceum in London on 29 January. We were second on, after a band called the Innocents, who had joined up for a few dates. I really hit it off with their American guitarist, Greg Van Cook. We seemed to have a lot of madness in common. We'd run around from bar to bar, and one day thought it would be fun to try to inhale exhaust fumes from the bus. Drunken, desperate stupidity.

When the tour finished it was time to work through the songs and prepare to record the first Slits record. We had done some earlier sessions with two guys at the old Decca label's Threshold Studios, which was like travelling back in time. The place was full of Leslie cabs and Hammond organs belonging to ex-Yes and Moody Blues keyboards man Patrick Moraz. Hailing from the same time zone were a production partnership named 'the Two Nicks'. They walked us through a demo recording session, like two halves of one person, each finishing the other's sentences. They were very old-school and would say things like, 'Yeah, Viv, that's really hot!', which didn't go down at all well. Ari hated them and Tessa, in her best 'Winnie the Pooh' Eeyore impersonation, said, 'Oh dear, is this what we have to deal with?' I became their go-between because I was male and played drums in a way that they understood. Together they asked, 'Budgie, could you talk to the girls about timekeeping?' Suffice to say, I couldn't, wouldn't and didn't.

The Nicks gave *me* some old-school tuition that would serve me well later when stepping into the rocksteady world of reggae. They drilled it into me to keep everything constant all the way through, to hit the snare at the same point and with the same weight when changing from a disco beat to swing. We spent days and days on 'Typical Girls', trying many different approaches until either the two Nicks or the girls threw their hands in the air and walked out, leaving me sitting there surrounded by the ancient gear from the prog-rock glory days of Yes.

After fine-tuning beats and arrangements with musicians from Jamaica sitting in with us at Island Records' HQ in St Peter's Square, we left for Ridge Farm Studios in Surrey, to begin recording what would become *Cut*. Ari could sing anything, yet often it seemed like she didn't want to. She would play with the ridiculous high notes she could reach and scream, but everything was always within her control and comfort. She would just pick up the bass guitar in the studio and, once she'd figured them out, play the most extraordinary basslines. It was a lot to do with attitude and character. Ariane had an unbridled character and an as yet untapped musicianship; it was that combination that attracted me and made me want to stay.

Ari had a disdain for the entertainment business like nobody else. She was young and she just didn't care. She had no respect for any of the rules, and it was infuriating for everybody. Before I joined, Palmolive would fight with her on stage, make up, then start the song again. Tessa would just keep calm. Viv always became infuriated, but loved Ari like an older sister would. I was in awe by the time we got to the studio to do *Cut* because it was so obvious that Ari was simply meant to be there. The recording studio was where she shone; it was her playroom. I was very fortunate to be with her in the right place, at the right time, with my receptors tuned in to the right frequencies.

I became good friends with the studio engineers, Brian Gaylor and Mike Dunne. They told me where and how other drummers had set up, like Paul Thompson from Roxy Music, and Simon Kirke from Free and Bad Company. I chose a position in the main room rather than in an isolated booth. I thought the whole experience should be about becoming a better drummer, absorbing new rhythms fresh off the plane from Jamaica. The first beat on *Cut*'s opener 'Instant Hit' is a direct gift from those final sessions in Island's St Peter's Square studio in Chiswick. Through a haze of spliff came the instruction: 'Here's a new beat, mon.' Telling me where the weight needed to be to make it work. It might be in a 5/4-time signature, but this was never even mentioned. Nobody knew, nobody needed to. I would get the beat going, Tessa started playing, 1, 2, 3, 4, 5 . . . then it goes into 4/4 and back into 5/4. If we happened to need a middle 8 and a chorus in a song they were there, but they just weren't deliberately constructed that way. I put this down to our reggae-schooled producer for the Cut sessions, Dennis Bovell and the girls being *atypical* girls. There was no intrusive patriarchal lineage saying: '*This* is how you do things.' We never talked about it, never thought about it as we rehearsed. Live, it might be chaos, and anything could happen. It usually did and it was usually good.

Dennis Bovell was the founder and guitarist of London-based reggae band Matumbi. He wrote and produced 'Silly Games' for vocalist Janet Kay, which was possibly *the* hit single in the summer of 1979. Dennis had the credentials the girls were looking for in a producer, but as well as this *Lover's Rock* chart hit, Dennis was also producing the simmering dub music for Linton Kwesi Johnson's 'Forces of Victory' album. He was working on both albums back to back, Linton in London and the Slits out on the farm. He even had time for phone calls, in which his voice oscillated between London cockneyisms and Jamaican patois, depending on who he was talking to, his mum or his mates. He was such a lovely guy, but I was beginning to feel uncomfortable. It could have been a simple musical issue, or it could have just been me not knowing what to do next and feeling I was not in the right place. There was a lot happening at Ridge Farm that had nothing to do with the recording of the album. The accommodation was luxurious and the catering was incredible. Brian and I would drive down to the local pub to sink a few pints after we'd done a day's work. They were such lovely people on the farm, yet it was all very odd, because it was such a different experience to anything we'd known before. The Slits were suddenly in the league of residential recording outside of London.

We'd completed the drum tracks and most of the bass parts and had started working on the guitars and main vocals, bringing everything up to speed, preparing to begin mixing.

For some reason I felt trapped, not by the situation, but by my world that had followed me. Jeanette had come to visit me at the studio, and I realised I'd been both ignoring her and dishonest with her about our relationship. To get my attention she was messing around with Brian. Nothing heavily sexual, but just enough to say, 'Are you jealous yet?' I was and I wasn't, but I felt I had to get out of the situation. Perhaps I also felt that I couldn't be there with Ari, Viv and Tessa without falling in love with one of them. Once again, my life was being shaped by my fear of relationships; the traumatic loss of my mother still resonating and disrupting my present.

I never wanted to leave the Slits until I did. I loved the Slits, and I loved the songs we'd done together. It wasn't like I had somewhere else to go, or anything else to do, but I made the decision to leave, even though I wanted to continue the rest of the session, to finish off little bits of percussion that still needed doing. I had to sit down on the lawn outside the studio with Viv and say, 'I think I've done what I need to do. I've got to move on. It's not to do with not wanting to be in the band.' It was very emotional.

Viv was really upset. Ari just shrugged. She wasn't nasty about it. I've often wondered what would have happened had we continued together. But they did two more albums and then it pretty much folded. Perhaps it was like a decision to leave home, having no idea what's going to happen next but knowing it's time to move on. It was becoming more and more difficult to understand Ari, and while I loved the intensity of her craziness, I couldn't stay for the next episode. There was something about the way it was going that didn't appeal. They'd probably agree now that it was disorganised chaos. They were already pulling away from their manager Frank Silver. I suppose there was a part of them that was unable to change, and that was Ari. She was always going to be Ari. They were still working on the album when I left. They hadn't done a lot of the over-dub percussion and probably hadn't done a lot of the main vocals at that point either. I didn't even visit afterwards, didn't even go back to say, 'How's it going? Can I come along to the final mix session when it's all finished?' I wasn't a part of that.

I had no connection to them or with them after that conversation with Viv. It still didn't sit well with me as a decision, but I'd paid my respects to Palmolive and made the best contribution I could have to the album and this unique collection of people. Perhaps I instinctively knew that after something so magical happens, if continuing doesn't feel right, it's time to leave. If only I had been able to apply that lesson in other parts of my life.

Cut was released on 7 September 1979; oddly, or perhaps even ominously, the same day as Siouxsie and the Banshees released their second album *Join Hands*. Something happened that same day, during a record-store promotion in Aberdeen, Scotland.

Whatever it was, Banshees guitarist John McKay and drummer Kenny Morris dramatically left the record store, the tour and the band.

They might have regretted leaving a couple of months later when Blondie had a party at the Notre Dame Hall in London. Banshees bassist Steven Severin recalls: 'He [Kenny] was with three or four other people so I walked up to him and whacked him. Nils [Banshees manager Nils Stevenson] had seen me approaching the table, and he was there in an instant, as was Siouxsie. Kenny half-fell off his chair and went to stand up and, as soon as he did, Nils hit him. He fell down again and, as he was lying on the floor, Siouxsie started kicking him.'

Sex Pistols drummer Paul Cook lived in the same building as Banshees manager Nils Stevenson on Bell Street in London. Nils called Paul, told him what had happened in Aberdeen and asked him to get up there as soon as he could. Paul had apparently heard about my leaving the Slits and told him, 'Nils, I'm not the right drummer for Siouxsie, but maybe you should give this guy Budgie a call.' John and Kenny's decision that day would change their lives for ever, and ten days later it would change mine too, irrevocably.

9.
Falling In

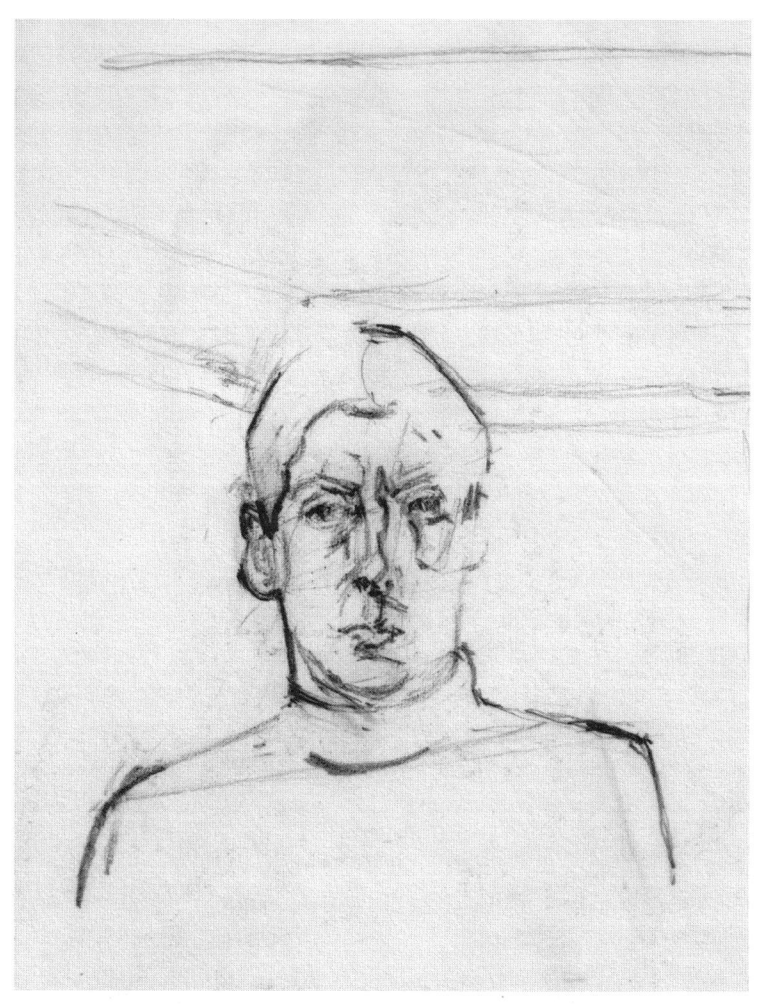

I'd seen Siouxsie and the Banshees play at the Greyhound in Croydon. I was hanging out with the Slits while Palmolive was still in the band, Palmolive wrestling with Ari at the side of the stage. We were hanging around while Siouxsie and co. were getting ready for soundcheck. I didn't get introduced and I was very much with the tearaways in the corner. The tearaways being the Slits, not the children who were charging around the venue, dodging Siouxsie, who was balancing on a stepladder in the middle of the room, maybe adjusting the lights. It was all a bit surreal. I didn't see much of the band, but I was fascinated by their equipment. They had everything stacked up on purple flight cases, rented from a company called Maurice Plaquet. It sounded very French, exotic and cute.

The Clash had pink flight cases; cute, it seems, was catching on. Siouxsie was wearing a sharp suit with a bolero jacket. She always seemed very upright before she went on stage, tall in stilettos, just like that little wax figure I'd made in Liverpool after seeing them at Eric's. I didn't feel an attraction to her then. It certainly wasn't fan-worship, not fandom or even groupie-dom, but I suppose somebody older than me would have said, 'Your gig lights were on!' Because there *was* a curiosity - *who are they and what are they like?*

I watched a later Banshees gig at London's Hammersmith Odeon and was very impressed. Kenny Morris was like a marionette sitting behind his kit, his arms exaggeratedly going up and down, even his knees popping right up above the bass drum. He really did look like a Woodentop, as if he were on strings with everything bouncing. John McKay was still and statuesque on stage. Dressed in a Japanese Shinto-style robe, with dark hair and a strong jaw, he had a striking presence. Hardly moving, he filled the theatre with swathes of noise from his guitar. Above it all was Siouxsie's voice, and her presence onstage, now in striped baggy trousers beneath the brown mac she almost always wore around that time.

After I left the Slits in the studio at Ridge Farm, I didn't have an inkling that anything was coming up. I was lost, wondering if I should even stay in London. For a short while I joined Glen Matlock in a new band he'd put together to play his new songs live. With Steve New and Danny Kustow on guitars, the Jimmy Norton Explosion was a straight-ahead rhythm and blues affair with a Small Faces twist. We recorded a session for John Peel, who complimented my harmonica playing by citing Captain Beefheart's 'Gimme Dat Harp Boy'. I could die happy with that accolade. Steve New was living with Patti Palladin when we arrived to pick him up for gigs. He'd always jump into the van, hair immaculate, with a big smile on his face and a huge love bite on his neck. Steve was such a sweet person and, like Danny, just too delicate for this world.

The London scene was still quite factional, but the Slits were close with both Malcolm McLaren's circle and Bernie Rhodes, manager of the Clash; they straddled both camps. Viv was with Mick Jones and had acquired the fabled ivory Les Paul guitar from Steve Jones. Palmolive had wrangled her first drum kit out of Malcolm, so it was all mixed up with stolen gear and an attitude of 'anything you need, girls'. I was becoming familiar with everyone, but the Banshees remained quite aloof.

I was still moving out of Sara's flat on the Cromwell Road, when Nils Stevenson called me. Nils had a soft London accent; his voice sounded like he was smiling. 'Hello, Budgie, it's Nils. I need a drummer for my band.'

I asked which band he was referring to because I presumed that, like Frank Silver, all managers had a few bands on the go.

'It's for *my* band, Siouxsie and the Banshees, you know them?'

Know them? Of course, I know them!

I thought he was joking. 'Sure,' I said, 'but they're on tour, right?'

I knew they were on tour because there were full-page ads in all the papers.

'Yeah, but something's happened. Are you doing anything tomorrow, can we meet?'

I'd done a wax effigy of the singer when I was in a cruddy Liverpool bedsit, and here I was in a cool London flat with their manager asking to meet me. My mind was racing. *They've got a manager, they're on tour, they've got an album out, and they need me. I'm good at doing that. I am good at no fear, and I will have no fear of stepping into an established band, even one that's just done an album.*

'Okay, tomorrow's good. Whereabouts?'

'The pub on the corner opposite Mornington Crescent tube. Can you be there about five o'clock?' He had that planned. Of course he did.

Talking recently with Echo and the Bunnymen's guitarist, Will Sergeant, he told me how shocked people in the Eric's scene were when I left Liverpool. It would be easy to think I'd considered many options: 'Yeah, I realised it was time to move on.' The reality was, I was winging it. The impetus to keep moving away from home was still strong. To stay would have meant contemplating what was missing, the absence within that I couldn't face. It's a trait I share with others who have made many career steps into the unknown. What appears to be pure serendipity may be the result of a fearless action. The path of opportunity appears to many but is taken by only a few, yet I could always say yes without thought of consequence. What did I have to lose? It would take many years for me to realise that what I had to lose was my sense of self. When David Bowie's long-time guitarist Earl Slick, summing up his illustrious career, was asked, 'Anything you wish you could have done better?' he replied, 'I wish I'd learned to say no.' Earl also lost his mum when he was just nineteen. No illness, no warning, she just died. He was there. Like I was when my mum died.

*

The meeting, in the pub across the way from the old Music Machine in Camden Town, was strangely formal. Siouxsie and Banshees bassist Steven Severin were drinking vodka and orange juice; I probably had a half, it could have been a pint, but it wouldn't have been bitter. It would have been mild, which was cheaper. They were smoking. Siouxsie was on Rothmans; Severin was a Marlboro man. These were both considered choices. Mine – the mild and rolling my own unfiltered 'Old Holborn' roll-ups – were probably just as considered. We just talked. I don't recall Siouxsie saying, 'Can you do this type of music?' or 'Are you any good at that kind of beat?' Instead, it was a formality. I already had a solid reputation as a drummer. The Slits was not a straightforward gig – other drummers could have tried and would probably have failed, but I'd now set a precedent for assimilating myself into a band and making it work. Perhaps it was more simple than that – the Banshees were on tour, the gear was sitting in trucks, the crew were being paid, they were haemorrhaging money and they didn't have very much time to get this thing moving again. Nils was probably thinking, *Please, just say yes. Please!* Even so, I wondered what was going on subliminally between the two of them. I wondered if in Siouxsie's mind, there might have been a bit of, *Hmm, I think he's cute. But I'm not going to tell Steve that. Because Steve might get jealous, and then he won't go for it, and he could be good for the band, and he's cute.*

Steve could already have been preparing his own version of events: *Let's get him in the band. I can then use Siouxsie to dominate and steer him.* Of course all of this is after the event, there wasn't time to consider motives or options. We certainly didn't discuss terms of employment or pay. I just didn't want to stand still as an artist. I wanted to move forward, and I was fully aware that this was the perfect opportunity to do so. I used all my chameleon powers to be exactly what they wanted me to be, without really knowing I was doing it. And then I had to prove that I really could do it.

We went down into a Camden Town basement rehearsal room, where their crew had set up equipment, including a guitar rig for original Banshees guitarist Marco Pirroni. Marco's presence relaxed me. He'd played with Siouxsie, Severin and Sid Vicious at that first gig at the 100 Club, but hadn't played with them since. I first met Marco at the same house that I'd met Steve Strange and Ari's German friend Nina Hagen - Barbara's house in that leafy Wembley suburb was becoming quite the hub for future stars. Marco went on to co-write many of Adam and the Ants' big hits. He was lovely to play with and we gelled quickly. This would have helped Siouxsie and Severin to forget at least one of their immediate problems. I gave my best rendition of the recently dethroned Kenny Morris, with a twist of the Velvet Underground's Maureen Tucker and a big drop of Palmolive thrown in - no cymbals, 'four on the bass drum', riding on the floor tom, not on the ride cymbal, snare on 2 and 4. We ploughed through 'Jigsaw Feeling' and all the other songs from the first album that didn't require Marco or me to learn any tricky arrangements. I just had to get the feel right, and the feel was good.

I don't know what they were expecting, but with Marco, I made a convincing sound. It must have worked because that night I left with vinyl of *The Scream* and *Join Hands*, plus a rare South American version of 'Hong Kong Garden', which I still have - thank you, Nils. I only had a few days to learn the beats and arrangements from those first two albums and a few singles. This wasn't familiar rock territory, hardly ever a simple verse/chorus/middle 8/chorus and out, which was fortunate because I'd already lost interest in formulaic rock songs. The Banshees' songs seemed to have storylines, with mood swings and tempo changes. There was more room for interpretation. They seemed to have subverted the rules of punk, rules which had only been drafted recently. They passed over even post-punk and into something of their own creation. Which is probably why they didn't get signed immediately.

I sat at home and listened and listened and listened, drawing little maps and diagrams. I analysed and began to incorporate the hand percussion parts, which Kenny would have done as an overdub in the studio, into my drum patterns. Joining an established band is a bit like riding a bike: the body must make many minor adjustments, each small repositioning being dependent on the previous imperceptible shift. These manoeuvres become second nature, necessary to maintain balance and to keep everything in line. Drummers make very good cyclists.

Today a drummer would just trigger a sample, of course, but I wanted to understand what I could make using this new kit I'd adopted. For example, 'Switch' has a cabasa motif, combined with an open hi-hat. I couldn't play the cabasa with a stick in each hand, so I transferred the cabasa part to the hi-hat and *voila!* Like Palmolive, Kenny used the floor tom the way others used the hi-hat. Kenny admired Maureen Tucker from the Velvet Underground, and it was also a sound familiar to a lot of seventies glam rock - think the Glitter Band. The floor tom played what would usually be played on the hi-hat, with the bass drum simply marking time, not much weight and no syncopation. I started to introduce these little elements that hadn't been played live before. I could reflect on when I first heard Kenny live, very light with no powering down on the beat. It's a good way of letting the drums do the work, but there was no weight in the kick drum. That's what I wanted to introduce, just like when I first started playing drums in St Helens.

I was influenced early on by John Bonham, inspired by the amount of weight he put into the kick drum - that's what I thought it should sound like. As soon as I started rehearsing with the Banshees, Nils noticed that the band now had a driving beat. He took me aside and told me, 'That's what the sound needed. That's brilliant.' Siouxsie and Severin only heard what they needed to hear: the arrangement was right. They certainly wouldn't have liked the suggestion that they now had a Bonham bass drumbeat. They'd have said, 'Ooooh, too Led Zeppelin, we don't want any of that!'

So, I was in, but as Marco was never intended to be a permanent replacement, we now had to find a guitarist. This was when I got to know the crew and everybody else involved with Siouxsie and the Banshees. The Cure were there too because they were the support act on that tour. Robert Smith, Michael Dempsey and Lol Tolhurst were waiting to see if the Banshees could pull this off and re-form a band in ten days. There was a real sense of urgency to it all because nobody could afford a month off. All the gear would have gone back into storage, the crew would have disbanded or gone on tour with Motörhead. (We shared our security, sound and lighting crews with Lemmy, Phil Taylor and Eddie Clarke, aka Motörhead.)

Here's the picture: dark rehearsal room, central stage, black drum kit, stage right, bass rig, stage left, guitar rig. Hopeful guitarists were escorted in and asked to play. This was part of the test – they had to use John McKay's setup, Fender Twin Reverb amp with an MXR flanger.

Some came in and just wailed. Some came in and showed off all their licks. Some soloed. Others turned up and thrashed away because they thought we were a punk band. Some thought it was dressing-up time and arrived in make-up and heels. Most of them couldn't play, and the ones that could were stylistically awful and wrong for the band. The Cure were there throughout, sitting cross-legged on the floor, facing my drum kit, like little gnomes in a row, three judges taking notes. After about the sixth dismissal Robert began scribbling something on his card – 'Nil points'.

By the end of the day, having failed to find a single potential candidate, Siouxsie and Severin realised they were unlikely to find anyone in time. That's when Severin went off and had a word with Robert, suggesting he become our guitarist. Robert wore a mac in the Cure, so when he played with the Banshees he just took it off and tucked his shirt into his leather trousers. Instant transformation.

My first gig with Siouxsie and the Banshees was at Leicester's De Montfort Hall on 18 September 1979. Just ten days after the band had split, and I was in trouble straight away. I had unknowingly changed the drum arrangement in 'Switch' and the audience knew it - of course they knew the drum part better than me and took great delight in keeping the beat going when I had mistakenly stopped. Siouxsie did not miss a beat; she spun round on her heel and gave me a stare that pinned me to the back wall. It said, 'You can do that tonight but do not let it happen again.' It was almost a friendly stare, but even Paddington Bear can give you one of those evil looks. I got that stare only once more, at the beginning of the endgame, many years later in Vancouver. That time it meant, 'That's it, it's over!'

The 'Switch' bitch became a little bugbear for a while, but aside from that, the feeling at that first gig was great. Robert was quite chaotic. At De Montfort Hall he had his notes perched on a lectern, like a choirboy. It was an ornately carved wooden lectern - very Goth, before Goth was even a word (which it certainly wasn't in our world). Everything was going fine, until the crew switched on the fans to circulate the smoke haze. Robert's sheet music was hit by the blast and all his carefully prepared guitar notes were scattered to the four corners of the stage.

Of course, Robert didn't scramble or bend to pick anything up. That would have been way too uncool. Instead he simply left them to blow across the stage and wandered around looking for the next song, and wherever he found it, that's where he played it, even if it was off in the wings. Robert had adopted John McKay's position stage left, from where I could see him looking at the floor and then up at me, as if to ask, 'I don't know what's coming next, do you?' It was one of those rare magical moments, when you're expected to just know, so you just step in and do it. The audience had that expectation, and they urged the whole thing to succeed. It was momentous in its own way.

The atmosphere on that tour was insane. They'd been losing thousands of pounds, and risked losing a whole lot more, so they were relieved to have a chance to complete the tour. Any reservations had evaporated. All those things you're not supposed to do, you can do them now. It was a big party, we got drunk a lot, and that licence to drink, so long as you turned up sober for stage, is all I really remember.

I was starting to get to know the band a little more, figuring out things we might have in common, and I certainly had more things in common with Siouxsie than I did with Severin. I still saw those two as a couple, but then I also saw Nils and Siouxsie as a couple, which of course they were. Nils's job as manager was also to look after Siouxsie in this collective drinking frenzy. I still felt like a bit of an outsider, which after the Slits tour was a familiar feeling. Back then I was the one from the north of England and the only guy in the band. This time around I was still the only one from the north of England, but I was hanging out with Lol and the crew - it was the first time I'd been with a band that kept the same crew on each tour, as if they'd sworn an oath of allegiance to the 'Ice Queen of Goth' in waiting.

There was also a deep loneliness to it all. I never knew what to do when I arrived at the hotel. All I could see was a TV and a minibar and a bathroom. I thought, *Which one? Bath? TV? Minibar? Minibar? TV? Bath?* I would usually have a soak in the tub because that was a luxury and television was never really my thing. The minibar, though, was very much my thing. We'd all dip into it, not pre-gig, but often after, when everybody was expected to empty the contents of their minibar into a plastic bag, bring it down to reception, and dump it into a big pile of ice cubes in a bucket on the carpet. It all meant that there was much silliness to be had while it lasted.

We finished the tour and Robert and the Cure left to go and be the next big thing. Siouxsie and Severin went off to the writing rooms of their publisher, Chappell Music, to begin writing what would become the songs for *Kaleidoscope*. I didn't see them after the tour. I'd done my job, and that was it. They never seemed very sociable, but being on the tour and part of the Banshees meant I'd started to meet more people and go out to clubs like the Blitz in Covent Garden. Severin may have taken me down there when he wanted to introduce me to some people. That's where I met Princess Julia, Boy George and Steve Strange again. Steve was one of the taste police, so despite my comparatively workmanlike style, I always got in. Brian Gaylor, an engineer on the *Cut* sessions with the Slits, was one of my few London friends. Brian was from a different part of society and a different era of London. Well educated, mad as a hatter, lost in fun and not a care in the world as he drove a big old army jeep around London. He and I would meet up and go to the Blitz despite not really being dressed for it. I didn't have the money for Vivienne Westwood, so I dressed as if I was going on stage, with a T-shirt, black jeans and Lonsdale boxing boots, which were light on the feet and soft, so I could float like a butterfly, sting like a bee. Just like the dancing Muhammad Ali.

Behind the scenes, I was being traded, though I wasn't party to any discussion. Nils bought me out of my management contract with Frank Silver, reimbursing him for the money he'd laid out on my future - £25 a week and greasy-spoon breakfasts up on Royal College Street. Nils had basically bought me into the Banshees. I don't recall any kind of commitment contract, but that was to be expected, and, in a way, it was quite nice it being so casual. I was now leaving behind my London-Liverpool connections and I moved into a basement studio in Shaftesbury Mews off Stratford Road, just north of Earls Court.

The word 'studio' was significant. I thought I'd made it! But really it was half a basement, one room with a little kitchenette, a bedette and a living-roomette. However, it was the first time I'd had my own front door. I adopted a dog from Battersea Dogs Home and loved to walk with her up to High Street Kensington and on into Kensington Gardens. I would always stop by the bronze figure of Peter Pan in his little enclosure, and marvel at the scale of G.F. Watts's rearing horse sculpture *Physical Energy*. From this crossroads the view east was downhill over the Serpentine reflecting Henry Moore's Arch, and looking south along Lancaster Avenue, through tall trees framing the Albert Memorial with the Royal Albert Hall beyond. I aspired to the Albert Hall rather than the Henry Moore, and a few years later it did, indeed, become the Banshees' preferred London venue. I may have visited a gallery now and then, but I didn't do much between obligations because it felt like I had to compartmentalise, do one thing at a time, which fitted with the recording of *Kaleidoscope*, a very intense run of sessions over just a few weeks.

We were recording down at Nigel Gray's Surrey Sound Studio, where he'd just been working with the Police on their first couple of albums. There was a lot of experimentation expected. Siouxsie and Severin had recorded some basic demos, but with no indication of what the drum parts should be. As soon as I got to the studio, I decided I wanted to make my mark. I listened to 'Red Light', a drum-box-driven, simple three-note synth pattern. I was inspired by Lou Reed's *Street Hassle*, and its version of 'Real Good Time Together'. Halfway through the song slips seamlessly from being a studio recording into a live recording with the drums fading in on a fill. I thought this was not only a great way for the drums to enter a song, but also a great entrance into the band, charging into this song on a wing and a prayer. They'd done this very simple studio version of 'Red Light', and I just picked up a beat I wouldn't usually play. It had a jazzy feel, in 6/4 time, coasting in on the ride cymbal.

From then on, I was on an equal footing in the studio. I was certainly treated that way by Nigel. It was such an intense process that it all feels like a blur now. It was like my brain was so focused on the job in hand, or maybe I was just high on life. It's as if I was playing a game, testing myself.

The studio itself was quite an old-school place. Bands would be in there for months, and you'd see boxes of two-inch tape piled up, all with the same song title, marked 'Take 20/21/22'. We might have done two takes of a song, but usually we kept the first to retain a slight looseness to the feel. With the Slits we had rehearsed a lot, working out the new beats for the old songs, and then I went in to play the drums with either just Tessa on bass, or Ari singing a guide vocal. *Kaleidoscope* was different, and much more experimental because we hadn't yet found a fixed way of being this version of the band.

Take 'Desert Kisses', for example. Siouxsie and Severin had made a demo with bass, vocals and just a little suggestion of a beat. This left a lot of space for my drums, to suggest a stretched languid 8/4 feel, and for the guitar to transform it into a lush paradise with everyone singing 'Aaahs'. They'd written most of the songs with beats from a Roland CR-78 CompuRhythm, which contains pre-programmed bossa nova and samba beats among others. It's what Roxy Music used on 'Dance Away', a shuffly, squeaky, drumbox. If you pressed more than one button at a time you got a strange mix of bossa nova, samba, foxtrot and waltz. These drum boxes began as self-accompaniment for home organs. I love them because they're not trying to sound like acoustic drums, which leaves space and options for my drums in the mix.

I still had to push for more space. When everybody was saying, 'Great take. We've got it. We've got the whole thing,' I'd ask Nigel for another pass on the drums. I'd add another drum track, so on the song 'Skin' you get this answering of two kits, with one beat, mirrored by a second, giving the impression of two drummers, but at the same time all a little bit ragged. I was trusted and allowed space to experiment and to grow as a musician.

The guitarist situation was a bit more complicated. Sex Pistols guitarist Steve Jones came to the studio to add some power and swagger to proceedings. Severin showed Steve the bass notes, Steve figured out some chords and, fuelled by copious amounts of red wine and stamping out of cigarettes on the carpet with his motorcycle boots, he confirmed all suspicions of him being a filthy rotten scoundrel. His reputation as the 'out of control Sex Pistols guitarist' preceded him, but he wasn't like that at all. He got the job done without any fuss and with amazing results.

He *was,* however, all about driving Siouxsie out to the airport to see if she'd snog him in the car. She said she didn't. He says different, but he would. Steve said to me recently that he doesn't remember much about playing on *Kaleidoscope*. At that time he was being vilified by the music industry and the tabloid press, and he had a growing problem with drugs and booze, so he was not in a good place. Testament then to Steve's innate talent, that his playing on the album still sounds amazingly fresh and spontaneous.

Eventually, we formed ourselves into a real band. John McGeoch became our permanent guitarist and a strong camaraderie started to build, but it took a while. I always felt that the age difference between me and Severin and McGeoch made them seem more worldly, a little superior. Siouxsie was a further mystery. What did she do after the studio? I soon worked out that she just went home, read and watched films. If she had owned a cat, she would have happily sat with the cat, on a mat. She really didn't enjoy going out, partly because she was so recognisable and she'd be pestered everywhere. Severin, on the other hand, didn't mind being seen and noticed. Guys in bands seemed to soak up every opportunity and Siouxsie had to have that inner self-confidence in such male-dominated environments.

If I think back to Siouxsie at Eric's or when I was hanging out with the Slits, what I had seen was a young woman who was aware that she was being watched. She was already well known, there on the front page of the *Daily Mirror* with the headline 'Siouxsie's a Punk-shocker'. I got that from Siouxsie before I even knew her, and perhaps that was part of the attraction, the way she handled who she had to be. What other people didn't see, until Siouxsie dropped her guard and allowed them to, was the cackling, crazy tomboy Susan from Chislehurst. She was hilarious and completely wicked; not in a dark, bleak way, just wicked. She would laugh along with the dirtiest, meanest, un-politically correct 'Derek and Clive' humour, the crueller the better. She refused to kowtow to what you're supposed to be as a singer in a band, as a female in a man's world. The Slits had this same aloofness, and Viv especially had similar attitudes and assertiveness - yet behind the veneer, they were frivolous, free and fun.

The Absence

In August 1980, there was a photoshoot of the women in punk titled 'A Ladies' Tea Party', with guests Siouxsie Sioux, Viv Albertine, Poly Styrene, Pauline Black, Chrissie Hynde and Debbie Harry. I like to picture how they would be talking. I can just imagine it - 'Yeah, yeah, yeah. Mick, he's a right one, isn't he? He's up his bum, he is!' 'Mick's just like Severin really!' Cackle, cackle, cackle. When the camera appeared, or somebody from the magazine or the record company, an air of 'fuck you' would descend. It'd still be fun, but the masks were on. They'd still play the same roles, but on their own terms. It would be okay, until somebody tried to push them too far, to do something awkward or some gesture that could be misinterpreted.

Siouxsie took a different stance from other female singers like Toyah Willcox or Hazel O'Connor, but also from most male singers. The 'boys in the band' would usually wearily agree, saying, 'Yeah, okay. Same old, same old.' We 'Banshee blokes' could feel empowered as a band by supporting Siouxsie's attitude. The strange dichotomy, though, is that a male in a position of power will tolerate, even relish, being put in his place by a strong woman. Shades of 'sub-dom' psychology, perhaps? Should, however, a 'bloke' in the band make a similar suggestion, the gauntlet would be thrown and it would be sex pistols at dawn.

This strength of unity and being led by a female vocalist gave us a sharp edge over a regular rock band. In interviews, we could talk about art, architecture, politics or football - our songs were not about being 'back on the road again'. Our songs were not about 'girls' and 'love', well, certainly not in any normal way. There was a sense of humour, often black in nature, and a shared attitude, which meant that my friendship with Siouxsie was growing, although at the time I felt I was only ever joining Nils and the other established males in her circle. I was merely the latest curiosity to be discovered.

Everything really came together when we were figuring out how to play *Kaleidoscope* live, trying to find our way into a record that had been started by Siouxsie and Severin but finished by a band. Would we use the drum-box or ditch it, like it never existed? We decided to stick with just bass, drums and guitar - no keyboards. This was when John McGeoch came into his element, using his guitar to augment that basic three-piece sound. Because of this process our sound developed and we came together as a band very quickly. The crew, realising that something exciting was happening, became a part of it. I started to build a close relationship with my drum tech, the band's driver, Joss.

While relationships became stronger on tour, this was also when the foibles, tics and undesirable characteristics would manifest: drinking to excess, not going to bed, not getting up, mood swings - all the things that went unnoticed in the studio became glaringly obvious on tour. We had the long drives, the days of nothing, the boring days off. Although we were getting closer as a band, we were not like the Cure, old school friends who had grown up together. For me and John this wasn't our first band adventure, although it was for Siouxsie and Severin. On the flip side, this probably meant we wouldn't kill each other, not immediately anyway. Yet there was enough dislocation happening that only added to my feelings of insecurity. 'Where's John today? What's Severin doing?' Just wondering what everybody did on the days off and in the weeks when we were *not* touring. I wasn't doing all that much, aside from looking after the dog. But our downtime was growing less by the day - we were on a very steep uphill trajectory.

Things were further complicated by relationships outside of the band. These rarely lasted long. Unspoken allegiance to the cause was sacred, and tolerance for anyone outside of the band clique was extremely limited. I felt this tension when we were on tour in Germany, early on, when I met a girl who spent the night with me in a traditional German hostelry, where depositing two pfennigs into a bedside coinbox started the built-in bed vibrator. It was nothing pervy, more of an old folks' thing for bad backs. Sadly, we didn't get to try it, as at the time I didn't have two pfennigs to rub together. There was no sex. I just felt the need to look after her. We were both very young. She left in the morning, and I waved to her as our bus pulled away. The lads gave me knowing looks and smirks: 'Bet you were up all night, weren't you?'

I was very awkward about it all. I didn't want it to be sullied by lad-speak and I also wasn't sure if I was required to stop this kind of activity. It was never spoken about. I suspected that perhaps it was not the best thing to be doing – what does it say about Siouxsie and the band? A one-night stand is very public.

I didn't like the blokey banter from the crew that morning in Germany, but I also wondered if Siouxsie, as a woman, would perhaps have a different perspective. I thought about what it must be like for her to see the guys picking up a girl in Wiesbaden and then dropping her off at the train station. The usual exchanges, 'Yeah, she was all right! Anyway, where are we tonight? I've got a lovely one lined up tonight!' A girl in every port, so goes the cliché. I was uncomfortable with the idea of it.

Groupies, obsessives, camp followers; different roles, all part of the same play, the game of the live gig. I saw it on tour in America. When we arrived at the Whisky a Go-Go in LA, the girls would circle in Cadillac convertibles: 'Hey, you guys want to come to the beach?' I was leaving the club in the afternoon sun, holding a bowl of tropical fruit like it was plundered treasure. I had never seen so many pineapples, guavas and mangos in my life. *Beach*, why would I want to go to the *beach*? You see what I mean? I was a wet-behind-the-ears English boy. I'd heard stories about other green British bands, someone gives them their first blowjob and, Oomph! It must be love, love, love! They get married, then they find out that fellatio in the USA is akin to a handshake in the UK.

We went to America for the first time in 1980, and in LA I was greeted by Lydia Lunch and her friend Marcy. It was one of those dalliances outside of what was deemed correct within this newly formed quartet of Banshees. I had my mind, and everything else, blown in America, because there were so many ways to have it done. In England I'd had very little experience of losing control and it tended to be very domestic - in a bed, in a bath, on a train, and that was that. But in America it could be many things in many ways and places.

New York was our first major American party city. Towards the start of that first US tour, we played the Palladium when it was still a cavernous old cinema, and the old Irving Plaza when it was still in a rough part of town. Sometimes we met the locals from the music and art world, who revelled in showing us the delights of the seedy paradise that was New York City in 1980. I met a wonderful woman named Rhonda, part promoter, part gallerist, perfect company. She took me up to her Manhattan apartment and showed me the delicate art of inhaling the final fumes of a pure marijuana reefer from a tiny roach clip. Rhonda exuded elegance and experience. She draped me in a blue silk dressing gown - 'It matches your eyes,' she purred. 'Just lie back, and relax.' That night with Rhonda changed my world. It took a long while for me to realise, but she gave me so much - so much love. Her parting gift was a foil wrap of MDMA, a psychedelic precursor to ecstasy. This, of course, had to be consumed before I boarded the band's midday flight to San Francisco. The streets of NYC would never again be as soft and as pretty as they were that morning. I was a giant, tiptoeing though spongy canyons of cuddly cartoon buildings. And then came San Francisco.

My guide was Jorgé, a friend of Rhonda's. He provided a much-needed escape from the boys-on-tour masculinity of McGeoch and Severin, which I didn't really feel comfortable with. Heaven was expanding! America was just so alien, so seductively exotic. Today the Tropicana Motel on Santa Monica Boulevard, West Hollywood, is a modern Ramada multi-storey car park affair with adjoining suites. Back in 1980, it was a small two-level motel surrounding three sides of a kidney-shaped swimming pool and a small wooden fence. Security and privacy were not an issue, as there was a full-size boa constrictor living in reception. Opposite the hotel was Palms, a heavy-duty lesbian cocktail bar. After a two-week tour taking in Toronto, Boston, Philadelphia, New

York and San Francisco, we landed in Los Angeles for our first LA shows at the Whisky on Sunset Boulevard. We were staying at the Tropicana while playing two shows a day for three days. We were dazzled by twenty-four-hour TV, no sleep, but a lot of drink, drugs and sex. We had arrived in heaven! Hadn't we?

American girls seducing the latest British boys in bands wasn't a story that stopped with seventies rock 'n' roll. It continued into the eighties with punk/post-punk and new romantic bands. On the surface I was in my element with all this wild behaviour, but there was also, already, a real loneliness to it. I still didn't know how to shape a relationship, especially one outside the world of the group. Even the basics felt beyond me. I was a kid in a sweet shop back in St. Helens, trying to find his way around the bright lights of the working men's clubs. I never knew when to go home. Or even if I *should* go home. I woke up in nice but strange apartments in New York's Soho or London's Marble Arch, but none of it lasted very long. There was no big deal to it for most of them. But I'd always fall in love. I say fall in love – I presumed that's what happened if you fell into bed with somebody, you're going to have a relationship and you work it out. But no, apparently not for the music scene around Siouxsie and the Banshees in the early 1980s.

Having a strong woman singing and fronting the band made the romantic dynamics different from all male or even all female groups. There would sometimes be a big end-of-tour party to which all the girlfriends came, but it usually ended in tears. Siouxsie could push it by taking a dislike to one of them, or the girls would be made to feel second in line. Everything deferred to Siouxsie. Even if there wasn't a subservience required from us to her, there was to 'the cause' or what she represented, and nobody was allowed to get in the way of that. If they tried, and the male was defending his girlfriend's right to receive their full respect, to be valued within context, it was difficult. Severin tried it several times and it never worked. There was always the possibility of an argument brewing with the queen bee.

John was very open with one-night stands; back on the bus, he was very much king of the road. Severin would be a little more discreet. He would have a girlfriend for a while, but I wonder if that was an unspoken source of annoyance and conflict, or even a trigger for Siouxsie. Together they carried the mantle, having formed the band and done most of the writing together. If he wasn't available when she wanted his input, was he being disloyal? Was Severin driven by a commitment to himself or a commitment to the band – or by his own desires and needs to be accepted and acknowledged as a writer and a musician in his own right?

I never had that need in me. I never thought of myself as a musician, ever. I was the drummer in the band. It's not that I had low self-esteem or lacked self-confidence, but I struggled with the deep-down belief in who I was as Budgie, the 'character' who played drums. As if I had some faulty mental connection. I was drawn to people who were full of themselves, who would know that they were the best, and they'd tell me that I was too – that I was with the best and that they were with me. But deep down inside would be that insistent little voice saying, 'You know you don't really believe that. I know you're struggling, but it's okay. I'll stick with you. I'll go along with this fabrication because I'm also struggling to hold it together.' I was trying to fill the emptiness inside with so much hot air, I needed help.

10.
Creatures Kissing in the Rain

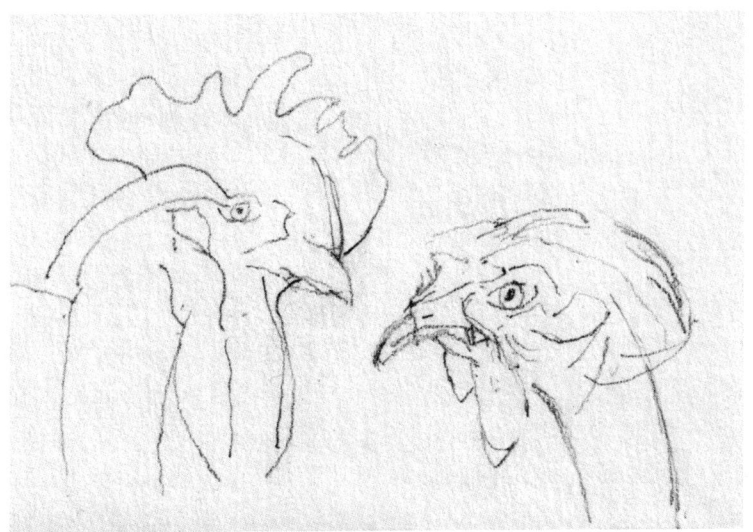

Although touring meant that I felt a little more 'with the Banshees', I still found myself wondering what on earth everyone did when we were apart. Why didn't I know?

The band was very London-centric, or at least very southern, as Siouxsie and Severin had grown up in the London suburbs of Chislehurst and Bromley. Banshees tour promoter and fellow Lancashire lad Dave Woods jovially and perhaps knowingly said to me very early on, 'Aye, lad, you have to watch those southerners.' There was always a feeling that I was a long way from home. When we went on tour, that was when *they* left their home patch. I had already left mine. My sense of where I belonged was tenuous, both geographically and, even still, within the band.

We were in the Ritz rehearsal room, writing songs for the album that would become *Juju*. Like most creative spaces, our Ritz (in name only) was tucked away underneath the arches of a railway bridge in Putney, with District Line trains rattling by above. Thick grey carpet on the walls and arched ceilings helped to absorb and diffuse unwanted frequencies *and* the accumulative, *creative* cigarette smoke. Thick brown carpet on the floor helped to absorb everything else.

After the play for the day ended, Siouxsie, Severin and McGeoch would take taxis home. Did they have a secret number? I was never offered a lift and certainly couldn't afford the fare. I would walk or take the underground back across the River Thames to my flat in Earl's Court. I presumed that Siouxsie and ex-boyfriend Severin were still best of friends, and that their manager Nils was also very much another ex-boyfriend of hers. It was Nils who brought me closer into the fold, suggesting that I, along with John

McGeoch, became equal partners in the band. We were writing in a newly formed collaboration, and John and I had to be open about our strengths and limitations. We also learned how we could best put our creativity into the band, without crossing an unspoken boundary that would have Siouxsie and Severin thinking we were overstepping the job description. John especially loved the challenge of trying to make something sound different to what was ordinarily expected, and I found that I had to ask myself, 'What would a regular drummer do here?' and promptly do the opposite.

We were back in Nigel Gray's converted dairy, the same Surrey Sound studio where we had recorded *Kaleidoscope*, but this time a different daily delivery appeared. Cocaine had arrived. It's strange to look back because they were happy times - a photograph of me with Nils, Siouxsie and Phil Oakey, singer of the Human League, backstage in a dressing room full of happy faces is testament to that. Nils has his arm around me, and I've got my head against his side. It's all very friendly, and in the beginning it was very much a family affair, but the insidious malevolence of drugs quietly slipped in through the backstage door.

It was cocaine at first. Nigel had the connections and the money, and a steadily debilitating habit. John and Steve used to 'Hoover up' the mixing console at the end of the day. It began as a bit of a comedy sketch but soon became something darker. Drink was mostly conducive to relaxing tension, creating the right mood, and sometimes helpful for promoting understanding in a relationship. It was a communal pastime. But we were not prepared for the effect that drugs would have on our tight little circle. The dynamic changed. Drugs bred secrecy and quickly took precedence over the expected 110 per cent loyalty to the cause.

It wasn't just drugs that were fracturing that loyalty; there was soon to come a song to send Siouxsie and me on our own way. The rehearsals for *Juju* gave us an excuse to be in each other's company with a bottle of wine in the evening after the band had finished. The feeling during those *Juju* sessions was 'Are you going to eat me or am I allowed to get closer, enter the inner, unknown territory?' The bait, perhaps mutual, was a track called 'But Not Them', written during the *Juju* sessions in early 1981. It sounded complete with just voice and drums – McGeoch and Severin didn't feel the need to add to it, and Nigel felt it shouldn't be part of the album. 'But Not Them' could have been taken as a very loaded song title to the other two Banshee boys, but they never took it that way. It was well rooted in the poetic and humorous lyricism of R.D. Laing's *Knots*. Severin's lyric for 'Mirage' also contained a knowing *Knots*-ness. At the time this book was a badge of tribal belonging, akin to Jean Paul Sartre's *Nausea*, which was another slim volume to accompany a pack of Gauloises cigarettes for the barstool existentialist. I'm sad, no, make that happy to say that I speak from personal teenage experience.

We had enough good material for *Juju*, so 'But Not Them' was shelved to focus on the tracks that worked better as a full band. Siouxsie and I began to have an increasingly devil-may-care attitude. We were less *obviously* serious than Severin and McGeoch and younger than them, so perhaps we enjoyed a playfulness that they never quite shared. That there might be something outside her usual sphere of the Banshees was perhaps a first for Siouxsie. John McGeoch had always been active in other projects (Magazine, Visage) and was very much a gun for hire at that point. Severin had really wanted to get him in the band, and that united them, so Siouxsie and I had more reason to be together.

Making a song with only a drummer and a vocalist was quite a heady experience and a process which led us to realise we had an understanding far deeper than the sound we were making. Nobody said anything because, essentially, that's what you do whenever you write a song. But during the rehearsals for *Juju* this understanding became bigger than the original remit, and eventually bypassed McGeoch and Severin. We started to feed the needs and desires of our creative connection beyond the music we were creating as a four-piece. This shift of emphasis has happened many times within groups, and it doesn't always work out so well. We felt, and hoped, that we were keeping it hidden. It soon emerged, however, that the subterfuge was not so effective. The Banshees toured early that spring, playing 'But Not Them' as part of the set. While we were on the road there was a certain amount of teasing going on. Do you? Would you? Was everyone complicit in our affair?

I consulted my well-worn copy of R.D. Laing's *Knots*: '*They are playing a game. They are playing at not playing a game. If I show them I see they are, I shall break the rules and they will punish me. I must play their game, of not seeing I see the game.*'

It was playful, it was working together, full of innuendo. Of course, it reached a point where the desire swept in, the overwhelming possibility of it. The emotional charge was overwhelming in rehearsals and fully revealed in the studio that last week in May 1981. We had three days at the aptly named Playground Studio, the final day a celebration of Siouxsie's twenty-fourth birthday. I was still strictly the man behind the drum kit. But I was drumming and charming my way deep into a relationship: it was as exciting as flirting with a stranger.

With the Banshees I'd been *allowed* to introduce new musical parts and play other instruments. The experience with the Creatures was different. Siouxsie didn't play an instrument, apart from a few chords on the guitar, simple melodies on the melodica, a little percussion. It was expected of me to do almost everything else on Creatures records. I organised them. I ordered them. I structured them. We didn't do a lot of arranging or linear editing of multitrack tapes. I performed everything from start to finish. I had to learn marimba parts, tuned percussion, Jamaican steel drums. It was so fulfilling, finally unleashing my musicality, and it felt tremendously exciting. We worked fast because I was confident in my ability to play, and Mike Hedges was very much a fly-by-the-seat-of-your-pants producer. We had two songs written, 'But Not Them' and 'So Unreal', and had been playing some other ideas on the Banshees tour earlier in the spring.

The idea to cover 'Wild Thing' by the Troggs came together in the studio. It was a powerful, risky and blatantly sexual statement. We both knew the Chip Taylor original, but I was channelling my love of the Jimi Hendrix version from 1967. Hearing his arrangement in my head, making the drums create the tune, but adding British swing. Siouxsie shifted her vocal style and emotional focus with each verse, creating a constantly shifting, intense and dynamic delivery. 'Wild Thing' gave us the title of our first recordings as a duo, as did our mutual affection for Maurice Sendak's *Where the Wild Things Are*. All in all, we had revealed our infatuation. I entered willingly.

'And I find more bitter than death the woman who is a snare, whose heart is a net, and whose hands are chains. The man who pleases God escapes her, but the sinner is ensnared.'
Ecclesiastes 7:26

The five tracks on what would become *Wild Things* by the Creatures were conceived in the same way as the Banshees worked on B-sides: fully engaged and, due to time constraints, quickly produced. We usually had three days to produce two to three tracks. There would be a germ of an idea and the three of us, Siouxsie, Severin and I, would flesh it out. Then any one of us would pick up and play guitar, keyboards or whatever instruments were around. Siouxsie would be furiously writing lyrics in another room. I quickly realised that with the Creatures, I was able to play the drums in a melodic way, rather than simply providing a tempo and a beat, with bass drum, snare and some tom-tom fills.

That said, my first love of the drums was as beatmaker. I love the release, the signal to dance that comes when the bass drum finally ends a long musical intro. In today's dance music it's 'the drop'. It's what the dancefloor crowd goes crazy for.

The drum kit in pop music is rarely considered as a melodic instrument, but with the Creatures that's what I wanted to explore, although I wasn't at all sure of what could be achieved.

I'd recorded *Juju* on Kenny's old standard-size Pearl drum kit. With 13/14/16-inch toms, 10-ply wooden shells, and a 22-inch bass drum, it produced the preferred drum sound of the 1970s – differing degrees of 'thud'. For the Creatures rehearsals I'd acquired a selection of lighter, 5-ply maple-wood Gretsch shells. Fitted with powder-coated Remo Ambassador drumheads, they created a more 'tuneable' melodic sound.

We set up my new kit at the newly opened Playground Studio in Camden Town, where Mike Hedges had been working with the Associates and the Cure. The sound of the oversized (14/15 and 18-inch) shells of the Gretsch kit in the small drum booth was cacophonous. The tuning of them, the *live*-ness and the ability to sustain a note, were so different from that seventies sound of the drums on *Juju* – they were also tuned, but had a fatter, muffled sound.

The open ring of the Gretsch created a sound like the single-headed drums that Phil Collins was probably experimenting with at Virgin Records' Townhouse Studios in Shepherd's Bush, during sessions for Peter Gabriel's third solo album. The drum parts and treatments on the songs 'Intruder' and 'No Self-Control' reveal what would become the quintessential drumming style and sound of Phil Collins. Of course, it was strictly forbidden to express a love of Phil Collins back then, but I just couldn't deny his influence. I literally bumped into him in the BBC loos when we were appearing on *Top of the Pops*. Phil was in the all-singing, all-dancing phase of his career, not a drum in sight. He was very polite, and we probably exchanged drummers' toilet jokes – or maybe we didn't.

Peter Gabriel's third album was a touring accompaniment in late 1980. We had just written our song 'Israel', but still needed a mid-section. During a TV studio rehearsal for a performance, the drums of 'No Self Control' inspired my first middle-eight drum break. The new kit allowed me to pursue a more musical approach to drum-tuning, bringing melodic arrangement into our songwriting. The Creatures songs recorded over that weekend were mostly formed around notes and chords suggested by the drums. I enhanced these suggested notes with tuned percussion, like the marimba and the vibraphone. I was always able to create melodies and harmonies from the most unlikely of sources, the drone of the Xpelair fan in the pub toilet, or the minaret-like hum of our Kelvinator 'Magic Defrost' refrigerator. As a boy I would drone myself to sleep at night, which used to scare my sister. Siouxsie and I shared a lack of musical education, but we always sought advantage in adversity, and our lack of formal education didn't hinder the creative partnership we were nurturing.

We quickly realised that the songs we were writing as the Creatures just wouldn't have worked within the Banshees. With the marimba, vibraphone and tubular bells following drum patterns, we were operating away from a fixed tuning. Humidity, heat and overtones played a huge part in our melodic choices. It also meant that Siouxsie's vocal styling was not limited by tuning accuracy or subservience to concert pitch. When the band formed, they just tuned to whoever had managed to be in tune, so if the E on the guitar was in tune, then the bass followed (just about), though never in a regular tuning and there were always overtones, atonal chords and drone notes. It was probably hard for Siouxsie to pitch her own tuning because McGeoch played with lots of harmonised reverb and digital delay, so those notes would oscillate and wobble. As the notes were always approximate, it wouldn't pin Siouxsie to hitting them, and there's a style in her singing which slides around the note. She could hold a flattened tuning just under the note that most singers wouldn't even consider correct. She was completely comfortable doing that.

Perhaps that was a characteristic of untutored singing. Most people wouldn't have a clue how to sing with drums only, it would be a huge obstacle. But Siouxsie was different; she could zone in and pitch a song to the drums with all their overtones. It gave her a lot of room to be simply a voice, unfettered. It seemed obvious to me - if you really wanted to hear her natural vocal you would free it of all restrictions, like relative tuning. I've always thought that 'Mad Eyed Screamer' demonstrated this more than any other song, when Siouxsie found a freedom, and a different voice, both in vocal and lyrical style. 'Mad Eyed Screamer' was about the crazies at Speaker's Corner. A strange and dark lyric but also full of humour: 'His balls are freezing in the breeze'. Bom bom bom!

We were overwhelmed by how easy it was. 'Thumb', the last track on the EP, happened incredibly quickly in the studio, and the whole thing was recorded and mixed in that one weekend. The creative connection and the speed with which it had all happened made us realise that there might be the possibility of more between us. We had created something very personal and professional, yet also almost sacrosanct and we could no longer deny we had a chemistry outside of the Banshees. And, of course, it had the added bonus of carving out some time for us that was ours alone. It perhaps appealed to Siouxsie's sense of disdain for everything *normal*. Her natural inclination was to disregard such conventions: on record companies, she was known to exclaim, 'I wouldn't piss on them if they were on fire!' Siouxsie would usually announce this live onstage, especially if company reps were in attendance. She always preferred to do what was most contradictory in terms of business, from the way we wrote the songs to having an alternative project outside of the main band, still centred around her unique yet contrarian position. Iconic, aloof, playful and enigmatic.

After *Juju* was released, we spent the early summer of 1981 on the road, often including two Creatures songs as part of the Banshees setlist. Our attraction was getting stronger but it probably wasn't evident enough to arouse curiosity. Our gig at Liverpool's Royal Court on the August leg of the tour was cancelled because the venue had been damaged by flooding. With the night off, I grabbed an early bite to eat then left the hotel and walked towards Mathew Street, in the direction of some old memories. I remembered the bust of Carl Jung, below a sign proclaiming 'The Liverpool School of Language, Music, Dream and Pun'. It's all gone now, no Probe Records, no Armadillo tearoom. I heard more recently that the name Budgie appears on a brick among many bricks bearing names of musicians and bands who performed in Mathew Street. So, is it my name or is it the heavy rock trio from Wales again? It could be mine, but it's probably theirs.

Humming the riff of 'Guts', I ended up by the Pier Head with the Royal Liver Building silhouetted against a dramatic Turner sunset. All the crimson-yellow hues of a drunken docker's bruise. 'A big fuckin' glow' was the description I scribbled on a student sketch I drew here in 1976. 'Written with freezin' fuckin' fingers in a freezin' fuckin' Norwester'. (Dr John Cooper Clarke and I were obviously separated at birth.) In a hotel room not ten miles from where, as a small boy, I had laid my face on the smooth stone pavement, I had a fitful sleep dreaming of the River Mersey bursting its banks, St Helens flooded with only Beechams Clock Tower visible and a liver bird perched on top.

Leaving the Irish Sea behind, we took the trans-Pennine motorway to Newcastle. It was an unusual schedule that day. An early afternoon concert for local children organised by MENCAP and the Paralympics. The venue was the large function room of a city centre hotel, usually reserved for wedding receptions. In keeping with the spirit of weddings and children, we opted for a one-off setlist of the band's singles, from 'Hong Kong Garden' onwards, with no dark, disturbing album tracks. The concert was a first for most of the children so it was gloves-off time. So much energy was unleashed, the kids running around the dancefloor, some whizzing superfast in their wheelchairs. I remember one cheeky, hyperactive little boy at the front of the stage, gyrating and trying to put his hand up Siouxsie's dress. All very innocent, but the atmosphere was charged and stimulating. By mid-afternoon it was all over, but the switch had been thrown, the feelings and that post-gig void had to be filled. We hit the bar, and one thing led to another.

Siouxsie and I would often telephone each other from hotel

room to hotel room, and on the *Juju* tour she would call me in my room and, if it was quiet, I'd pop round to hers. We would usually sit having a drink, enjoying each other's company, but that night there was an unspoken suggestion to let things go further. Siouxsie was wearing a black flamenco dress, and she allowed me to lie with her. *Allowed* is such a loaded word, but that's what it felt like, from when I was first allowed to contribute to the Banshees, then allowed into her hotel room, and allowed into her bed. I was the one for whom she'd let her guard down, while everyone else was kept at arm's length.

There was no semblance of morning-after regret, when one more drink tipped the scales, after everything repressed was liberated. Was it a consummation of a desire? Or just a brief taste? It wasn't like we ran downstairs into the hotel lobby shouting, 'Hey, everybody! What you suspected is true. Our secret's out and we just want to let you know. Sorry if it's all a bit weird, but we're caught in the throes.' Which would probably have elicited a response of, 'Yeah, okay. See how long you last.' But there was nothing like that. It was never spoken, but it became obvious when we were back in Newcastle for a Banshees gig later that August.

In the same hotel as that first fateful night, we had arranged a photoshoot for the cover of the first Creatures record. The resulting pictures later became notorious for capturing what was obviously going on between us. It certainly wasn't me who suggested that we get hot and wet in the hotel shower. That would have been Adrian Boot, who was a good few years older and a very experienced photographer. I still wonder if he could believe his luck when Siouxsie and I put ourselves in a compromising setting, doing more than we had perhaps really intended. He might even have read the chemistry and wanted to bring that into the artwork, or maybe there wasn't anywhere more exciting to shoot a photo in a hotel in Newcastle than in a steamy bathroom with the temperature rising. The Creatures, near-naked in a shower.

I have always suspected a connection between this image and Robert's opening line from 'The Hanging Garden', 'Creatures kissing in the rain', which surfaced a year later in 1982. Was Robert in some way infatuated with Siouxsie? His image changed radically after being so 'close to Sioux'. Somewhere between the white 'London' jacket, the black Ray-Ban Wayfarer shades of the Glove, and the backcombed, crimped Siouxsie hair and red slash lipstick, Robert had morphed into a strange amalgamation of Siouxsie and Severin. I could posit another lyrical reference to Robert's fascination with Siouxsie. The opening line to 'Just Like Heaven', 'Show me . . . how you do that trick'. I remember during the *Hyæna* sessions, hearing Siouxsie scream with delight when Robert made a strange sound with his tongue and lips. It tickled her almost as much as Robert creating 'Love Cats' - a nod to one of Siouxsie's favourite Disney cartoons, *The Aristocats* - with a video containing her constant and ultimate dream of fondling tiny kittens. I could be stretching it, but I don't believe I'm *that* far off. It was a highly formative and career-changing time for Robert, and the air was thick with passion and plunder.

When the shower shoot started it was intimate but careful. We had to get through the tentative stages: 'How close shall we be? Do I touch you? Do I hold you? If I hold you, am I holding you like an animal that wants to pull away, or am I holding you like an animal I care for, one that doesn't mind?' Of course there was alcohol involved, and gradually more of our baser instincts began to surface. It was fun and playful, and we were laughing. The role-playing switches between each shot as it gets wetter, literally as well as metaphorically. I was wearing dance tights so it may have looked like I was naked, and Siouxsie wore a sheer camisole that, once wet, was virtually not there. I was aroused and thinking, *Do we kiss?* We got within millimetres, almost sharing a breath. It oscillated between playful and intense, silly, arty and sexual - and as soon as it got closer to sexual, it quickly shifted back to silly.

This was where the play-acting came in. We *were* laughing a lot because it was quite ridiculous, slipping around in a bathtub with a shower curtain, a shower pipe in Siouxsie's hand and another one growing in my tights. But it was inevitable that we would want to go further. The very nature of the photoshoot, even with an underlying feeling of trust, could have resulted in regret afterwards.

We'd revealed so much, yet the photos were never just a proclamation. We could always hide behind the fact that we'd had a few drinks and were trying to achieve a look inspired by Man Ray, who was a huge influence on Siouxsie, how she perceived herself and how she wanted others to perceive her. There were two models Man Ray often photographed together. They were close friends, Lee Miller and Anouk Aimée. One image of them shows a quiet moment, both in soft angora sweaters, looking askance. It's such a beautiful, intimate picture, it almost feels like an intrusion to be looking at it. That's what we were aiming for, that same defiance. We could have hired professionals to take our place, but it would have had less impact. Maybe that's why actors in intimate roles often think they've fallen in love. Maybe it's difficult to act being in love many, many times. Maybe it's hard to risk the possibility of falling in love, giving yourself to somebody in that way, only to have to leave when the job is done.

I wonder who I was pretending to be in those photos. Peter would never have been able to do those photos, he'd have been too embarrassed. Yet I can also look at those photographs and see them as purely intimate. Maybe I don't even see myself. I can see what we were hiding, and how the images that went on the cover of the *Wild Things* EP were not as intimate as those marked with a red pencil, ones that were far more revealing, literally and emotionally. There is a vulnerability in how we kept those feelings of intimacy concealed, like in the early days of a love affair. There are photos from the shoot that are very funny and silly. All aspects of a relationship were present that afternoon in Newcastle: aggression, passion, love, humour, silliness, clumsiness.

Along with the fun and the frolics, we were also focused on the technical quality of the finished image. Though colour film was used for quality, the finished images were always planned to be printed in black and white; the colour images that appeared in an Australian magazine were used without permission. Our goal was an amalgamation of the silver gelatin prints of Angus McBean and the *Solarisations* of Man Ray. This was not tabloid titillation; it was an homage to the photographs of the artists we admired.

But the art of it did not sit well with Siouxsie's manager. Nils took it as the undoing of the collective band name, the insistence of all billing being as Siouxsie and the Banshees, not *Siouxsie* with the Banshees. One name, equal focus. And though the principle was admirable, the reality was that it had always been too much for Siouxsie to do everything. McGeoch and I would take care of the drums and guitar magazines, and there was always an exception made for Siouxsie and Severin, the founder members, to do interviews together, with photos to accompany them. But with the Creatures, everything changed. Joint interviews, front-page photoshoots, joint TV appearances. Suddenly, despite all objections, it was Siouxsie and Budgie, but not as part of the Banshees.

Nils, and perhaps the record label, had never promoted Siouxsie as a solo artist. Siouxsie had not wanted this, and Severin would not have stood for it either. But here she was, Siouxsie the icon, playing a very feminine role in a duo with me, her drummer. In truth, his professional reaction to the photographs was perhaps more a smokescreen for Nils's true feelings - enraged and extremely upset. He guarded her jealously and was maybe still holding a candle for her. She had already moved on from Severin and then Nils as boyfriends, and now *I* was the catalyst for pushing further away from any lingering vestiges of those early influences and their male dynamic. The photographs said it all: the chemistry was strong, we were more than just fond of each other. I couldn't hold back the fact that I desired Siouxsie and just wanted to be with her.

I've since thought of the Creatures as a threat to the security of the main project, but at the time Siouxsie and I had no thought or fear of it. We felt very secure within the Banshees and what we were doing felt like a new band. We were so confident. Before anyone had time to think, or perhaps reconsider, the photos were out in public. The vinyl was pressed, and come October, six short months later, we were on *Top of the Pops* performing 'Mad Eyed Screamer'.

Siouxsie was way more up front sexually and sensually with the Creatures. There was a lot of press, including the front covers of *Sounds* and *Smash Hits*. We were suddenly a public couple, cited as the 'Richard and Judy' of punk. During an interview, a journalist asked Siouxsie if we were in a relationship. 'We're in love!' she sighed, followed by an immediate dilution of that proclamation, in a voice like a little girl introducing her teddy bears. 'And I'm in love with Steve, and I'm in love with John . . .' to which I felt obliged to add, 'And I'm in love with them all.' Siouxsie concluded her answer in a matter-of-fact voice: 'No, seriously, we're just good friends.' It was very much Siouxsie's way: in short, denial. It was hard to know if it was said purely for business reasons, or if it was to keep me in my place. It was how we were when out together, in denial, maintaining it was all just high jinks.

But I *did* gain a privilege. I was now *allowed* – there it is again – to use the band's taxi account. And taxis became a ridiculous part of the game. During the recording of *A Kiss in the Dreamhouse*, our affair reached ridiculous routines of subterfuge. Before leaving the studio, Siouxsie would give me a surreptitious signal if my company was expected later. All taxis were hired on account, pick up and destinations logged. Suspicions would be raised if I booked a car from the studio and it ended up at Siouxsie's address after midnight. So, a cunning and devious plan was hatched.

I would order a cab, picking up from Playground Studio, destination: my flat in Wandsworth. Mid-journey I would redirect, 'Oh, sorry, mate, I've got to stop here. You just go on, thanks!' and then wait and hail another cab. Not on account, not traceable from the monthly invoice. The cabs were booked to take me home, but I never got there. I was allowed to be with Siouxsie, but only in secret. I presume we were still protecting the innocent from our entanglement. To add complete disclosure to this nocturnal farce, I must add that Siouxsie and Severin lived at the same address, she on the first floor and he in the flat above. Like Dracula, I had to leave the scene of the crime before sunrise. I also had to get out without being seen or heard. The staircase was too risky, doors opening and closing, thin walls, footsteps on creaky floorboards, and the chance that Severin might be an insomniac staircase-watcher. As a boy I never had a front door key, but if no one was home, a bedroom window would be left slightly open, with just enough gap for small fingers to slip through, ease open the window and climb in. I reversed the vaguely remembered routine, dropping down to the dividing wall just a few feet below, and in my still trembling, sexed-out, post-trip, pre-hangover state – with a rising vertigo that usually only comes when looking up – I would be on my way. Of course, it's one thing climbing in through an upstairs window as a ten-year-old; it's an entirely different prospect climbing out of one when you're twenty-five and a little tired and emotional. Adding to the difficulty of my planned descent was a complete lack of knowledge of vital foot-holds and finger jams next to the pipework and washing lines on the north face of 34 Croxley Road. On my first descent, I made it gingerly down to the top of the wall only to find it a crumbling crescent of moss-covered brick. I summoned the spirit of French highwire artist Philippe Petit, slipped silently along its length and dropped down into the back entry without mishap or discovery.

The traffic lights changing through a timed sequence for another empty night bus added some colour to the empty grey streets. And with the sound of the dawn chorus still a few hours away, I would walk slowly and silently home. In those eerie early mornings, I slipped into an altered state of relaxed exhaustion, my body on autopilot but my mind awake. The night's ordeal and the escape sobered me up. The last vestiges of stimulants had been flushed from my system. I was a temple of purity in tune with the universe, trudging the streets of West London. It was a five-mile walk home to Byam Street, SW6, about two hours. Perhaps walking home was my penance for my errant ways. Perhaps part penance for who I'd become, part remembrance for who I once was. I walked to remember; I walked to forget.

Mostly, I remembered the walk from Morley Street to Pimbo Road, Kings Moss, back in St Helens. It was about four miles, over steep hills and low-lying farmland, and my dad and I walked to Grandma's house there every Sunday. I have many fond memories of those walks. My dad and I walked for comfort, and for company. Standing at the centre of a stone bridge, one foot in St Helens, the other in Billinge. Collecting chickweed for the budgies. A pint for him in the Colliers Arms, a dandelion and burdock for me, to feel grown up. Together we were forging new happy memories, while silently sharing an inability to understand our mutual loss, of his love, his wife, our world, and my mum.

11.
Cherries & TCP

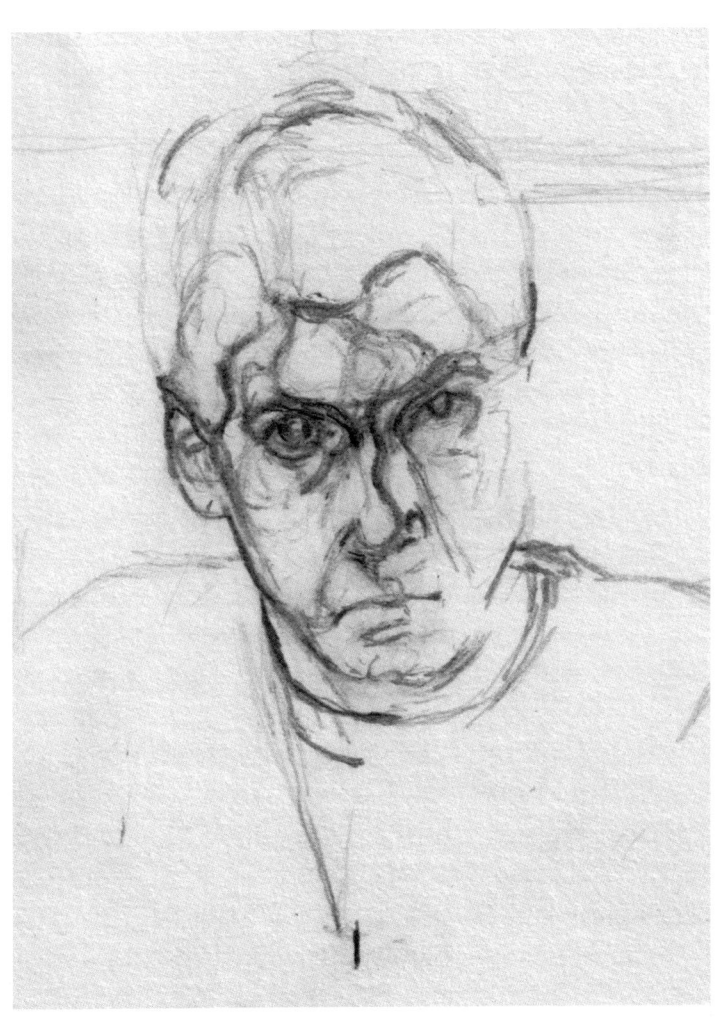

It was 31 October 1981. New York City was celebrating Hallowe'en. Fire trailer rigs, with sirens screaming, through red-light intersections. Firefighters in costumes with feathers on their helmets, a Wild West backdrop to the ghouls on the streets. We'd been on the road since February touring our Hallowe'en opus *Juju*. We'd be home by Christmas, but that night another surreal 'Lullaby of Broadway' was in the making. I had been on many tours, and even though I was more than familiar with the routines, certain aspects of hotel etiquette were still problematic. I always felt unsure when the adjacent room had a *connecting door*. Should you lock it? Or is that rude? Does it mean you're uncool and don't want to hang out? Are you hiding something? It was a dilemma when it was one of the crew, or, God forbid, someone else in the band. If they took the decision and locked the connecting door that could be just as bad – what did *that* mean? That they didn't *like* you – or worse – they didn't *trust* you?

Maybe this dilemma was mine alone. Maybe it exposed my need to be both gregarious and private. The clown and the clam. Did it expose an undeveloped sense of personal space? Maybe the sudden death of my mother erased all sense of security, so that nowhere ever felt safe, like home, ever again. It was hard for me, as Peter and even in the guise of Budgie, to find a place where I felt settled. That connecting door represented a security breach, the absence of a safe space. That absence had become more acute on the *Juju* tour, as the feelings between Siouxsie and me began to unfold and escalate.

The band became separated from the grounding influence of the road crew; we began staying in separate, more luxurious hotels.

Checking in should have been a leisurely mid-afternoon affair for just the group and our tour manager, but I'd be hovering at the reception desk, listening out for Siouxsie's room number. We were not usually near each other, as quite often everyone was on different floors. Siouxsie might get special treatment – she never demanded a 'diva suite' – but the hotel manager would make sure that she was looked after, with something fancier than the rest of us. The tour manager always had the presidential suite, but the price to pay for that dubious luxury was no privacy, because that's where the after-show party would be. Then I'd get my key. What's my number? Are we on the same floor? And if we were, how far away, how many doors to sneak past? Where was the fire escape? My thoughts were focused on the possibility of clandestine meetings, without the risk of an unwelcome, awkward meeting late at night.

On the *Juju* tour, Siouxsie wore Indian dancers' ankle bells on her wrists. They always travelled in her suitcase. And as her suitcase was trundled along the hotel corridors, the bells would ring. From the quiet of my room, I would listen out for them, a muffled but distinct *ching, ching, ching*, and from the volume and direction of the bells, I could gauge how far away my quarry lay.

I was on eggshells the entire time. The urge to be close superseded all notions of what was correct, even the need to go to bed and get some sleep. Architecture also played a part in making the whole experience more surreal and bizarre. We spent many nights at the Gramercy Park Hotel in Manhattan. Built in 1883 as a modest ten-storey apartment building, it was at that time double the height of its townhouse neighbours. New York had since expanded in a boom of buildings for wealthy bachelors and entrepreneurs who needed space for entertaining and rooms for their valets and butlers. The Gramercy's huge apartments filled the entirety of each floor, connected by lifts and staircases for the maids and staff. This quirk of social history and apartment-building design meant that there still existed many connecting stairwells between the original floors and mezzanines. Fast-forward a hundred years, and a few Manhattan cocktails after midnight, Siouxsie and I would leave the party for our respective rooms, hers on the tenth floor, mine on the third. Somebody would ride the elevator to the same floor with Siouxsie, and I'd get off at the third floor.

'Goodnight.'

Quick phone call: 'Shall I come round?'

'Yeah, but don't use the lift.'

I was never allowed to use the lift in case I ran into somebody. I'd have to find the nearest service staircase or fire escape and race up more than half the height of the building. These were high-ceilinged apartments with two or three long flights of stairs between each floor. This was way beyond the call of duty, but it certainly kept me fit, although I never really thought about that as I ran up flight after flight of stairs. It was automatic. I never questioned the summons, or whether it was expected of me. It seemed straight out of a movie, and squarely in my role as Budgie I felt smart and sneaky; the fact that nobody knew was all part of the fun. But it was also exhausting.

It was often my choice not to stay until morning, which per-haps revealed a lot about *me*. It was good for me to receive an occasional rebuke from John about my drinking. Severin said as much later one night at the King's Head pub in London, 'Why do you have to drink to just be normal?' And later still, 'You know she loves you, don't mess it up.' Hearing that put the onus completely on me, both as a lover and as a member of the band.

It also felt like a warning; there was no discussion.

But then, I was terribly jealous of how Siouxsie was able to show affection for the crew in a way that I never received myself. These guys were extremely good-looking, shirts off all day, bronzed and sculpted, scars and tattoos, whereas I was white and skinny, with no tattoos. She liked drinking with the crew, and they loved it when she stayed up partying with them. She could easily become '*slugger* Siouxsie', just one of the lads. Maybe I was being too judgemental, or perhaps too distant. The crew were like brothers to her, they entertained and protected her. I had to go along with it, but my mind played tricks - imagining she was having more fun, too much fun without me. This was worse when my self-esteem was low. Just one of *many* reasons why I got drunk.

From the start of our strange relationship this power imbalance got in the way. Siouxsie could click her fingers and what she said went. She was uncommunicative in the morning and nobody could do anything - after all, she could not be left behind. In autumn 1981, on tour in the USA, our driver was a quiet type from Texas, known by his CB call sign WC. British toilet humour was not lost on WC. Long night drives would be punctuated by truck stops, to pick up fuel and cigarettes, and to use the bathroom. Arriving in town in the early mornings, we'd park up outside the venue and take a dayroom at a nearby motel, a place to rest and shower during the day. We didn't always jump out of bed the moment the engine stopped. After the constant manoeuvring and heavy gear changes of WC's old tour bus, the sudden quiet was a welcome relief and perfect for a little extra snooze.

This morning our nap was interrupted by our tour manager Tony shouting, 'Has anyone seen Siouxsie?'

Her bunk was empty. WC was still in his seat.

'Hey, WC, you seen Siouxsie this morning?'

WC said, 'Sure did - right after we pulled in - 'cept she didn't look so happy, ah figured she needed the bathroom.'

'Did she go to the motel?' Tony sounded worried.

'Nope, she went off towards downtown.'

It was 10am. We split up and searched the nearby streets, shops, diners, cafés and even the early-bird bars. And that's where we found her - in a bar, hanging out with the locals. (Siouxsie on this tour would often prefer local bars and on this occasion was 'determined to get fuelled up and beat the shit out of someone'.) We helped her to the motel room and made coffee, like they do in the films, and walked her round the room. We kept her moving, like she'd overdosed. McGeoch took the lead: 'Come on, Siouxsie, take a sip, we've got a gig tonight.' She struggled weakly, protested a little, then lay down on the bed to sleep it off.

We were coming to the end of a gruelling six months of constant touring. The UK, Europe, and now North America. The last run of shows began in Vancouver and had taken us to New York via New Orleans. We then played Toronto and, en route to Chicago, we stopped just west of Detroit for a gig in Ann Arbor, Michigan. Eighteen shows in twenty-six days, and a drive of over five thousand miles. It was no wonder Siouxsie hit the bar for breakfast; we would all have probably joined her had we known. But that was it. That need to get out. Not just to 'get out of it', but to get rid of everything, and everyone, especially the all-male company. It was the first time I'd witnessed this unrest in her.

It was showtime at the Second Chance club on East Liberty. The microphone stand was downstage centre. Siouxsie was seated on the front of my drum riser. McGeoch broke the ice with the shattering intro to 'Halloween', Severin set the tempo, and when the beat kicked in, Siouxsie got up, took two steps, and swung her hand cartoon-like, at nothing. We all shared the same thought, *Oh fuck, this is not good.* John and Steve powered on through the opening sequence - then Siouxsie grabbed the mic, bull's eye, the adrenaline kicked in, and there she was. We were a better band than we knew and could adjust quickly to any adversity. Siouxsie rarely drank before going onstage, but we had to be good at quickly changing tack mid-song to accommodate an attack of brain fog. McGeoch, Severin and I would meet at the hotel bar for a quick shot before leaving for the gig - Siouxsie was always last-minute and straight onto the bus, make-up perfect, sucking on a Strepsil throat lozenge. The danger point was if Siouxsie felt frisky, especially in interviews; she would throw down the 'drink-challenge gauntlet' at any time of day, particularly with female journalists. 'Let's have a drink. What shall we have? We're in Sweden, vodka shots.' Neat vodka - and all bets were off. The journalists loved it.

All this meant that as the *Juju* tour went on, I was having to play different roles. On the one hand, I was still the new guy, joining the old established relationships between Siouxsie, Nils, Severin, sound guys, security and crew. Then there was me as the new guy in another role: Siouxsie and I as musicians, writing together as the Creatures, outside of the Banshees. Then there was my secret role, the relationship we were guarding and the responsibility to keep it quiet. This should have meant equality, stability and a level of influence, but my insecurities ran deep and to presume any power would have been viewed with almost mutinous contempt. It was a strange, passive position to be in.

This feeling of impotent power gave me more reason to focus on the power of the Creatures, on my drums and Siouxsie's voice. We quickly became inseparable - intimately symbiotic, she became like mistletoe on my tree. Mistletoe doesn't kill the tree, but it weakens it, makes it vulnerable, and ultimately competes for resources. Siouxsie as parasite, me as willing host?

I felt excluded from the camaraderie of the band and people became suspicious of me; it was as if I was Siouxsie's eavesdropping elemental. This, of course, pushed me closer to her, where I had - I realise now - the additional role of alleviating some of the stress she was under. I could do things for her, so she didn't have to ask a stranger or someone to whom she didn't want to reveal how she was feeling. But Siouxsie didn't confide in me. There was never that emotional connection that comes with true confidence in another, especially a lover. She never once asked, 'Budgie, can you come see me? I just need to talk to somebody. I've got a situation and I really don't know what to do.' This is a conversation I might have had with others, but never with Siouxsie. I wish we *could* have shared in that way; it might have changed so much. Those moments of sharing are perhaps what make best friends out of lovers, someone to trust and be trusted by someone, who cares and is cared for. It's said that the post-coital cigarette is the real offender in the extra-marital affair because it goes with the conversation afterwards. It consolidates the intimacy.

Those stolen moments; shorter than a mayfly's breath.

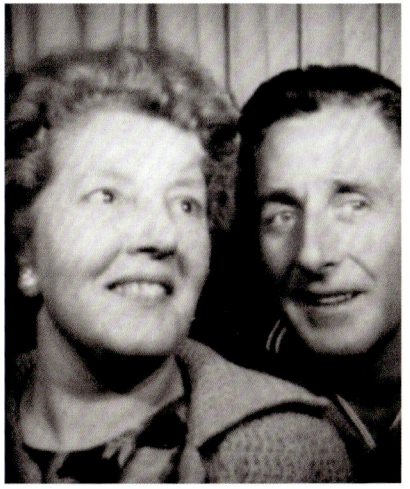

Mum and Dad

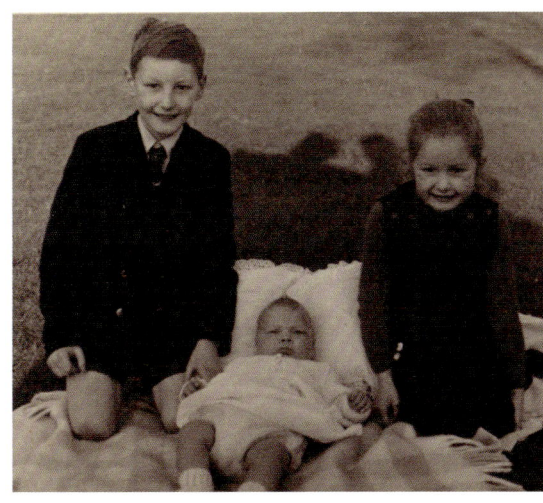

Michael, Linda, me and Mum and Dad shadows

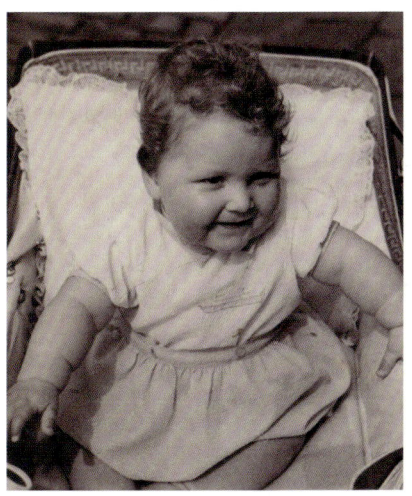

Isn't she lovely?

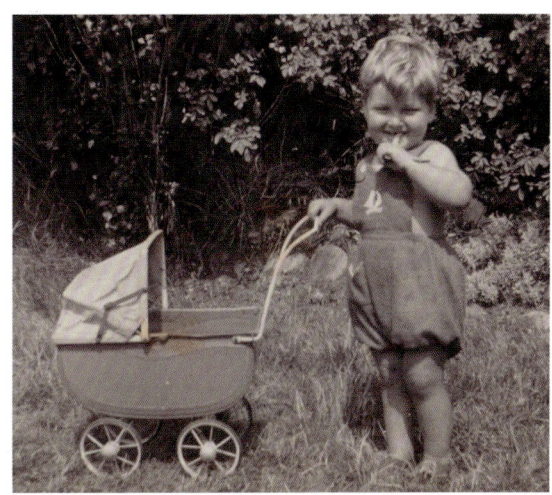

Peter and Pram

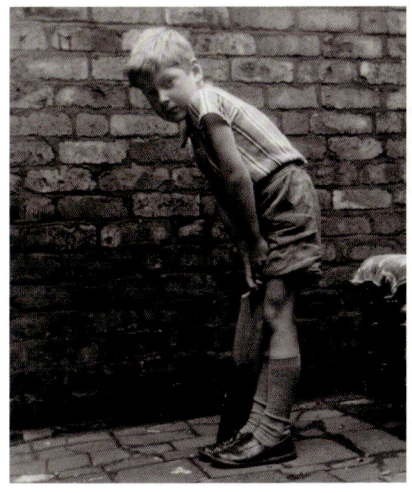

Peter the Cricketer

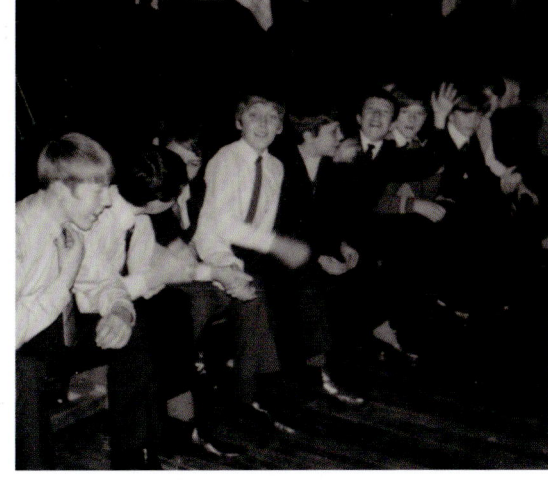

St Alban's school dance, 1970

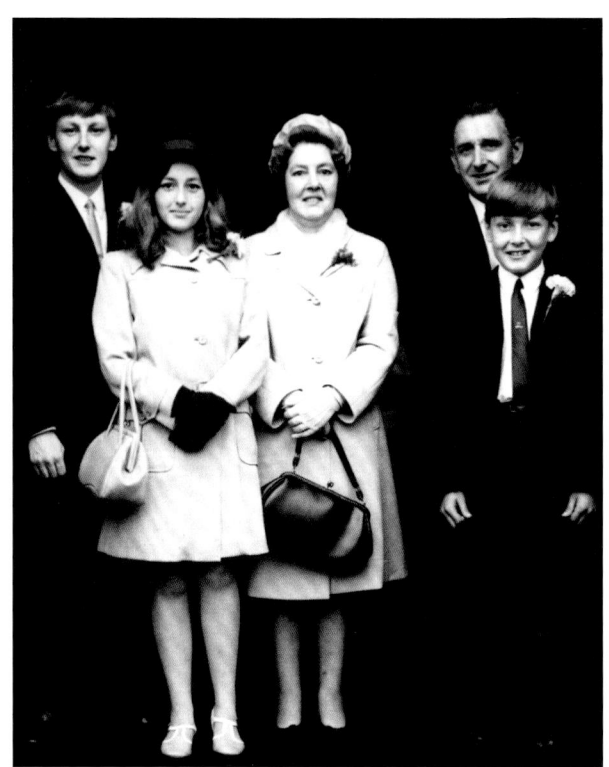

1 July 1968

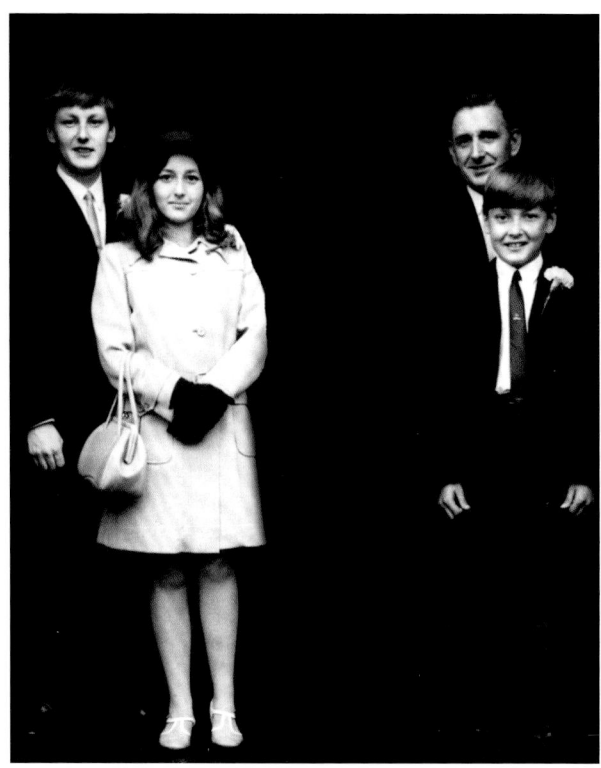

Ethel Clarke (21 May 1924-13 April 1970, age 45)

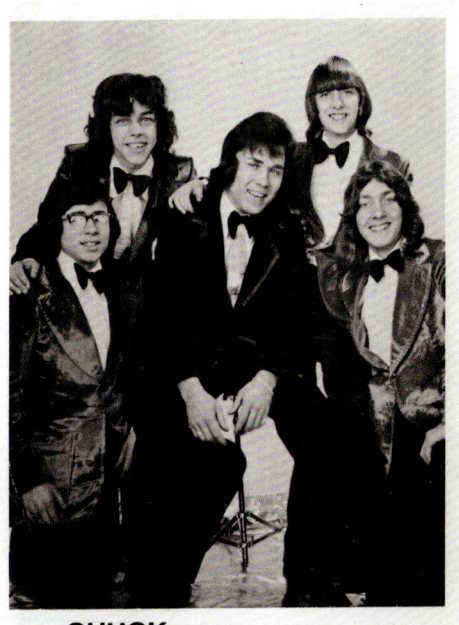

Salvatore, Colin, Chuck, John, Peter,
1971

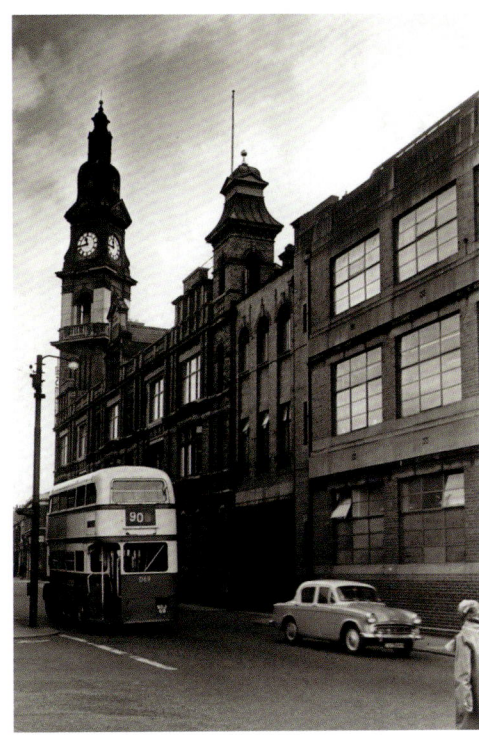

Beecham's Clock Tower

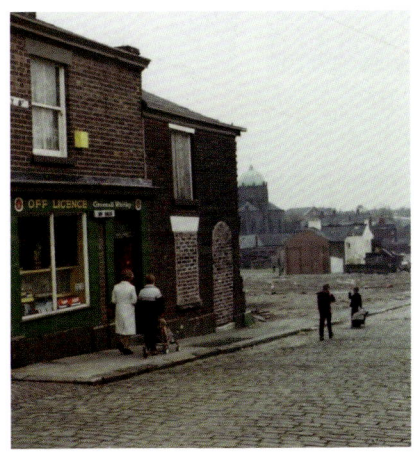

The off-licence on Morley Street,
and Lowe House church

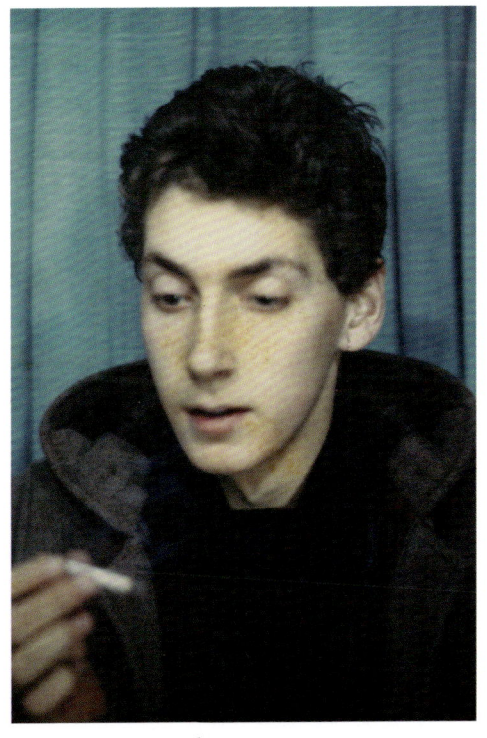

Liverpool Lime Street, 1976

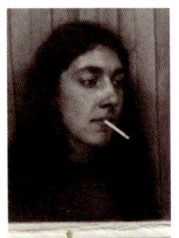
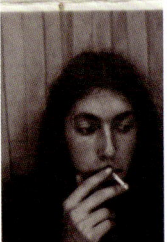
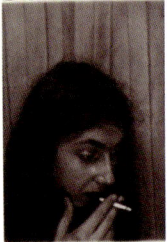
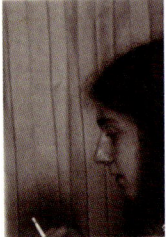
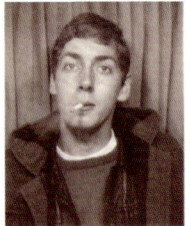
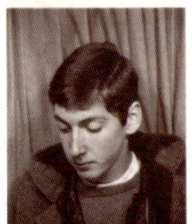
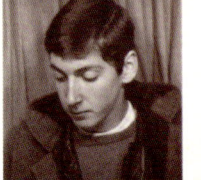
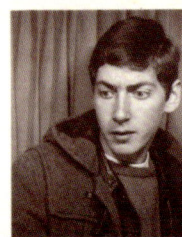

Liverpool Lime Street, 1975

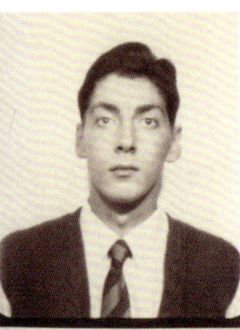
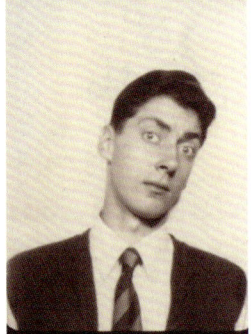
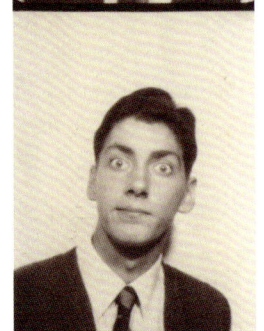

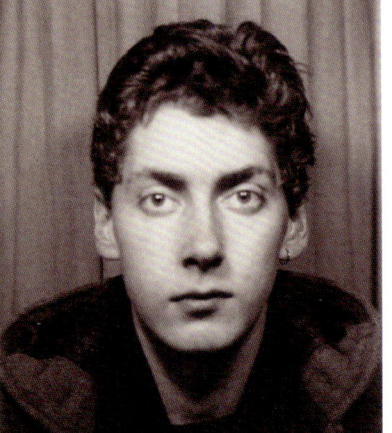

Liverpool,
November 1975

Liverpool Lime Street,
December 1976

Liverpool,
October 1977

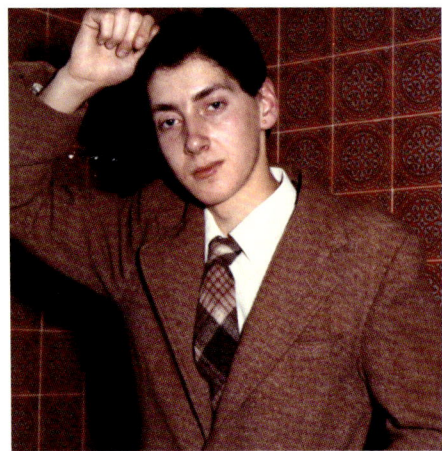

Harris Tweed, Pips, Manchester,
October 1977

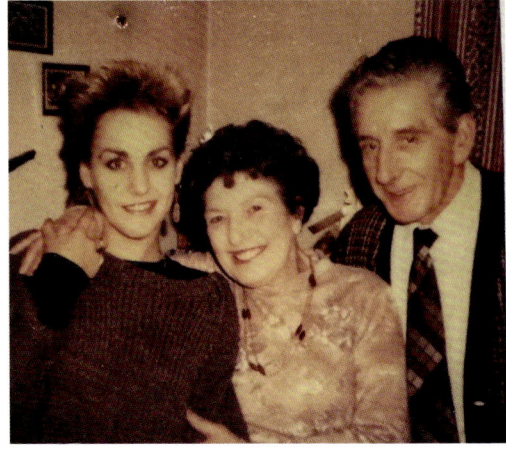

Jeanette, Elsie and Dad, St Helens,
1978

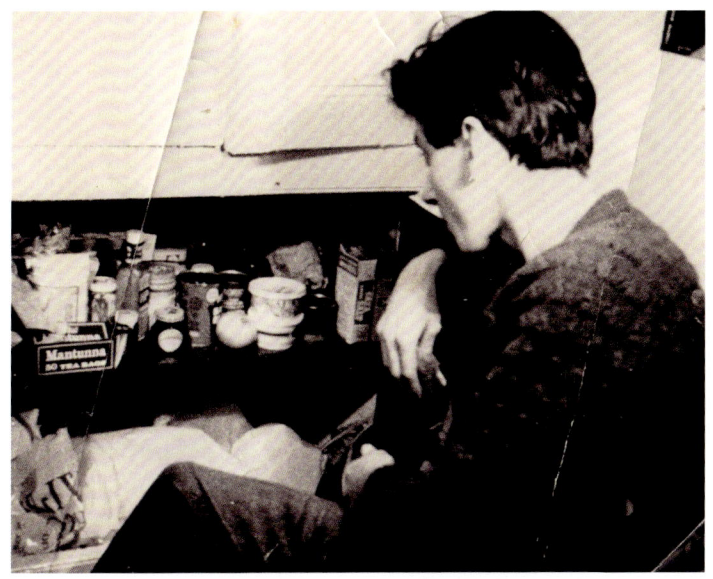

The Green Cardigan, Ampthill Rd, Liverpool, 1977

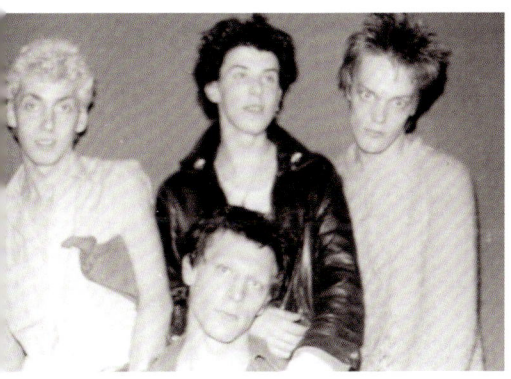

Spitfire Boys, 1977 - Budgie, Griff, Paul and Dave

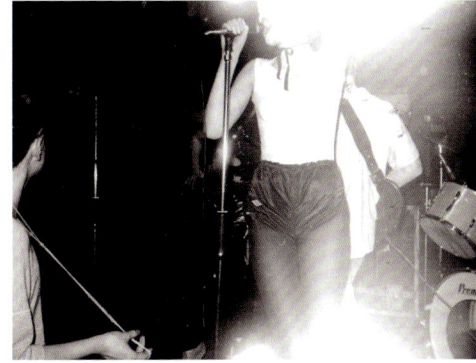

Siouxsie and the Banshees - Eric's, 1977 (with Holly Johnson and string)

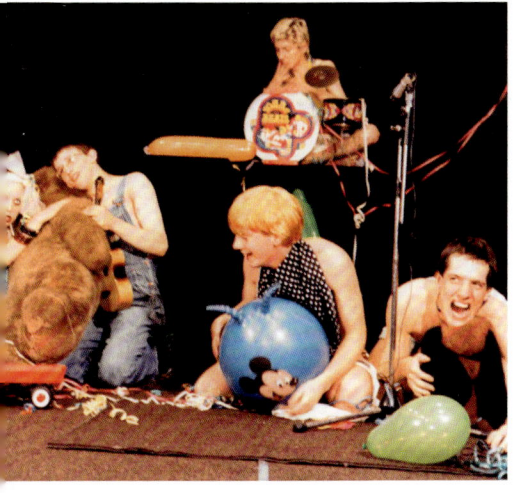

Big In Japan, 1978 - Jayne, Ian, Dave, Bill

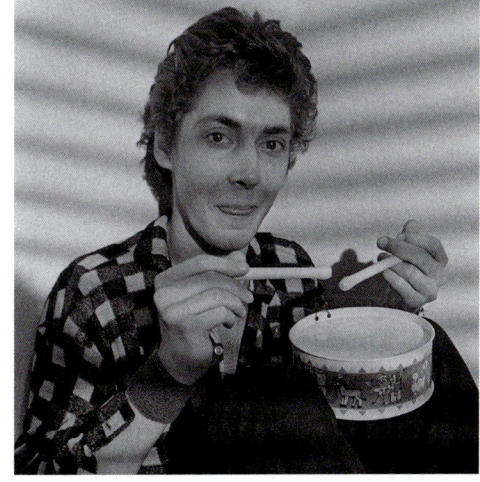

Happy House - video - London, 1979

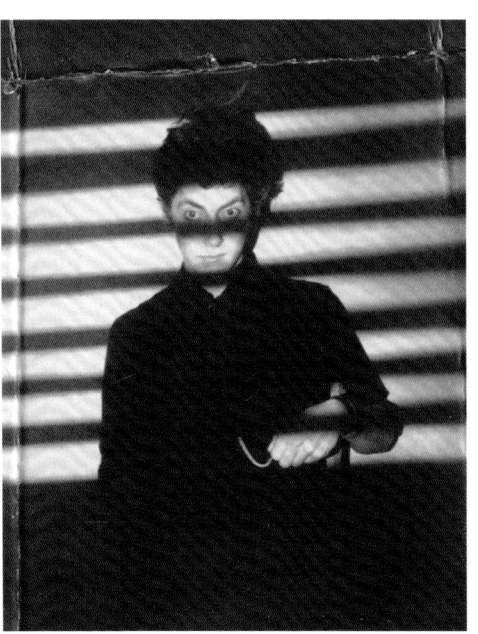

Kaleidoscope - London, 1979

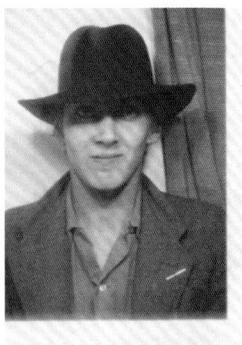
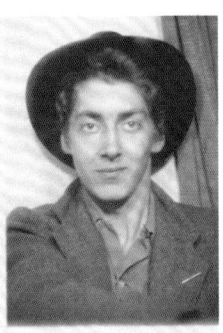
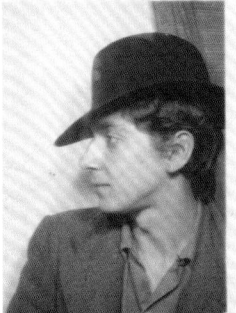
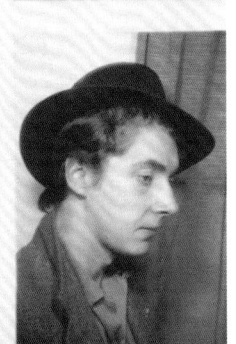

Earls Court Tube station, London,
8.30pm, 30 November 1979

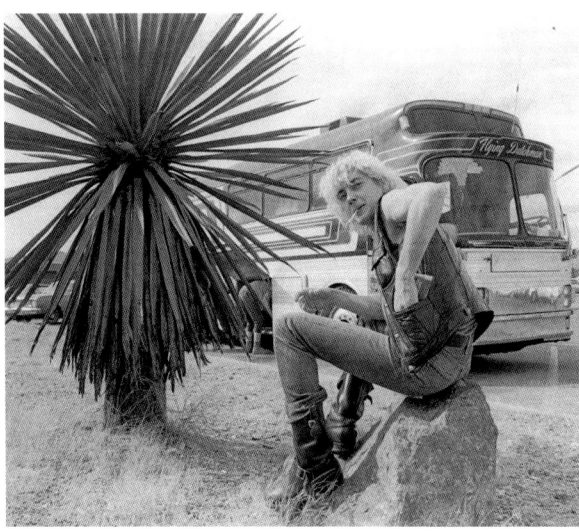

Yucca, me and The Flying Dutchman - USA, 1980

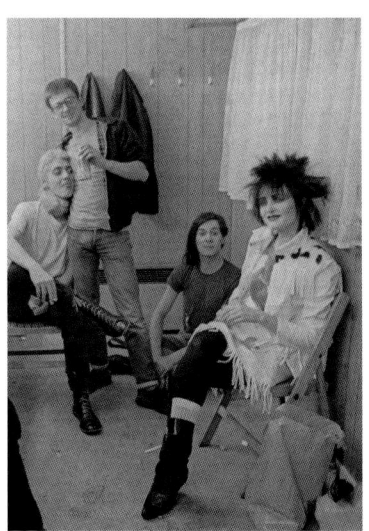

Nils Stevenson, Phil Oakey,
Siouxsie - London, 1980

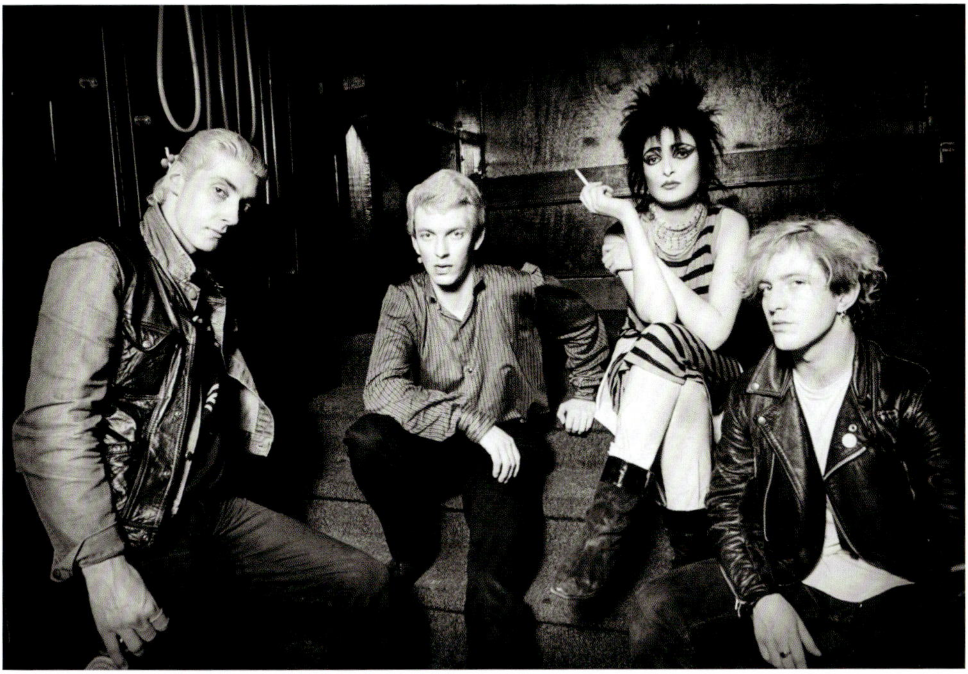

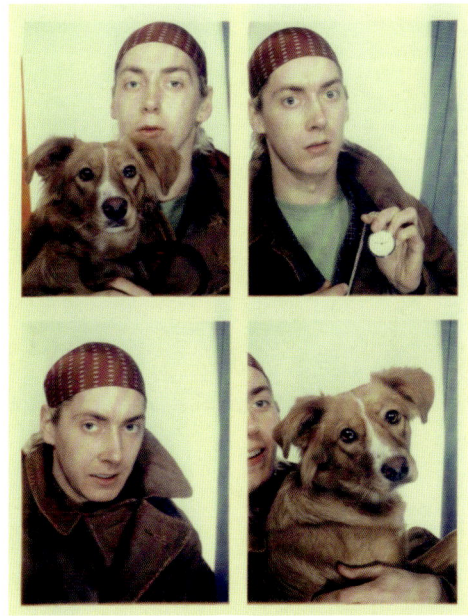

Siouxsie and the Banshees, Boston, MA, 1980 - the eyes have it!

Earls Court Tube station, 5 June 1981

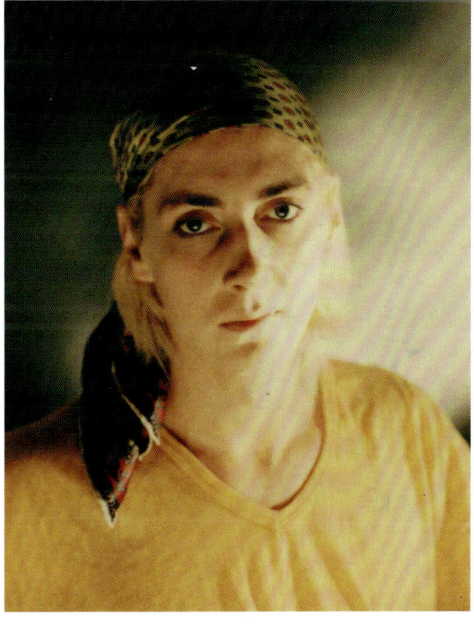

Juju, London, 1981

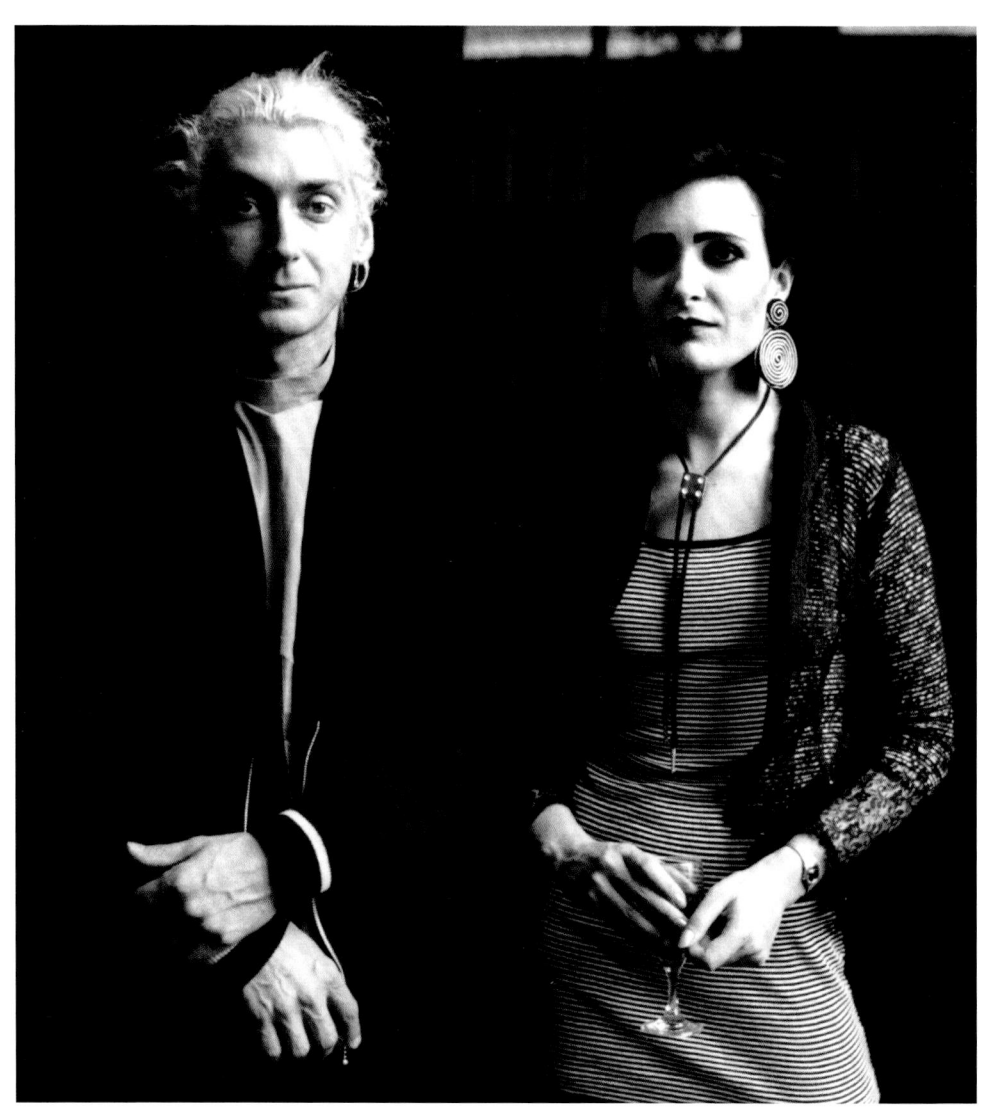

Que sera, sera . . .

We rarely had those moments. We drank, we had sex, she fell asleep. Before the room-service breakfast-request forms had been collected, I was back in the service stairway, asking myself, 'Is it up or down to my floor?' My suitcase would be lying in my room where the bellboy had left it, towels still neatly folded at the bottom of the oversized bed. Next to the pillow a 'goodnight mint' sat on a little card, its handwritten message promising fine weather tomorrow. The next morning it was always just business as usual. Any love, care or affection would be expressed solely in our music. Music is the most honest expression I have. I can't fake it behind the drums.

The start of the *Juju* tour, and the dislocated intensity at the beginning of this affair, are associated for me with the sounds and smells of New York City and especially those of the Gramercy Park Hotel. The leather of the barstools, the waxed wooden counter and the Brasso-polished foot rail produced a powerful sensory connection to Morley Street, and a world with my mum still in it. The pervading smell of beer and sawdust was as comforting in New York as it was when I was a three-year-old in St Helens, dancing on the bar countertop to the sounds of Motown playing on the jukebox. Siouxsie and I would spend hours chatting to the cocktail waiter, or whoever happened to drop within earshot as the conversation got louder and more animated. When we were staying at the Gramercy, their Manhattan cocktail was our preferred poison – always garnished with a glacé cherry on a cocktail stick. Just the fragrance whisked me back to memories of being a small boy in bed, not quite asleep, when after a night out at the pub, my parents would come to kiss me goodnight. I remember my dad's low soothing voice, and the faint aroma of cigarettes on his warm cherry-breath.

Good-time alcohol was advertised on TV in the 1960s. Drinks like Babycham, Cherry B and Pony (*'The little drink with the big kick!'*) promised parties, colourful celebrations and fun to brighten a grey world. I associated the warm liqueur-flavoured atmosphere of the Gramercy hotel bar with that affectionate goodnight kiss on my forehead, a subliminal feeling of comfort conjured up in the warm sweetness of bourbon, vermouth and a maraschino cherry. Then I floated off, into my own staircase mystery, feeling like the invisible man.

TCP is a liquid antiseptic with an odour synonymous with hospitals, cleanliness and healing. TCP diluted with water was what Siouxsie liked to gargle with, and as it wasn't available outside Britain, a large bottle of TCP was a required purchase at Boots the chemist when departing from London's Heathrow Airport. She used it to stave off the risk of a throat infection, although I imagine an ENT specialist would recommend something less aggressive.

I still associate TCP with her, almost as a favourite, familiar fragrance. Siouxsie was never one for perfume, it was all about the image and make-up. Intimacy with Siouxsie is, in my memory, an olfactory experience. Odours more reminiscent of artist's materials. The freshly sharpened lead of an eye pencil, the nutty oil of foundation, the dusty spice pigment of eye shadow, the waxy fragrance of lipstick, the sweet dry perfume of loose powder and a lingering bass note of TCP. For both of us, separated by only a few months in age and geographically by the length of England's M6 motorway, TCP and Dettol were the scents of our childhood, both far harsher in tone than the cherry sweetness of my parents' goodnight kisses. My mum used to put Dettol, another generic antiseptic, in the bathwater to keep us 'germ-free adolescents' - what was good for cleaning floors was good for cleaning us too. Although you couldn't gargle with Dettol - even diluted. Dettol smelled equal parts protective and lethal. An empty bottle of Dettol could be reactivated by adding water. It turned a cloudy white colour, and the same happened if you peed in it - trapping air in a facecloth bubble and peeing into an empty Dettol bottle, both favourite bath-night magic tricks of my little boy self.

These are the things of memories: Dettol, TCP and that smell that came out of the old coal scuttle under the stairs; old leather boots covered in a thin veil of mould, and the washing box with its hinged wooden lid that I used to hide inside.

Now, if I recall those smells, Dettol, TCP, the family wash basket, the cherries, it's like returning to those early days with Siouxsie and our oddly linked childhood memories of scents, and for me, back to Morley Street. I wasn't aware of this at the time on the *Juju* tour, because it was much too painful and I had hidden it all away. Thinking about it now, I feel sad that I went to such extremes to show a love and affection for Siouxsie that I couldn't commit to. I couldn't love anybody else entirely because I still hurt too much from the loss of my mum. It would be so easy to say that it was all Siouxsie's fault and her being unable to connect or to be present, but there was something deeper that I couldn't let go of. The unrequited love for my mum and her absence. I think I went looking for someone who couldn't love me back. I put up barriers against the world, with booze, art, music, and by becoming Budgie, to defend myself. In Siouxsie, I found someone coming from a similar place of absence, with the loss of her father, through both his death and, before that, to his alcoholism.

Siouxsie told me a poignant story of her dad reading her to sleep with Rudyard Kipling's *Just So Stories*. This was the hole that *she* could never fill. She loved him dearly, yet he infuriated and embarrassed her. She would say she hated him - or, as she would say in later interviews, that she hated his alcoholism. But what I realised later, working through my own alcoholism, is that alcohol and drugs just delay investigation. Being angry at alcoholism - 'It's the alcoholic I despise; not my father, not Budgie' - is well intentioned, but like a diseased tree, the problem lies hidden deep within its core; without treatment the disease will kill. That's the saddest part of the alcoholic's story.

With Siouxsie I found someone who had that same pain and had found the same way of trying to deal with it, both of us pouring booze into the hole that the death of a parent had made in our lives. We connected on a deeper level without realising it, like animals having an instinctive understanding in another's presence. I believe that seeing Siouxsie for the first time, sculpting that little figurine in copper wire and red wax, started a conversation, if only with myself. It was an act of awareness, a spontaneous rendition of feeling. I'd never experienced a need to acknowledge a moment of connection. It was as if that animal instinct had brought us together.

Sitting with my pint of IPA and Old Holborn roll-ups, I sensed our class and background differences being disregarded. I would soon be smoking the same cigarettes, drinking the same drinks. Our similarities ran as deep and as dark as the mines below St Helens and Chislehurst. We were as different as chalk and coal, but I instinctively knew that this was it. Still, I often felt that I was conceited and arrogant - that I manipulated and orchestrated the whole thing. That's a lot of power to take credit for. Who had really been the cat, and who had been the mouse? Would a calculating manipulator be running up and down the service staircases of the Gramercy Park Hotel in New York, following the scent of TCP and the sound of jingle bells?

12.

Eat the Sleeve – Find the Blotter

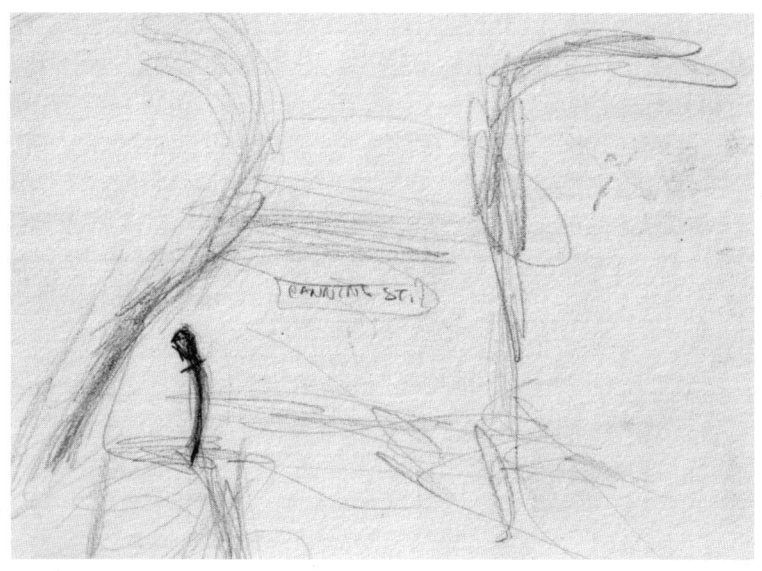

A Kiss in the Dreamhouse was a very apt title for what was to come next. Things were starting to get weird in the Banshees. 'Fireworks' was mostly written during soundcheck while we were touring *Juju*. It was a song for 5 November, or Bonfire Night, a British celebration dating back to the seventeenth century marking a failed Catholic plot to kill the king. Admittedly, it was limited in its global appeal, but we didn't care. My drum part was hatched from Neu!'s 'Hallogalo' and Klaus Dinger's motorik bass drum pattern. I wanted to play all the 8th notes in the bar - so adding weight to Dinger's unaccompanied snare beats on notes 3 and 7. Like bouncing a basketball close to the ground, keeping a constant tempo and weight, using your toes instead of your fingers! It posed a bit of a technical challenge; easier to pull off when you don't think about it too much. I mirrored these 'driving' bass drum notes with the ride cymbal, Severin swung a pendulum bassline and McGeoch played a nod of respect to Keith Levene and his guitar phrasing on PiL's debut single, 'Public Image'. When all these elements collided, the song probably had even less global appeal than Guy Fawkes and the Gunpowder Plot. The same went for the B-side of this non-album single, which required another technical challenge. On 'Coal Mind', I played a slightly lazy behind-the-beat shuffle on the snare. Siouxsie had some very dark lyrics and McGeoch created another signature 'riff' by detuning his low E string down to D, reminiscent of the Beatles' 'Helter Skelter', recreating that low buzz 'drone'. As was usual with songs predestined to be 'extra tracks', we worked quickly - freed perhaps from the traditional songwriting techniques of verse and chorus imposed on potentially 'radio-friendly' songs. We were down the Old Kent Road, at Manfred Mann's Workhouse Studio in

Southwark, south of the River Thames. This was unknown territory for me, but the evening takeaway gave me my first experience of traditional pie and mash with that lovely liquor sauce.

The day's recording completed, we left with a rough mix and headed north of the river to make a late-night call to RAK Studios in St John's Wood, where the Cure were recording music for the album that would become *Pornography*. We would often drop in on the Cure at work or at play. We were hoping to partake in some illicit substances, 'little pepper-uppers', but when we got there, the cupboard was bare. Still, it was nice to see Lol and Robert. Robert hardly lifted his head from the mixing console (he may have been deep in thought or simply sleeping) and Lol was having a quiet moment on the ubiquitous studio couch. There were, as always, an engineer and an assistant – like elves in a goldmine, checking the machinery, facilitating new ventures into unknown seams. Robert was in the deepest depths of the Cure, his personal sea of dreams. Their new music filled the room, like an iceberg, pushing mere oceans aside, informing every particle of how to behave in its presence. This was something immense, the weight of sound so intense. We left while we were still able to breathe.

The experimentation of 'Fireworks' was developed further when Mike Hedges came in as producer. This seemed like a logical step after his creative and inventive approach to recording the Creatures' *Wild Things* EP. He came in for a try-out, and we got on like a house on fire. Mike had organised a string quartet for an intro to 'Fireworks' and to play the song live in the studio with the band. String sections are usually an addition to the main track, and so recording together with four heavy cellos really changed the feel. It was an unconventional approach and a prelude to the way in which the *Dreamhouse* sessions would develop. Scratched into the vinyl run out of 'Fireworks' was the line 'Eat the Sleeve and Find the Blotter', a reference to a form of LSD on the London scene at the time. We half seriously wondered if anyone might find and follow those instructions. If so, might they have had a placebo-effect kind of trip?

Mike effectively became an additional member of the band, and with him at the controls the studio became *his* instrument. We had moved into Playground Studio in Camden Town where writing and recording sessions were aided and abetted by that unpredictable muse - heavy drinking. The studio was on the corner of Bayham Street and Camden Road, just a ten-minute walk down to Mornington Crescent tube station, surrounded by Greek restaurants. We used to meet for dinner, talk about plans for the evening, eat a little, drink a lot, and make sure we left with enough wine for the long day into the night session. Retsina quickly became the drink of the album. It was getting serious - the fridge was always full with bottles of this amber-coloured resinated wine, with an acquired taste not too dissimilar to that of TCP with a hint of Wright's Coal Tar Soap. Each bottle was labelled with a name, and a mark to show the level of consumption. The mark was never needed for mine as I never left a drop.

This was just the start of the chaos. We always mused on using LSD as a recording experiment. 'Wouldn't it be great if we got some California Sunshine, some Windowpane or Purple Haze?'

I'd dabbled with LSD a little when I'd just started at art school and had the house on Morley Street to myself for a couple of weeks. We'd go to the pub, get drunk, drop half a tab, and marvel at the imperceptible transition from being drunk to tripping. After a night of nonsense - a few devilish encounters, nothing too bad - came the comedown. I never quite knew where the trip ended and the hangover began.

We never did take acid while trying to record, although there was one session when we were all pretty far gone. Mike, evidently having some fun in the control room, sent a slowed-down version of the track to my headphones, then without my knowledge sped it up slightly, and slowed it back down again. I was trying to keep in time, thinking, *What's going on?* I'd get the instruction to do it again and hear laughing in the background as they opened the talkback switch. There's a tape of it somewhere, with my voice through an Eventide Harmonizer saying, 'What's going on?' and,

'Hey, it's not funny any more.' Because I'd never really learned to grow up, I found it a bit traumatic when I was under pressure, vulnerable or had had a few drinks, like a kid being teased who didn't understand. At the same time, I often feigned to find it all very funny.

The overriding feeling at the start of the *Dreamhouse* sessions was one of frenetic fun; the owner of the studio was having financial problems and expensive equipment was disappearing daily, piece by vital piece, the facilities being dismantled around our ears. The first thing we noticed was a large gap where the Dolby noise reduction units used to be. We liked noise so the Dolby wasn't missed. The studio was being repossessed, and Mike seemed determined to go down with the ship - the doors and windows would have gone too if he'd had his way. For 'Fireworks', we recorded hundreds of Chinese firecrackers exploding in the studio. If asked what a triangle sounds like underwater, Mike would put a microphone inside a Durex condom, plunge it into a bucket of water and press record. What happens if you set off a fire extinguisher against somebody's clothing? The fabric freezes and then falls to pieces, which is not advisable if the clothing is still being worn - which it always was. The drinking and late nights led to high (and low) jinks, and the occasional visits from 'the dealer' didn't help.

I had started getting incredibly powerful headaches, growing tensions in the back of my head that made me want to physically break something. I attacked the fridge with a hammer. I have no idea why, but it was a big fridge and I had a big hammer. I'm not a violent person, but one day I just flipped out on that fridge full of Retsina.

I went to visit my friend Sara's old family GP in Earl's Court to explain about these crippling migraines and how I'd never felt anything like this before. The doctor asked me how much I was drinking. 'Oh, a few glasses with a meal,' I lied. Then they asked me what I was drinking.

'Mostly white wine, Greek Retsina, Italian Frascati.'

'You could try switching to red wine.'

What a relief. Why hadn't I thought of that? In the waiting room I'd been looking at the wall charts showing the recommended daily intake in alcohol units. I was preparing to confess the whole truth about how much I was drinking, and all the drugs too, but no need. 'Try red wine,' they said. I skipped to the chemist for some migraine medicine thinking, *I've got it beaten, yes!* Then off to the 'outdoor' - the off licence - full of beans, thinking, *No more Frascati for me, I'm going for Beaujolais!* Pop some pink and blue migraine tablets for good measure.

Prior to the doctor's orders, I always tried to drink away my headaches and quite often it worked. I didn't want to lose the buzz, because I thought it helped me achieve a better performance. It meant that I'd be walking this terrible tightrope, trying to stay primed in case I was called upon to deliver. I never realised that it might not be the best idea for me to try and do that performance at 2am, when I'd been juggling my demons along with all their swords and knives.

'This might not be the best time, Budgie.'

Because it was him in those moments. Peter wasn't available for comment.

One night, before starting the recording session, I was opening a bottle of warm champagne. The cork popped suddenly, and champagne spumed all over the mixing console. We needed a new studio, and quick. Mike called an old friend at EMI's Abbey Road Studios, and the next day we relocated to the famous Studio 2. It turned out that my impatience to get stuck into the booze was a blessing in disguise; moving to Abbey Road gave us a much-needed change of scene, and a smarter postcode.

Siouxsie would take time off to think about lyrics while we were letting off fire extinguishers and drinking. She worked alone with Mike on the vocals, always open to trying out new ideas. It wasn't so much about getting a perfect vocal, but finding a perfect moment. Mike was a good interpreter and very encouraging to us. He had lots of his own ideas about what we could do with effects, and you can hear a lot of them on that album. There's a lot of invention that you might not hear on casual listening. For instance, on the track 'Cascade' the drums sound staccato in the verses, developing into a full kit sound for the choruses. They were not played this way; the effect was achieved by using a crescendo played on a ride cymbal as a switch to open an audio gate. As the cymbal swelled, the gate opened, allowing more of the recorded music track to become audible. The cymbal itself was also recorded and phased, an audio version of the magician's cape concealing the illusion. There was method in the apparent madness. It was a creative process that fully embraced the studio as an instrument.

It was also great fun. We often worked through the night, sometimes until eight o'clock in the morning. We would emerge like moles, out onto Bayham Street with the London commute in full swing, into the early-morning rush hour and the belching exhaust smoke of old London buses and lorries. It was Camden Town as advertised: grey, wet and grimy. No chance of secret assignations after those early-morning finishes, we just wanted to get home to our own beds. Later, as the sun went down over Camden Town, we would return to the studio, and enter our very own psychedelic *Dreamhouse*.

Siouxsie and Severin would talk very intimately when they were discussing songs, and I was never invited into that discussion. Severin wrote a lot more lyrics then, and a lot of his lyrical ideas on *A Kiss in the Dreamhouse*, songs like 'Melt!' and 'Cascade', were very sexual. Siouxsie's words were if anything perhaps more post-coital ('Slowdive'), or post-trip ('Cocoon').

It was a late evening in Abbey Road's Studio 2 when Siouxsie and I recorded 'Obsession' together, and for a moment it felt like the Creatures had infiltrated the *Dreamhouse* sessions. I was standing on a small wooden riser in my Vivienne Westwood Cuban heels (I always thought it was the most wonderful shape for a man to have, Cuban heels and a tight waistcoat), stamping beats with my heels and clapping flamenco style. A steady 3/4 - pom-pompom: 1, 2, 3 - 1, 2, 3.

'Can you feel this beat? It's an obsessive heartbeat/Waiting to be joined with its obsession'.

These lyrics were not about us: it was a story Siouxsie had heard about the nature of obsessive psychotic desire. Yet with all the references to a beat, a furtive relationship that's a game in some way, perhaps her creative subconscious was being fed by what was going on between us. I was utterly oblivious to any personal meaning in the lyrics, but there was a moment of intimacy for me in the recording. Mike had tied long paper chains to Siouxsie's mic, so it made a fluttering sound as she stood on the same plinth that I'd been tapping out the rhythm on, swinging the mic in a huge circle. We did more clapping together, and as the track ends you hear a giggle followed by some sharp inhalations – air being sucked through pursed lips. Swedish slang. Our secret sound for 'Yes'. Siouxsie giggling was, to me, wonderful confirmation that we'd touched some deeper point, or at least lifted the need to be utterly in denial. It was a moment of frivolity that connected us. There were more of those looks and I felt as if we were almost telepathic. I wanted it to be that close.

From that point on, we would laugh and giggle knowingly about nothing, usually a sign of growing intimacy, particularly among adolescents, apparently. It could have been cute, or infuriatingly tiresome. Mike would have been part of it too because he somehow enjoyed that moment of 'We are now outside of normality - we are pushing through into another realm'. This helped make the record what it is. Some producers tried to search for the real Siouxsie. Mike Hedges didn't care. He just accepted everything she presented. Others would say to her, 'I'm not sure about this lyric. How are you singing that? What do you want to do when we get to the middle-eight?' Siouxsie's response would be, 'Fuck off! Just record it.' Mike never asked those questions. He was just totally in the moment. I tried to be that way too, even when I was in the studio surrounded by seasoned professionals. I must have driven them crazy. I tried to be patient, to give more time, especially to Severin, as it took him longer to formulate his ideas. But a more patient approach was difficult because I was always wanting to get things done quickly or spontaneously. In those sessions, there were many moments of genuine and wonderful group harmony, but there was far more going on behind closed doors. Things were starting to fracture.

Severin was distancing himself, formulating a closer friendship with Robert Smith, who visited the studio a few times. He'd already worked with Mike, so it was kind of 'under the guise' of seeing him, sitting on the ubiquitous couch at the back of the control room. Robert was mostly quiet, laughing with Severin. I remember one day, when I had just completed the drum track for 'Slowdive', and Robert, unprompted, said, 'I really liked that drum fill you just did.' I knew exactly the one he meant; a fill of 'note subtraction' rather than 'addition'. No one else had mentioned it. No one else had ever said anything like that to me. Robert was always listening, so intently.

There was a closeness developing between people inside and outside of the group. John McGeoch was working with Visage and had secured an 'endorsement' from Yamaha – not that I really knew what that meant. But, as well as new Yamaha guitars, there was a glowing Yamaha motorcycle downstairs in the car park next to Mike's white Porsche 928. Robert, it seems, had already set his sights on a Porsche like Mike's. John was also the first Banshee to buy a house, so it seemed he was moving quickly through the echelons of achievement.

Meanwhile, the studio was literally falling apart, and the drink and the drugs were having a similar impact on the band. Everyone was hiding how much they were consuming, nipping out of the room to indulge, thinking that the others didn't know. Similarly, Siouxsie and I continued our deception, taking separate taxis then jumping out halfway across London, or spending the night then walking home. We didn't think they all knew, but of course they did. *Didn't they?*

If you live so closely and intensely together, as the Banshees did for *A Kiss in the Dreamhouse*, you always know what everybody's up to, but nobody wants to rock the boat. Because if somebody does, we all sink. How could we recognise an unhealthy relationship in a band with a history of unhealthy relationships? None had been mature, considered or even loving relationships. Everything was tumbling together. Nils had left in a way that was very traumatic, especially for Siouxsie and Severin. He had succumbed to the bad drug scene in London at the time, hanging out with people like Johnny Thunders and the Heartbreakers, and heroin drove him off the rails. His departure, and subsequent fall from grace, were perhaps also fuelled by feelings of rejection and betrayal. How much did it hurt seeing the photographs for the Creatures EP? Siouxsie would have swept aside any accusations of a relationship. Severin would have probably protected Siouxsie and himself by pushing Nils away. Severin's primary purpose was ensuring that the band he and Siouxsie had started together would survive.

With Nils gone and *A Kiss in the Dreamhouse* finished, Dave Woods, who was until then Nils's right-hand man *and* the band's agent, assumed the role of manager. Perhaps because 'Woodsy' was now both manager and agent, we went out on the road again, and again and again, and again. Same old crew, same old routine, same old random tours. *A Kiss in the Dreamhouse* was a traumatic album and was pivotal in terms of laying bare the chaos of the time, reduced in the run-out groove of the vinyl to the whimsical lyric sung by the twelve-year-old Mandy Miller, 'Nellie the Elephant packed her trunk and said goodbye to the circus'. Of course, we never discussed the real elephant in the room. Any work that you feel achieves perfection is often a by-product of many accidents and near disasters.

'If I ever find Heaven, it will be by backing away from Hell.'
Father Edward Dowling

13.
Empty Vessels

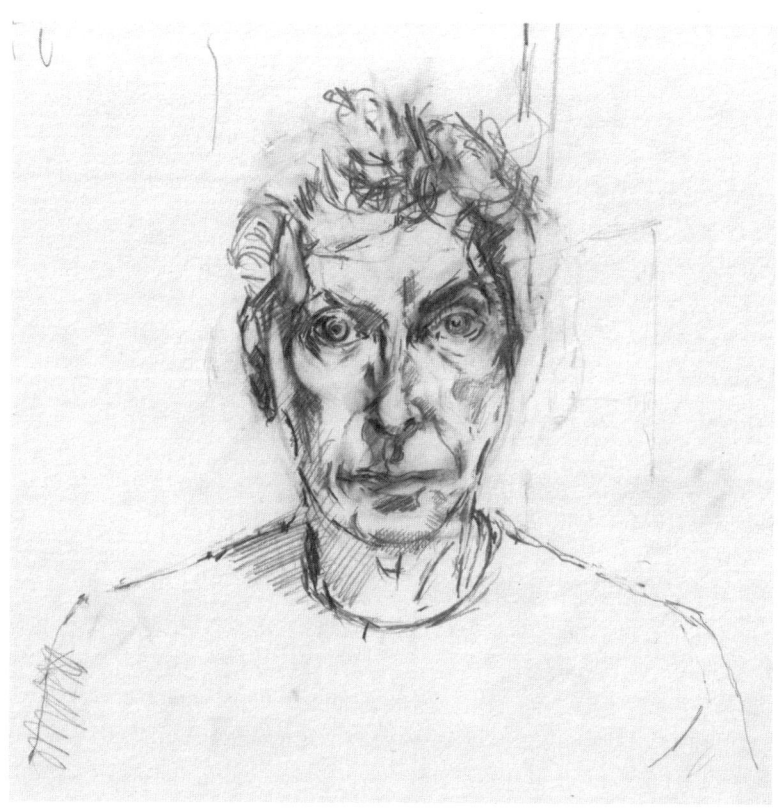

The madness of the *Dreamhouse* sessions continued when we took the record out on the road, and it quickly became clear that something was very wrong with John McGeoch. For our first gig he arrived in Spain with Russell Webb from Skids. Severin and Skids vocalist Richard Jobson used to share a flat, so we all knew each other. We presumed Russell was just along for the ride. It turned out that he was basically there to look after John. We didn't know how bad John's drinking problem was and, in a way, he became the scapegoat for the collapse of the band during *Dreamhouse*. At that first gig in Madrid he got totally confused and started playing the wrong song. John was summarily fired.

I had - and still have - to live with the unresolved guilt that I didn't stand up for him and instead just went along with the group-speak. My own guilt is further exacerbated by knowing that John had previously tried to help me confront my own drinking. One morning he turned up unexpectedly at my flat in Shaftesbury Mews. Perhaps I'd had a night of it and word had got back to him, but John greeted me with a smile: 'Hey Budgie, surprise - something tells me that, apparently, you've got to watch your drinking.'

I thought to quip back, 'Hey John, you've got some need to talk.'

But I didn't. His concern was genuine, and it hit me hard.

Unfortunately, not hard enough, because I ignored his friendly warning and was never brave enough to say the same to him. I was perhaps part of the reason for his collapse, complicit because I failed to be as supportive as I might have been, instead contributing to a band dynamic that had been mutually toxic.

Perhaps we were all in too deep to admit that we had a

problem in common. I was too busy forging a romantic link that was getting stronger, and I didn't want to jeopardise it by saying, 'Hey, perhaps we should all take a break and reassess all these crazy things that are going on?' I didn't feel I had the ability or the maturity to do that, and I certainly didn't want the responsibility. The situation wasn't handled at all well. No one thing ever happens in isolation, and while everyone has expressed their own opinions in interviews, there is little consistency between our answers.

Was Severin pondering a new plan? He got on well with Robert, and I imagine he would have considered him a good balance to Siouxsie and me – if he could just persuade Robert to join the Banshees. But McGeoch was always pulling in a different direction. He was strong-willed, knew what he wanted and, most importantly, he was a superb musician. He was also a brilliant ally and never musically demanding. He never required the rest of us to improve our game to match his, but instead spurred us on to greater musical achievements. His input was on a different level. John wasn't complicated but he was compulsive. He loved Siouxsie, and the pair of them got on famously. He was one of the few men that Siouxsie would take criticism and advice from. It was sad to see that dynamic turn sour, primarily because of John's insatiable need for girls on the road. That's what undermined Siouxsie's respect for him, and subsequently his position in the band. The girls and, of course, the drinking.

Siouxsie hated the girls he chose to be with, especially if they were loud, full-on, trying to 'out-Siouxsie' Siouxsie. She hated people's misconceptions: 'So you're Siouxsie Sioux of the night. The Goth legend and the Ice Queen.' Siouxsie would respond wearily to anyone regurgitating lazy journalism. She had no time for them. She might play along for an evening, almost as a game, but most times she would get irritated, snap, and tell them to fuck off. John could end up defending someone who, in Siouxsie's eyes, was just another nobody, not a woman with integrity. It was also perhaps the fear that a member of the Banshees bringing another element into the inner circle might be destructive to the purity or safety of the group.

John seemed indifferent to all of that, or perhaps he had a more relaxed attitude to it. He maybe felt that such control and restriction was crazy - in his mind, he was just being himself, and suddenly there were a lot of rules. We had many guitarists, and, without fail, they were required to change their clothes and hairstyle, to adapt their playing style and create suitable parts for all the songs they had to learn. But the biggest requirement for each new Banshees guitarist involved accepting a whole new way of thinking and a loyalty that most found beyond the call of duty. 'Outsiders' were to be kept at a distance, and even getting too familiar with members of the crew was not encouraged. That's a big ask of anybody.

I, meanwhile, just accepted my position and continued to develop that role, the path of least resistance for Budgie, fitting in with what was required. I was with Siouxsie for the next seventeen years. I still think it's an achievement to have lasted so long - much longer than many musical or personal relationships I know - and to be continuously prolific. Perhaps being continuously prolific is a clue to our longevity as a couple.

> *'Don't stop to count the years, sweet songs never last too*
> *long on broken radios.'*
> 'Sam Stone', John Prine

It didn't take me long to understand why Siouxsie was so protective of our little world. She once told me that she was attacked on Chislehurst Common, near a place called Pickend Pond, which was notorious for flashers, and that someone had cut her with a knife, leaving behind a scar. But the real story, which came out later, told of a surgical scar. She was seriously ill when she was still a young girl, not long after her dad had died. The procedure was for a condition called ulcerative colitis, which can be brought on by trauma or serious upset. A colectomy is an operation not usual for someone so young. As a young girl, she and another girl were sexually assaulted, but the adults they told only made them feel responsible for being in the wrong place. The trauma and repercussions of the attack and having life-threatening surgery were perhaps too much for a young girl to process, so perhaps the two incidents morphed into one attack involving a knife.

At the time, I thought, *She has been through the ringer. I should look after her.* Not because she was delicate, but because she was using the Siouxsie persona to hide something serious. It would be too easy for me to paint a bleak picture of a malicious Siouxsie with Budgie as the innocent who got tangled up in the mess. That would be too unbalanced a vision of it. Perhaps our deeper connection was that we were both hiding behind our respective personas to avoid dealing with the trauma of our dead parents. Siouxsie's persona had been created by the press, and while of course she had a good hand in developing it, the glamour soon wore off. It felt like it stopped being fun for her quite quickly. When we got together, I joined her in hiding from the world. If you're in a relationship with the star of the show, you don't go out much. If we were going to meet, we did so at a dark restaurant, or at somebody's house, or in our own flats. It was very private. We didn't go out clubbing, except maybe to Heaven on Saturdays, because there we could just vanish.

We got to know Marc Almond in 1981, soon after he arrived in London, probably at the Limelight and a post-*Top of the Pops* party celebrating the success of 'Tainted Love'. Marc was obviously attracted to and perhaps empowered by Siouxsie's image. He already had the black eyeliner, red lipstick and leather look, but where Siouxsie would wear studded cock straps as accessories, Marc fully embraced the S&M scene and presented its style full frontal in Soft Cell videos. The excessive drinking and drug-taking went hand in sticky hand with the rubber-clad cabaret. I don't know how Marc handled it all, but he did as we all did, until we couldn't. He had gravitated towards sleaze, landing a flat in the middle of Soho right opposite Madame Jojo's, where he lived with a python - 'Come in and meet my pet snake.'

Siouxsie and I became close with Marc, and after many nights out on the town there would eventually be a musical collaboration with him on 'Threat of Love' in 1999. Marc's other writing partner outside Soft Cell was pianist Annie Hogan. She was also smitten with Siouxsie, and I quite fancied Annie, but of course Annie wasn't interested. I was still naïve in many ways. There's a Soft Cell lyric from *Non-Stop Erotic Cabaret* that sums up how things were: 'We could go out to dinner but we're always on drugs'. I don't recall Siouxsie and I having many quiet dinners together. We would occupy ourselves, but never sit down to 'have a chat'. We would just watch movie after movie after movie. I don't remember half of them. I wasn't a very good movie-watcher - it was more a way of getting close and being intimate that didn't involve communicating.

After the third glass of wine, we'd probably start making out. I didn't feel like I was an adult. We seemed to regress, and even when it became sexual it was still childlike and silly. Nothing was taboo and yet nothing was serious, so nothing was real either. What we were couldn't be disclosed because we didn't have a real relationship to talk about, not that we would have known how to talk about it if we did. We didn't know how to be a couple because we were not 'out' as a couple; we were in our closet. I always wondered what it was like for other people, to wake up in the morning and say, 'I'm going to work now. Maybe see you at lunchtime . . . or see you tonight . . . or see you at the weekend.'

Instead, Siouxsie and I did what reclusive people do: hole up and dial in food, drink and sometimes drugs. We got a dealer to send some round by taxi, in a cassette-tape box, with black cabs going across London in the guise of picking up cigarettes. It wasn't really about the drugs, rather the fact that it was so easy to get them. It became as easy as ordering in a curry. I wouldn't be paying for it, anyway. Drugs didn't really agree with me. If I had a line, I'd just talk all night. Really, I just needed a good bottle of wine. Make that any bottle of wine.

It had been another year of massive change in the world of Siouxsie and the Banshees: 1982 had started with two shows in Hong Kong and a glimpse of Kirk Douglas's dimpled chin – we were lunching in the same restaurant at the Holiday Inn, Kowloon – then five days of fragrant cherry-blossom sunshine in Japan. A final chilly month of fjord-hopping in Nordic, fishy Smörgåsbord-land left us all looking a bit shell-shocked by the end of July and Cornwall's Elephant Fayre festival. After a two-month late summer holiday, we almost had our land legs back, but sadly John was still all at sea. October ended with John McGeoch's last Banshee gigs and a sad farewell. And so it was that on 5 November, with the release of *A Kiss in the Dreamhouse,* Robert Smith was preparing to become our new guitarist. But our immediate future was two months of congested UK motorways and the German autobahn racetracks.

14.
Face the Feast

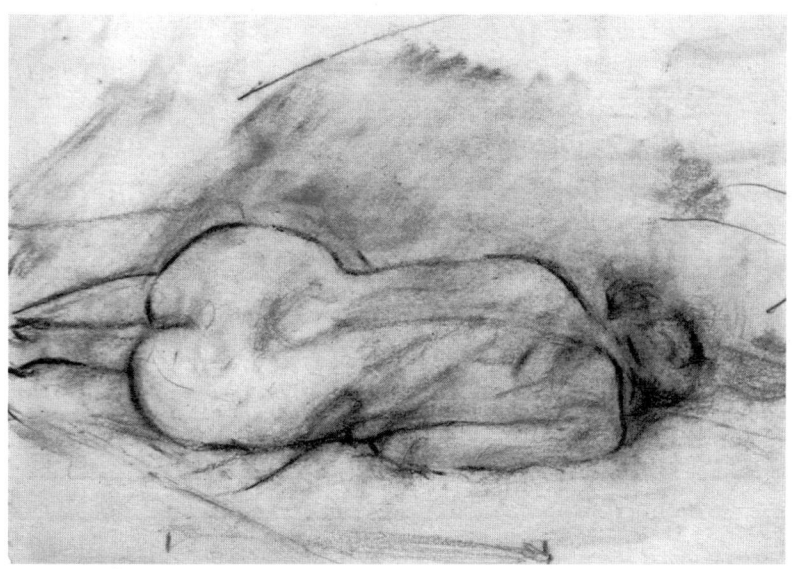

It was almost Christmas 1982, and we had all been working hard. Siouxsie and I wanted to party and had an escape plan. I randomly placed a finger on a map of the world and it landed on South America, somewhere in the middle of nowhere, so we moved the finger slightly and I phoned a studio in Mexico City. Nobody there could speak English, however, so they weren't quite sure what I wanted. We looked a little further west towards the Pacific Ocean: 'Well, Hawaii's not far. That would be a good ruse.' We investigated and found just one place - Sea-West Studios on the island of Oahu, in a place called Kuilima. There'd been some severe weather and the lady who answered said, 'We have no electricity at the moment, but we've got a lot of candles.' This was the perfect attitude. 'If you'd like to book some time in the New Year, we're free from January first.'

We gave it some serious thought. About a minute. It would be a great start to 1983. 'We'll take it from 1 January, we'll probably need about two weeks,' I said.

We didn't actually have any songs, but the Creatures had united us with such confidence that we didn't give that a second thought - this was about adventure!

It was just two days after the Banshees' last gig of 1982, at London's Hammersmith Odeon, so there was no time to repack our bags. We left London on 31 December on a 10pm flight west to Canada. Two hours later, somewhere over the Atlantic Ocean, the British Airways crew wished us all a happy New Year. When we landed in Canada it was still New Year's Eve, so somewhere over the Pacific Ocean, halfway to Hawaii, our Canadian crew appeared in the aisles, dressed as babies, wearing nappies and very little else - *not* the British Airways style at all. We toasted in a second New Year - with all the high jinks and abandon of a high-altitude party. When we landed in Honolulu it was *still* New Year's Eve, and the arrival of New Year was celebrated by a cacophony of fire-crackers exploding and falling from high-rise balconies. It was the loudest, most intense celebration I had ever heard. As we got out of the taxi, dense clouds of foul-smelling sulphurous smoke filled the air between the hotel towers. Without much thought, I said, 'Wouldn't it be nice if we had something other than champagne?' In London we would have telephoned a *friend* and sent a taxi over, but this overseas mission called for careful planning and cunning skill. I went out with $100, which counted for a bit more than it does now, looking for a likely character. I asked the first person I met if he could get me some coke, handed him the money and of course never set eyes on him again.

It was part of my enduring naïvety back then, but now I feel like I was being looked after, that my guardian angel was saying, 'No, Peter. You don't know what's going on. Listen, let me just take the hundred, put it in that man's hand over there and I'll just disappear him out of your life forever.' Meanwhile, Budgie sat there whining, 'Oh, it always happens to *me*.' The guardian angel guided Peter back to the safety of the hotel, because obviously Budgie had gone hunting for drugs without a map or a clue, and there were crazy folk all around.

The next morning, hungover and $100 lighter, a car arrived and we were driven over to the other side of the island. Though it was remote, and it felt as if we were on our own, the landscaped gardens of the Hyatt Regency Hotel were populated by fellow travellers. There were wicker chairs and ceiling fans to go with my touristy straw hat, which I wore religiously with my only white T-shirt. It was so hot and humid that the leather trousers I hadn't unpacked after the British winter were chucked into the bottom of a wardrobe, where they quickly turned green and mouldy. Mike Hedges arrived two days later, looking like he'd definitely had time to pack. It was time to check our list of ideas and ingredients.

I had written the words that would become 'Ice House', an erotic fantasy cum ghost story, based around an obscure TV play starring a Victorian icehouse in the garden of a big old English pile. Siouxsie had the words for 'Miss the Girl', her homage to J.G. Ballard's *Crash*. And that, along with some drumsticks and a few tins of Heinz baked beans (never leave home without them), was that. It wasn't that we were complacent; it was more that we were just curious and ready to see what would happen when we arrived.

To our urban British eyes, the studio appeared to be in the middle of a jungle – and a lot of jungle jingles made it into the recording of *Feast*. Sounds of us and of real creatures, thrashing around through forests of bamboo plants and the aerial roots of huge banyan trees. At night we would hear a strange and deep sonorous call coming from the trees and creepers around the studio.

'What *is* that?' I asked.

'That's a gecko lizard,' said our host and studio boss, Rick.

'But aren't they tiny?' These lizards were all over the outside of the studio windows at night.

'Not the ones out in the jungle,' said Rick with a smile.

The gecko's call, a deep two notes descending from high to low, 'Geck-O . . .' was amplified through the resonance of a big body cavity. We were constantly in awe of our surroundings, marvelling at how spectacularly deep and dark it was out there, and basking in the feeling of being lost in it.

I invented many different drum beats each day in the studio. We'd put them on to a cassette tape for Siouxsie to work on the following day, while Mike and I created more rhythms. Once Siouxsie had finished a lyrical idea to fit the beats, we listened to the melody and started to flesh it out on marimba and tuned percussion, building the songs from how the vocals had affected the drums. It was a 'suck it and see' procedure that worked.

Siouxsie had a musical idea for her 'Miss the Girl' lyric. She picked it out with single fingers on the battered old piano in the studio – it was very simple. She and Mike then said, 'Okay, that's it. We're going to the restaurant now. You stay here and figure it out on the marimba.' Fortunately, I was never too hungry in the heat, so I had no problem rehearsing the different parts ready for the evening recording session.

Along with drums and tuned percussion, the Creatures used other instruments that happened to be around. The desk was the conduit but also a musical instrument in the right hands. It was an MCI desk, custom made for Rick Keefer, the owner of the studio. It was finished without the usual numbers and markings around the numerous knobs, faders and switches. This was fine for Rick, as he knew it back to front. Mike was familiar with other MCI desks, but this was more of a challenge. Once he found his feet, he was able to creatively overload the microphone preamps and develop many different forms of harmonic distortion. This can be heard to best effect on 'A Strutting Rooster', a song that could only have happened within this Hawaiian studio. I had to take a totally different approach to playing the drums due to the hot and humid conditions – the drums had seen better days and the drumheads would easily lose tension during recording. It wasn't ideal, but with our need to work quickly a lot of the weird detuning of the drums was retained. We allowed the construction of song arrangements to be dictated by elements outside of our control. Drum takes lasted as long as I was able to hold the drumsticks before they flew out of my sweaty hands. With no air conditioning we would simply open the doors and ventilate between takes. Everything, including me, was a little wet. The conditions had a direct influence on the length of the heavier drum-led tracks.

The old marimba looked like it was close to returning to its natural form, but it had a beautiful rich warm tone that we exaggerated by layering takes recorded at different tape speeds. Imagine a song playing sped-up to double normal speed, then recording a single lowest possible marimba note on the 1 of every bar. When played back at normal speed, those single low notes become a deep sub-bass marimba sound. You also clearly hear the marimba's harmonic overtones, making everything more rich and colourful. There were big drums, little drums, bits of percussion, a conch shell - that was a new one for me. Oh, and for the song 'Dancing on Glass' we danced on broken glass - what else?

Mike Hedges played a huge creative role in cooking up our *Feast*. He would send me a repeat echo in my headphones. So, if I hit a cymbal once, ding, I would hear ding-a. If I played 8th notes I heard 16s - ding-a, ding-a, ding-a, ding-a. It created an illusion of me playing more than I was; an impression of speed while I was playing half-time. Mike also used the harmoniser to enhance the 'note' of each drum or give the impression of playing in a big hall, when the kick drum bounces off the back wall and sets up a tempo. In effect he was making me the metronome, a time-keeping constant that I was setting up myself. I could play behind it or in front of it.

The Creatures didn't do a lot of physical tape editing (cutting the two-inch tape to make a composite master from usually no more than two different takes) because we didn't have time, but also we didn't have the need. What went down on that day and onto the cassette was the drum take that Siouxsie would sing to and what we recorded everything else to.

We invited the singers of the local Hawaiian Academy to come in and add their voices. They sat in a little circle, three or four of them, and allowed us to record their family chants. These had been passed down as part of their oral tradition. We asked them to all sing at the same time, something that, apparently, they'd never done before. One would begin chanting, another would start their chant, and it sparked something very special. They all started to gel together, perhaps because they were trained singers and they pitched the keys correctly, as we didn't have anything tuned for them to pitch to. The Hawaiian words seemed to have a natural rhythm, and the recording became the song 'Inoa Ole'.

We didn't want *Feast* to be 'A Postcard from Hawaii', with

Hollywood ukuleles, pedal steel guitars and the swish of grass skirts; instead, we tried to let everything Hawaiian naturally suffuse and influence our musical decisions. Hawaii completely shaped the record and it would never have turned out as it had if we'd gone there with other musicians, or as the Banshees. Wherever the Banshees went, they would mostly sound the same.

I was like a kid in a sweet shop, thinking, *Just throw everything at me. Just pitch me as many balls as you can and I'm going to play with them. I'll figure out how to use them, and I'll bat 'em all back.* I sensed that this could be a trait I inherited from my dad. He relished having a problem to solve. It filled me with the challenge. When you don't stop to think about what you're doing and are completely absorbed by it, when you revel in running up a series of blind alleys, when you're clueless and knowing that feeling clueless feels good, then you can be sure you're onto something special.

It'd been a hard-working 'holiday' for Siouxsie and me. We were pretending that we were on our own. Mike was supposed to be in the room upstairs - who knows what he was up to, because I don't think he was ever there. If we weren't working in the studio, we'd have a drink at the hotel bar and just fall into bed or nod off on the sofa. It was all very hit or miss, no candlelit dinners or 'How are you feeling about all this?' It was very much a physical process, with an absence of 'grown-up' discussion.

We'd set ourselves a challenge, as if we were contestants in our own game show, like something you might find on Netflix now - 'Okay, you've got two weeks to write and record an album!' - only loaded with misbehaviour and ludicrous distractions as challenges. We went up in a glider whale-watching, towed up by a twin-prop aircraft that then released us to glide and float back down into silence. We rented off-road trikes, joining a group of tourists, all trundling along, trying to get used to the gears. The instructor said not to go near the cliff, but that's exactly where Siouxsie was heading. He had to chase her, lassoing her bike. We went to the peacock park. We drank a lot of cocktails. We went out with Mike, Rick and his wife Donna for a lot of dinners, eating in chi-chi American restaurants full of Japanese golfers. While Rick was busy in the studio, Donna was busy in her kennels as a breeder of American Boxers. Donna's first dogs, Irving, Sabra, Goody and Nuffy, get their own mention in the credits for *Feast*.

Like the traditional singers and the sounds of the jungle, some of this mayhem found its way onto the album. We invited Rick and Donna and all their friends and friends of friends for the big mad party recording of the track 'Flesh': 'Oh piggy squeals and donkey brays - at a sober party/Doggy barks and horsey neighs - try to shock the party'. Siouxsie came up with those lines and we printed them out, then went to the shops to buy five-litre flagons of 110 per cent proof rum, which went into a very sweet punch. The guests arrived and guzzled, saying, 'Ooh, this is lovely. It's like mandarin. Isn't it passion fruit and mandarin?' We said, 'Yes, that's what it is. Yes. There's a little bit of alcohol, but it's fine.' They all got completely legless, of course, and we got them to recite the lyrics over and over and over again, until by the time they'd had enough to drink they couldn't say it without laughing.

It was a suitably surreal ending to our Hawaiian adventure. Like Luis Buñuel's *The Exterminating Angel* and the party from which nobody could leave. We had recorded these affluent, middle-class voices, with loud American laughter collapsing into chaos. It was strangely alien to then play along with, and the mood of 'Flesh' became very mysterious. I was playing the marimba with my fingertips, very close to the microphones, a repetitive part dipping in and out of this crazy party mix. The drums were recorded with a fading repeat swamped in reverb, intentionally trying to disturb the flow and ultimately joining the cacophony. After that, we were done.

We were still mixing literally hours before we left. Mike had a flight out of Honolulu the night before us, so he did his last mix and then jumped in a taxi and went off to the airport and everything stopped. Rick was going, 'Is that it? He's gone?' And then we got very drunk.

I'd been getting very drunk most nights. There's a Polaroid of me sitting in front of this contraption for chilling wine as it's being drunk, a Professor Branestawm-type invention of curling glass laboratory tubes. Donna wrote on the back: 'What is it? It looks good, it works and it's full of alcohol? – Answer: Budgie!' At the time I thought it was funny. That was when I could drink all night, crash out, wake up the next morning and get on in the studio the next day, with none of the hangovers and headaches I'd had during the *Dreamhouse* sessions with the Banshees.

For our last night, Rick and Donna took us to a couple of bars and we had a few tequilas, and a few more tequilas . . . and I was never good on tequila. I get speedy and trippy, as if I'm someone else. A little sailor guy was being leery with Donna, and I thought, *I'll sort him out.* He was coming at me, doing all these kung-fu things, and I decided that I could do kung-fu too. Unfortunately, the little sailor guy was with a big sailor guy, who gave me a palm to the chin as if to tell me to shut up. I went over backwards, hit my elbows hard, and cracked my head on the ground. The big sailor guy then pulled up a shrub, roots and all, and it looked as if the little sailor guy was coming in to finish me off. But Siouxsie straddled me, took off both stilettos – she always wore stilettos if she was out on the town – and shouted, 'Come on then, who's first?' This was when Siouxsie showed her true colours.

Siouxsie was a ferocious ally and I know she loved me, and that I loved her. But I didn't know how long such an intensely symbiotic relationship could last. We were more Bonnie and Clyde than Richard and Judy.

If they wanted to get to *me*, they would have to go through Siouxsie. She was, at that moment, my guardian angel. Siouxsie always said that she rooted for the Native American Indians in old Western films. If somebody was on the back foot – or falling to the floor after being chinned by a big sailor – she would step in. I was out of control and these guys were going to knock my lights out. Siouxsie could handle herself. She could pack a punch - and did, on occasions. I was always attracted to the bigger guys in school and sat next to the guy everybody else was afraid could beat the crap out of them, because he would be my protection. In Siouxsie, I'd aligned myself with the harder woman, the strong woman. My dad was very soft with me, and I'm like that too. From what I'm told, I think my mum was more strident and more vocal. Easygoing, but with strong ideas of what was right and wrong. She was never violent, but her death left a gap that you could say I was looking for a strong woman to fill.

The sailors clearly thought that taking on a mad woman wielding stilettos was not a good idea, so the big guy pulled the little guy away and off into the night they ran. Rick and Donna decided it was probably best that we went home. The next morning, our beautiful Lincoln town car had to go back to the hire company stained with my dried blood. My right elbow had swollen up, my head hurt, *everything* hurt, but the return to England was calling. As I boarded the flight, I decided to spare Siouxsie and the cabin crew my moaning by anaesthetising myself with a few vodka gimlets until we got back to London.

Foolish feels like the best descriptor of those two weeks in Honolulu. Foolish only in the sense that we had no master plan - we worked hard, and we played hard. We started with so little, but we finished with so much more.

Hungover and battered as I was, we were still carrying the precious cargo of the two-inch master tape because it was too risky to send a courier. We'd heard that Severin and Robert Smith were working together at Garden Studios in Shoreditch, so we went along, merrily trotting down the steps into the subterrranean studio that John Foxx built. Everybody was expecting us to have a single, maybe a couple of extra tracks, because we'd only been away for two weeks, but here we were with the album mixed, the photographs ready to go. We played them some of it and there was just silence. They seemed shocked by what we'd done, and, in the case of Severin, no doubt concerned about what it meant for the Banshees.

Recording *Feast* had allowed Siouxsie to step out of being Siouxsie Sioux of Siouxsie and the Banshees for the first time, which meant she could loosen up and have fun. Sadly, this had to be reined in because so much had been invested in the Banshees. We never heard Polydor say, 'We want another Creatures record right now!' The feeling was always more, 'Don't let them do that again!' I still have the receipts from the time in Hawaii and it barely cost Polydor any money. Their reaction was probably more political than financial. As soon as we realised that Severin and Robert were still finishing their record, we went off to Wessex Studios in north London for a weekend and did a cover of Mel Tormé's song 'Right Now'. Released as a single, it made number 14 in the charts, higher than any Banshees single since 'Hong Kong Garden' back in 1978. Food for thought or salt in the wound?

I still have a sadness that we never sat down to talk about that time, to reflect on what we'd achieved and what it meant for us, both as the Creatures and as a couple still supposedly in the first flush of love. We just got on with it. I struggled to express the kind of emotions that might have been second nature to most people because I simply wasn't capable of doing it. I never said, 'I'm so happy and in my element, this is amazing!' I think the loss of a parent can create so many emotional barriers. Sharing moments with another, acknowledging achievements, being able to openly express something beyond words. Siouxsie and I rarely if ever held hands in public, but we did on *Feast*, at least metaphorically - we held hands and jumped off the cliff.

15.
Swimming with Flying Fish

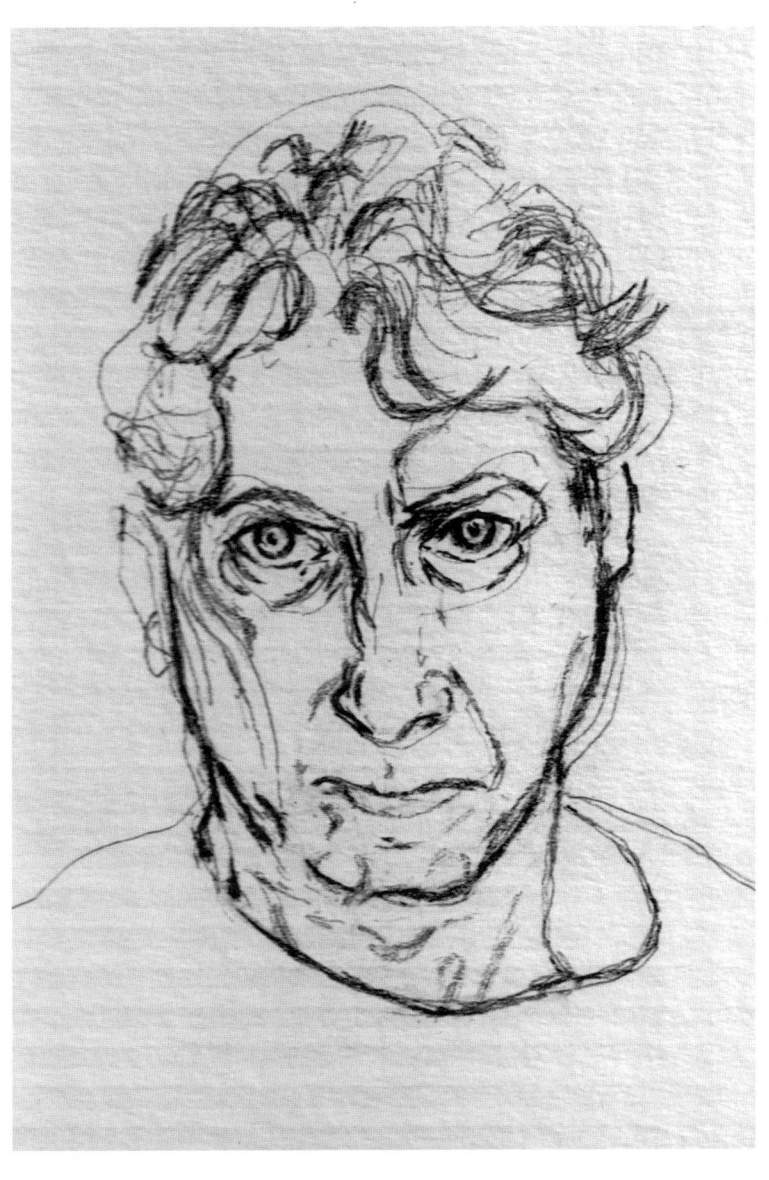

It quickly became clear that as long as the Banshees were around, the Creatures would always be a sideshow to the main event. It was also clear that the record company and management wanted us to put everything on hold outside of the main thrust of the Banshees. It was implied that we didn't have dedicated 'Creatures fans'; they were either Siouxsie fans or fans of Siouxsie and the Banshees.

But from the comments on the Creatures website (which existed some way off in the future at this point), it seemed that many preferred the Creatures' sound, finding it challenging yet perversely more accessible; playful yet still in touch with the darker subject matter that Siouxsie was known for in her lyrics.

Retrospectively, I think it was a good thing that Polydor didn't tell us to put the Banshees on hold for a year while we continued with the Creatures. That might have killed us. We were so high on the thrill of what we'd done that there was no thinking, just total abandon. The whole experience was oddly tactile - being infatuated and having an outlet for it. Being the Creatures was having our cake and eating it. We could have inhabited the same world as Chris Frantz and Tina Weymouth's Tom Tom Club, who were a bit like us in a way, but I think the spontaneous element of the Creatures would have had to change, returning to demoing songs before recording them. We did change our ways when it came to writing for *Boomerang*, but that was because for the first time we didn't have the Banshees waiting in the wings.

Feast had been a busman's holiday, an elopement for us and validation of our crazy idea of how a love affair might look. Many years later, at the end of our relationship, Siouxsie would tell me that the lyric 'Morning Dawning', the first track on *Feast*, was about me. It was more than likely assigned to me belatedly; she seemed to have been lamenting lost love long before I arrived.

As the Creatures, we'd worked in such a different way to the Banshees' usual process. When we recorded *Kaleidoscope*, Siouxsie and Severin had had all the ideas, but when I joined I was *allowed* - that word - to steer the recordings in the studio. I added live drums and a simple 'E' string bassline to a beatbox demo that became 'Tenant', in this case using a Boss MXR flanger to develop the sound of the track - and perhaps the band - in unexpected ways. There was still a lot of spontaneity in our process, but this began to disappear when more fixed band roles were re-established. Siouxsie would sometimes get on the kit, playing her own style to demonstrate what she wanted to hear from the drums. This was invariably more like Moe Tucker of the Velvet Underground. If I picked up the guitar, I'd use open tunings. Nobody was telling us, 'That's not how you do it.'

But the Banshees quickly adopted a more traditional group approach. Siouxsie didn't record guitar again after *Kaleidoscope*. If I suggested a marimba part it was usually frowned upon from certain quarters as being 'too Creatures'. So those elements of fun and experimentation receded and the recording process became more serious, with everyone sticking to their primary instruments. The Creatures never had those restrictions.

Maybe it hadn't gone quite as smoothly for the other Banshees side-project, the Glove. Perhaps Robert Smith and Severin had been a little over-indulgent with illicit substances during the studio sessions. The gossipmongers told of a non-stop party with an open-door policy. The Glove included my ex-girlfriend Jeanette, who excelled in a very difficult position as a 'first-time' vocalist. Alas, Smith and Severin sounded like they'd put the cart before the horse with their studio celebrations.

The Creatures and the Banshees would be waiting until Robert and Severin were finished. There was a collision of energy:

Siouxsie and I were still coming down from the rush of *Feast*'s success, so the 1983 Banshees adventures took a while to get going. We went to Sweden for a few days writing, and Robert, who had replaced John McGeoch on tour and subsequently in the band, suggested we record 'Dear Prudence'. It was a song we all knew and, having also played it live back in Liverpool with Ian Broudie as the Secrets, I already had my own approach to Ringo's multi-layered drumming on the Beatles' original.

We recorded the basics of the cover at the Europa film studios in Stockholm, and then back in the UK we set up at Angel Studios in Islington. Angel was an orchestral studio and as we were to be the first non-orchestral session, so the staff were a wee bit nervous - probably because unfortunately we had a bit of a reputation. Robert was essentially camping in the studio, sometimes with his wife Mary. His sister Janet came along to play the harpsichord - a very delicate instrument - on the opening motif that changed our version of 'Dear Prudence' into something quite different to the two-note intro used by the Beatles on the *White Album*.

In the video for 'Dear Prudence', directed by Tim Pope (who of course regularly worked with Robert and the Cure), you see three of the most inebriated musicians you are ever likely to encounter in a video. Venice was chosen as the location for the filming, and I self-importantly cast myself as St Sebastian, being shot full of imaginary arrows. I was dressed in a blue two-piece suit from the Tibetan shop near the British Museum. On my feet I wore Chinese worker boots, bought on our first visit to Hong Kong, the thin rubber sole of which offered little heel protection. This was bad news for me. At the end of the day's shooting and drinking, I fell from grace from the top of a very high wall. I landed heavily, with the heel of my left foot suffering full impact. The pain got worse by the hour, so by the time we'd eaten, I'd downed enough brandy to flambé a hundred Christmas puddings. But still, I was demanding more brandy, almost kicking down Smith and Severin's room door to get at their stash.

A local doctor arrived and shot me up with a sedative that

tipped me over the edge of my booze and opiate tolerance, and I passed out, comatose. I don't recall anything of my ambulance ride from hotel to hospital. Suffice to say, I was transported in a wheelbarrow. I awoke in a hospital bed in a room that smelled of boiled potatoes and Brussels sprouts: lunch was being served. My fellow inmates gathered around my bed dressed in white gowns with limbs missing and laughing like characters from a Breugel bad dream or a Goya-esque nightmare. My manager arrived to collect me, this time without a wheelbarrow; instead I had to unceremoniously hop back to the hotel in the midday sun – my gold lamé trousers split between the legs. I had become a mad-eyed screamer with my balls bouncing in the breeze.

It wasn't just my misadventure that should have been ringing alarm bells at this point. The video wasn't great – what worked with Robert and the Cure didn't really work with us. Tim was really focused on Siouxsie, but it wasn't just that. There was something else going on, a friction that went unacknowledged, especially by me.

We went to do a series of gigs in Tel Aviv just days before we were due to play London's Royal Albert Hall and make the live recording that would become *Nocturne*.

In my mind, we were heading not just to Israel, but back in time to the Holy Biblical lands. As nobody else could drive, Robert became our designated driver for a day trip to Jerusalem. We had only a little time before soundcheck, but we managed to walk through the market in the Old City streets and stopped for a while by the Wailing Wall. Robert then drove us back through the Judean Desert, alongside the Dead Sea. Siouxsie was hatching words for a song to be called 'Dazzle'. It was dry and airless, but the windows stayed shut; it was hotter than a kiln outside.

The laid-back hedonism of Tel Aviv took me by surprise. The sweaty club dates were fiercely chaotic and something that we hadn't done for years. There were a lot of local musicians who were keen on showing us a good time, hanging out and swimming at night. I didn't really sleep for days, and just went for it - these are the moments that you can't manufacture. After the gigs we'd go out into the city and then to the Mediterranean beach, where I learned to swim on an acid trip. There were flying fish which seemed to inspire me to swim, telling me, 'It's okay, just come with us.' I'd found my swimming credentials and a temporary Jesus fixation. The acid probably helped to get me to the peak when we arrived at Tel Aviv airport the next day. I was wearing the same outfit that can be seen in the 'Dear Prudence' video, complete with headscarf, calmly waiting for the plane, blessing people, thinking of Jesus. I had a mental image of peace, a peace that came from absolute exhaustion.

Flights were always quite fraught for me. At the airport I would always attach myself to Siouxsie. I don't know if I was keeping an eye on her, or just wanting to be together, feeling the desire. We felt the need to share everything, to go mad together up in the sky. Maybe that was the co-dependency. Sometimes, fuelled by the free wine, it would become a performance. I was often not sitting in my seat, especially if I was feeling frisky. I would be in the galley, hanging out with the flight attendants, who never said that perhaps I'd had enough and should go back to my seat and eat something. Food?

The most Budgie part of the Budgie alter ego was being given the freedom to act out this Keith Moon fantasy, but there was always something holding him back. I had Peter, the responsible voice somewhere, doing his best to hold it together. I could push it to the limits, and the Tel Aviv performance was close to it, but at that extreme I was always kept safe by the fragments of Peter who silently remained. The drinking and aeroplane antics were an extension of what was acceptable in the culture I grew up in.

The young Peter, who played drums, was shy. He had to turn up and be ready to draw on all his skills and capabilities just to get up on stage - I have often wondered if that was the reason for the obsession with extrovert characters like Keith Moon or Ginger

Baker, who lived so hard. I needed Budgie offstage, not behind the kit. I became both attracted to and fearful of outrageous, confrontational characters.

Could I exist in the same airspace as somebody like that? On stage I could, because that was demanded. It's not surprising, given that Peter Edward had adopted Budgie and Susan Janet had taken on Siouxsie, that these alter egos would become blurred when together. Was Peter with Siouxsie and Budgie with Susan? Who was with whom?

A couple of weeks after getting back from Tel Aviv, the Banshees played the Royal Albert Hall. It was an important gig, VIPs and film crews everywhere, but those big gigs never fazed me. After all, my drum kit was the same size whether we were in the Royal Albert Hall or the Royal Albert pub. It was a busy couple of days, though. We were all still frazzled from Tel Aviv and the lingering uncertainties around the Creatures and the Glove.

I did what I often did at big gigs and wandered out of the venue, into the streets of Kensington. I would do it as part of the game, a step into normality, the other side of the red rope, away from the mythical backstage. I wanted to try to feel what it was like to be a punter, to get out of the craziness of being stuck in the venue all day. Of course, I looked quite a lot like the punters and vice versa - you can see them in the film that we made of the *Nocturne* concert, all the happy girls and boys with the black mohawk spikes and bleached blond hair. I was walking along with them, and sensed them looking at me, maybe thinking, *He looks just like Budgie.* I met up with my sister, which allowed me to be myself for a while, then when I got back to the Albert Hall I discovered I'd forgotten my pass. I told security I was with the band and as usual they gave a sarcastic, "Course you are, mate. Everyone here is.' I gave them our tour manager's name, and, after a bit of an anxious wait, they appeared. 'Oh, hello Budgie, we were wondering when you'd show up.'

It was at the first of these *Nocturne* shows that my and Siouxsie's symbiotic entwinement came into play. Our soundman, Tony Selinger, came into the dressing room in a bit of a panic: 'We need some music to be playing when the house lights go down and you come onstage.' Siouxsie was putting the finishing touches to tonight's make-up, Severin was looking after his elderly granny who came to all the big London shows, Robert was busy pulling his leather trousers over his pyjama bottoms, the Woodentops were in the house. 'Budgie, do you have anything?'

Back when cassettes were the most portable format for music, I always carried an assortment with me. There were road favourites like David Bowie and Lou Reed. But I always had what Siouxsie might want to hear, Mick Ronson's 'Only After Dark' or Jim Morrison crooning with the Doors, but also her favourite classical pieces. Prokofiev's 'Dance of the Knights' from *Romeo and Juliet* was always good to get her into the party mood.

But tonight we needed something strident, something grand. I settled on Stravinsky's *The Rite of Spring*. I first heard this in secondary school when a stand-in art teacher put on a record and conducted an imaginary orchestra. I was mesmerised. We quickly cued the tape up at the passage I remembered with the timpani pounding like a giant demanding to be let in - the dramatic and frenetic 'Glorification of the Chosen One'. Tony fine-tuned the tape position with highly trained technical precision, turning the spindle with an old pencil. With no rehearsal it was going to rely on my familiarity with the piece to know when to count in our own opening glorification, 'Israel'. I had dreamed of being this close to heaven so many times, I clicked my sticks and they seemed to be in the same key, a perfect moment.

16.

Howling in Berlin and The Tokyo Telephone Incident

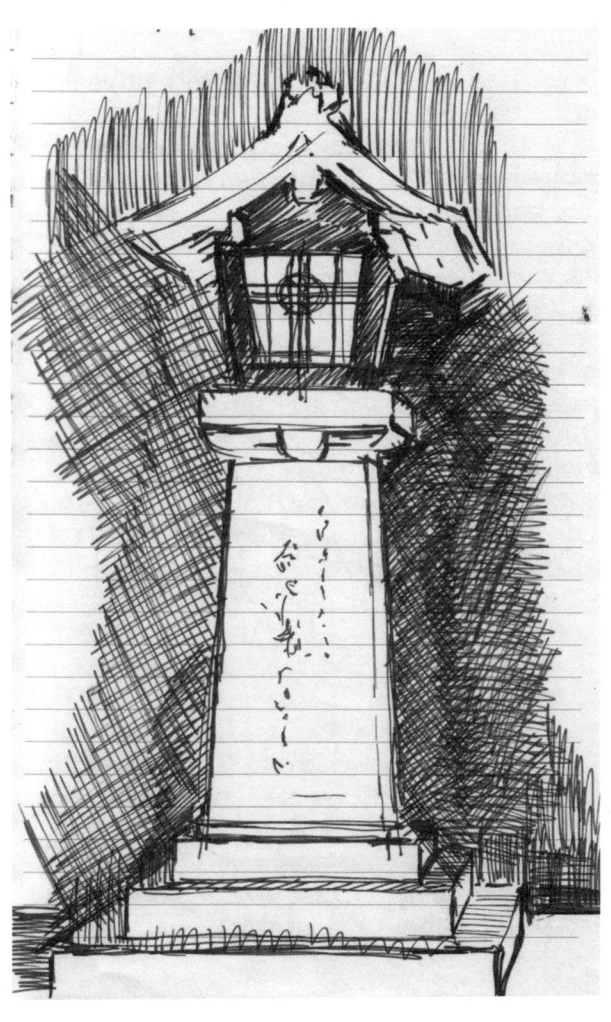

'Dear Prudence' and the Royal Albert Hall gigs had been a success, but they were papering over some very big cracks. We had nothing written and were bereft of ideas, so Siouxsie and I had to step in. The first track we recorded for *Hyæna* was 'We Hunger', initially with just drums and vocals, which meant, in many ways, it began as a Creatures track. We had fragments, demos for some tracks like 'Pointing Bone', but they were only half songs.

By August 1983, the Creatures' 'Right Now' had started its rise up the UK charts. The Glove's *Blue Sunshine* was about to be released, and the Cure were about to resurface with 'The Lovecats'. Because the Creatures had given us such a creative boost, Siouxsie and I were even more committed to the Banshees - it was everything to us, and though we were tired, we didn't feel burnt out in terms of musical inspiration.

During *Hyæna*, Robert was already reinventing himself as the Cure. This meant that he wasn't entirely present after the initial writing and recording sessions for *Hyæna*. The story put out as to the reason for his leaving the Banshees was that he was suffering from exhaustion, and perhaps we all were - but that isn't the whole story.

There had always been a level of chaos to the connection between Siouxsie and Robert. Even when it was playful there was an air of something odd to it - her pet name for him was Wabbit, after the 'kill the wabbit' refrain of Elmer Fudd in the Bugs Bunny cartoon, and Robert called Siouxsie by her middle name. I'd never heard anyone else address her as Janet, and it felt playful, knowing and testing. The edginess of their relationship affected our prospects as a band. People think of Robert as a quiet character, and of course sometimes he was. But he was also precocious and petulant, and with his tongue quite firmly planted in his cheek, he would create a situation then push it to breaking point.

Never was this more apparent than on our second trip to Japan. Throughout the tour, Robert was in a constant state of hangover and had figured that Japanese girls loved eccentricity. Combined, these might have explained his tour attire. He wore a large white bandage around his head and tied multiple scarves around the tops of his brothel creepers. It rather complemented his strange shuffling gait, all executed to such a degree of studiousness that one day at soundcheck, the crew took to impersonating Robert for the whole afternoon.

Arriving in reception for breakfast, the hotel lift doors opened on to a sea of young girls screaming, mobbing us, wanting autographs and photos; it was all getting a little intense. The record label had generously left gifts in our rooms: bottles of sake containing gold leaf flakes - if you shook the bottle, it became a luxurious golden snow scene. Siouxsie and I were doing a live interview with Kid Jensen for BBC Radio. It was early evening in London, late night in Tokyo. We were drinking our gold leaf sake, feeling very relaxed and very privileged. It was one of those surreal moments when we really felt like precocious pop stars.

Siouxsie would often and quite rightly complain about the lack of air in hotel rooms. Air conditioning was always a problem; it was always too cold and always too stuffy, both terrible conditions for a singer's throat and voice. She phoned reception to ask them to open a window. A polite voice said, 'Very sorry, madam, we can't do that, hotel *security* policy.' A not so polite Siouxsie replied, 'Come and open my window, I am not a security risk!' She was not happy, and eventually picked up the heavy old telephone and slung it at the window. The glass gave way under the impact and a cascade of dangerous shards rained down into the hotel's central atrium.

Now Robert, who'd seen the occurrence and thinking it all rather swell, took his phone with its heavy receiver and smashed his room window as well. Another sharp shower of broken glass fell dangerously into the space – but a canvas suspended above it caught most of the glass without trace. You could tell that the police didn't like it, as they eyed up the whole situation – shouting, 'Passports, please. You must stay in your rooms, you will all now face deportation!' We were saved by the intervention of the local promoter, but the incident was serious and it's no coincidence that we did not set foot in Japan again for another twenty years.

Siouxsie and Robert as Saboteurs?

We were oblivious to the effect that alcohol was having on our careers. It affected what we were doing musically, created internal tensions, and escalated minor problems into majorly destructive incidents. It was a tumultuous time for us all, and there were many times when it should have all collapsed. Yet an unseen force seemed to be keeping us all together. It made me question who or what this driving force could be. I hadn't stood up for John McGeoch and I certainly didn't for Robert – that was Siouxsie's prerogative. I was never the one giving the orders. I was subservient to the Queen Bee and her hive of workers. I was the one who would be sent to buzz her hotel room when we had to leave for the airport in fifteen minutes.

By this point I didn't fear dismissal myself, because of the Creatures and the feeling that I had somehow become indispensable. Somehow, I was still needed. And that's a funny way of putting it. I'm very clean and tidy – especially on a tour bus: if the ashtrays needed emptying and the pizza from last night needed clearing away, I would do it, taking great pleasure in making less work for the driver. It was probably because I had to grow up quickly after my mum died. Most musicians are terrible slobs, expecting someone to pick up after them, their socks here, their undies there, their glasses and beer bottles left all over the place. They might get a guilty conscience and clear up in the morning, but if not, it was Budgie to the rescue, whether Budgie felt like crap and hungover or pompously self-righteous. Either way, if I was up cleaning up it was a tell-tale sign that I was feeling really bad and was doing my penance, my Catholic upbringing coming through. I'd be polishing glasses, loudly putting plates away, wanting everyone to know what I was doing.

This desire to serve was perhaps a lonely attempt at trying to find a lost domesticity and sense of home, but it also became an inept way of trying to show affection. How else could I do it? Music was where connection happened, but was it affection? I certainly didn't know much about making love. Siouxsie and I drank together and, if enough of our inhibitions had been subdued, we would usually fool around. This had more to do with breaking down the pretence of always being strong or being in control of our lives. Which we were not. But to be gentle, to embrace, for sex to be about the intimacy of bodies and minds - we knew little of these things.

When I tried to be romantic, it was with gifts. Once, I commissioned a dress for Siouxsie from the fashion designer Colin Swift, of Monmouth Street: a dress a flamenco dancer might wear. It was typical of my extravagant nature at the time. As soon as I had a bit of money, I'd spend it on something expensive at Browns on South Molton Street, or something from Harrods or Fortnum & Mason. I considered these signs that I had arrived. I'd buy extravagant presents for people and then wonder why it wasn't reciprocated, especially when it came to Siouxsie, who could be very generous. My attempts at romance rarely went beyond the materialistic, however.

Siouxsie was having to deal with my increasingly erratic behaviour. I'd started 1985 with my usual weekly routine of eating out, gigs, cinema, snooker, hairdresser, gym, art galleries, then I got ill and quit drinking for five days. My health improved and I was in good enough shape to begin work on a new album with producer Hugh Jones.

It was April 20th and my friend Philip had invited me to go with him to Cardiff Arms Park to watch *a rugby international*, of all things. I grew up watching Welsh rugby union on TV, but this would be my first time watching a live match at the famous Cardiff stadium. The atmosphere was powerful, and as the crowd surged, my feet left the ground and I was set adrift in a powerful sea of singing and drinking. We drank a lot of Guinness, chased by even more brandy. Leaving for London and inspired by the day's sport, Philip picked up broken bricks and stones from a building site and began tossing them around like rugby balls. I wasn't aware that I was supposed to be catching them, and a heavy chunk of rock took me by surprise, smashing against my shin. It should have hurt more than it did, but I was anaesthetised by the booze. We got on a slow train back to London, totally unaware we were surrounded by the wrong supporters. There I was, with my bleached hair and earrings, surrounded by these brawny blokes who were not thrilled by our presence. We were noisy, rude and provocative. The police had to drag us away for our own protection. Always keen to continue the party, back in London we hit the Earl's Court Road and went to our favourite little restaurant, where I ended up crawling around on the floor and biting a customer's leg underneath the table. We were very politely asked to leave.

This was the Budgie that Siouxsie often had to open the door to. It's no wonder that once the physical lust had dwindled away, almost to nothing, all that was left was a professional relationship. Life with Siouxsie was one of extremes; she expected total commitment. This might well have contributed to the demise of the people who did come and go, certainly the guitarists. With Robert gone, John Carruthers, who had been in Sheffield band Clock DVA, joined.

From the off he could never live up to the Siouxsie image, and never seemed comfortable - it wasn't voiced, but he was very much thought of as the 'Sheffield tyke'. John always said he never understood why he'd been chosen as the next Banshees guitarist. I wonder if it was because Severin and Siouxsie felt less threatened by a seemingly simple Yorkshire man. But John was also smart, funny and mischievous. We were regulars at a huge subterranean snooker hall beneath London's old diamond district in Hatton Garden. John and I, two lads from 'up north', got on very well together, as pals and, more importantly, musically.

Working towards what would become the album *Tinderbox*, we started to write together. During a break from recording 'Cities in Dust' and after a couple of pints in the pub with Jameson chasers, we went back into the studio and spontaneously composed and recorded the guitar and drums that became the song 'Umbrella', a completely improvised track to which Siouxsie gently sighed a poetic octet. Sometimes the drinking worked. Severin, however, was too engrossed playing *Escape from Colditz* on his new Commodore Amiga, so he probably didn't realise that John and I had come back from the pub.

We started recording what would become *Tinderbox* in May 1985. It had been an album of false starts. Firstly, our new American label had put us with Bob Ezrin, who had produced two of my favourite teenage albums, Alice Cooper's *School's Out* and Lou Reed's *Berlin*. Bob came along to sort out the songs for what would be our debut album for Geffen Records. He turned up at John Henry's rehearsal rooms in North London wearing a real Canadian bear fur coat. Siouxsie and I supported the animal rights campaigns of Lynx and PETA, so the collaboration was already on shaky ground. First, Bob wanted to fire Carruthers - but only Siouxsie got to fire guitarists. He also had his keyboard at the ready. Some producers like to establish co-compositional writing credits, which for us was another reason to proceed cautiously.

We met again and for the last time in Madrid. Bob and I spent a day in the Prado museum admiring, among many iconic images, Francisco Goya's *Saturn Devouring his Son* and *The Garden of Earthly Delights* by Hieronymus Bosch, both paintings pre-empting the mood of the evening ahead. After a pleasant day in each other's company, we joined everyone else for tapas and slugged some vino. And soon 'Slugger', an affectionate name for Siouxsie, began to slip not-so-subtle jibes about Bob's furry dress sense into the conversation. 'Hey, how's it growing, Fozzie!' was the one that really got his goat. He left the next morning and we never saw him again.

He was replaced by Hugh Jones, who had enjoyed big success with REM. We worked with him in a way that we had never worked before. Writing sessions in London had an air of the classroom, complete with chalk on blackboard. He was suggesting changes of key and time signatures - discussing the technicalities of songwriting. Things we usually did instinctively. It took us a while to adapt.

We opted to record away from London and followed the path of Bowie and Iggy Pop into the hallowed rooms of Hansa Tonstudio in Berlin. Siouxsie and I shared a two-bedroom suite in an apartment building near the Berlin Zoo. Severin and Carruthers had an adjoining set of rooms across the entrance hall.

Each day we would be picked up and delivered to the studio by our driver, Jos - one of the most patient and forgiving human beings I've ever met. I don't recall Jos ever sleeping or eating, and he never drank alcohol. Jos only drank coffee and always had a wrap of what John Cooper Clarke referred to as 'Oliver Reed': rhyming slang for speed, amphetamine sulphate.

It was thrilling working in this tall building adjacent to the Berlin wall, exactly where Mr Bowie remembered standing in 'Heroes', even if it did remind me of the pubs in St Helens, where the buildings still stood amidst the post-war emptiness - like solitary stumps in toothless old gums.

Our apartment was on the Kurfürstendamm, one of the city's main arteries, a fifteen-minute drive to the studio by the Wall that encircled West Berlin. The Wall meant no through traffic across the city. On a sunny spring Sunday afternoon, a walk along the Ku'Damm was a pedestrian paradise. Everyone was walking. It was how I imagined the Promenade des Anglais in Nice in another century, when the tourists were Russian aristocrats and their debutante princesses stepped out to be seen.

This island of Berlin had a strange, timeless atmosphere. I found a wonderful old vinyl record store, and as Siouxsie was about to have yet another studio birthday, I bought her a box set of Wagner's *Ring Cycle*. I still have it. She never played it. It was perhaps just another expensive gift, lacking thought, or love. The gift of Wagner's music being rejected may have been an omen.

The nights in Berlin were like knives - bright and shiny, with dangerously sharp edges. For all its legendary status, Hansa was falling apart and so was our little band. It was a hot late spring, and Severin wasn't coping well, either with the heat in the studio or its effect on his equipment. He vented his frustration by smashing headphones. This only made things worse, as the studio had no replacements and we were behind the Berlin Wall.

The tension wasn't helped by how much we were all drinking at this time. Siouxsie was my main drinking partner, and most nights we'd find ourselves in the little bar opposite the apartment where the jukebox kept playing the big hit of that year, 'Live Is Life' by Opus. It was an awful song. It certainly didn't feel like 'live is life' to me at the time. There was a little Italian restaurant in one of the few other buildings still standing by the Wall. Severin and I went there one time, and one time only. It may have been for a missed breakfast or a late lunch, but I was still suffering from the night before and I felt exposed and vulnerable. An uncomfortable experience for me, perhaps for Severin too. I felt like I did back in junior school when walking into a classroom full of children. My head would be fixed, and I could only look in the direction of my chest, which was so tight that I couldn't breathe. Sitting at the table with Severin, every movement - fork to mouth, hand to glass, glass to mouth - was resisted by steel-like sinews. And yet within these restrictions, I was shaking.

We were working hard, but I was completely torn. I wanted to play the messed-up rock 'n' roll game in this place with such a history, but I felt like I was going insane. We'd hang out with the ladies of Berlin band Malaria! Gudrun Gut, Beate Bartel and another friend Silke. Silke had caught my eye and had become the sole focus of my attention as I drank my way into another night of oblivion.

In Berlin at that time there were many impromptu bars, one-night only affairs that appeared in a basement, only to dissolve in the dawn. That night, the bar could have been in Mitte, could have been anywhere. It was a small bar with a fridge full of vodka. Silke was serving. We were all having a good time until it was time to leave. In my mind, in my state, it was never a good time to leave, especially when it was really, *really* time to leave.

As soon as we got back to the apartment, I insisted that we go out again because I needed another drink. I could be very belligerent in those moments, times when Siouxsie probably knew me better than I knew myself. She knew exactly where I was heading, and why. I wanted to go see the lovely, smiling young lady who was serving the nice vodka behind the nice bar. I was deep in the alcoholic delusion that I must be in love - that's what I always thought. I certainly didn't need, and absolutely couldn't handle, another drink. We argued, I stormed out into the night and, wherever I got to, it wasn't the nice little bar with the fridge full of vodka.

I woke up in a bed with a catheter in a vein in my left arm. An apparition in white, stood in the dazzling sunlight streaming in through the white curtains behind them. I seemed to have landed in my very own version of Powell and Pressburger's *A Matter of Life and Death* in heaven's hospital, and I felt okay.

I came back down to earth with the interrogation from the doctor. I must have answered his questions with enough coherence to convince him to let me leave - or perhaps they just needed the bed. Before I was sent on my way, the doctor gave me his prognosis, in excellent English: 'Your blood alcohol level was .28 per cent. This is not so good. The good news is that your liver is okay. But if you carry on drinking like this, it will not be.' Much as had been the case when I interpreted the doctor back in England telling me I could carry on drinking if I switched to red wine, I heard only four words: 'Your liver is okay.' That seemed like good news; the other part I could dismiss.

I made my way over to Jos's place. He was shocked to see me. 'Budgie,' he asked, 'what happened?' I told him what I could remember, the row, the storming out and the waking up in hospital. He drove us over to the apartment on the Ku'Damm. We took the stairs to the third floor and quietly knocked on the door. There was no response, no sound of movement. All was quiet.

I remembered out loud that I didn't have a key. Jos did. The door dragged open across the thick pile carpet. The air inside smelled stale; not the sweet smell of death, but a close relative. The curtains in the living room were still tied open and the morning light picked out shards of broken glass beneath the smashed door of a drinks cabinet. A dark trail led into the bedroom. It ended where a bare white foot was resting in a pool of coagulated blood. She was lying face down on the edge of the bed. 'Oh no, Siouxsie, love, what have you done?' Jos said, not expecting an answer. It looked bad. We roused Siouxsie and drove her to the hospital, thankfully not the same one where I'd woken up that morning. (It was fortunate that Jos had a key. Siouxsie remembers being unable to stop the bleeding, so she locked the apartment door so that I couldn't get back in, and went to bed.)

It might have been a different establishment, but there was a humiliation in being subjected to the fallout and consequences of my actions. Progress through A&E was slow and reality began to emerge in the form of sweats, shakes and confusion. After her stitches were tied and cut, we paid the bill and got back to the apartment, both relieved to be alive.

17.
Bacon in Harrods

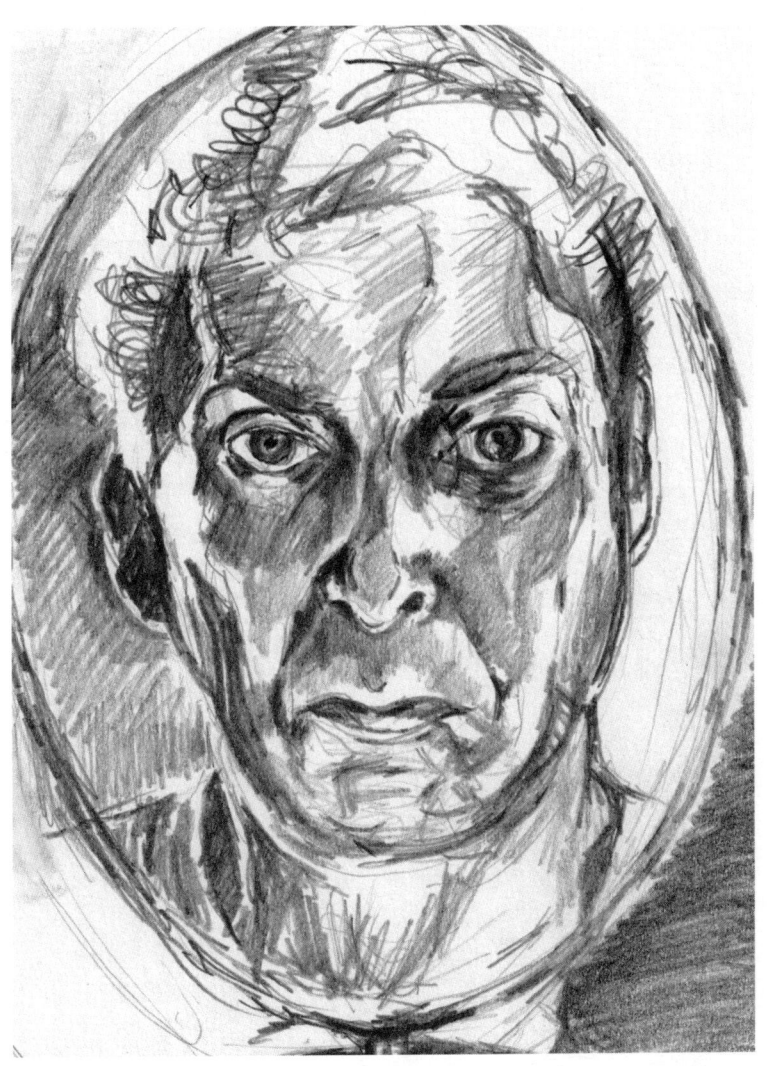

Drinking was not something I could do as a pastime or social activity. It had one purpose - to get me happily drunk. If I could have stopped at happily, I might never have had any trouble. I would be in bed recovering from the night before (or the two days before), and I would only surface after dark. This recovery process would involve about six to eight pint glasses of water, lined up by my bedside: my method of rehydration to cleanse me overnight into daytime and back into the following evening. I had to get rid of the alarm clock because the ticking would cause my heart to beat in time, and I became convinced and obsessed that that wasn't a good speed for a heart to beat at. I could only lie on my right side because I thought that my heart would be squashed if I turned over.

After all of this, I would still return to the pub not too long before closing time. This would be long enough to get a little lit up on alcohol, but not enough to require copious amounts of cocaine to power-bore me through the animated monotony of another night in the pub.

From a night in the pub aged seventeen, on my own in the Cotham Arms on Victoria Square, St Helens, to a night in the pub at the King's Head in the Barbican, London. Initially as a dreaming wannabe drummer, and later as a professional popstar. What is wrong with this picture? Everything. Especially me and my part in it. I would phone my brother Mike from London once a year, usually on New Year's Eve from the phone box outside the Devonshire Arms on Marloes Road, for the duration that a modest pile of 10p pieces would allow. Valuable drinking time, valuable beer money, not to be wasted. The picture in my head was Budgie, né Peter, in London phoning home from the big, bright lights of London, independent and happy. The booze fuelled the delusional fantasy.

The late eighties were spent trying to live up to some idea of what we should do, and be, as successful musicians. Liverpool and Eric's, those early days in London, were so very far away. Regardless of all the chaos around the drinking in the Banshees, the mutual, innate need for the band between Siouxsie, Severin and myself kept the show on the road. The *Tinderbox* single 'Cities in Dust', released by Geffen in the USA, became our first serious hit on the other side of the Atlantic, reaching number 17 in the charts. But we had nothing left in the tank. We had always talked about doing a covers album and this felt like it might be the moment, and also a way through a sticky patch for the band. It transpired, however, that things would just get stickier.

After recording *Through the Looking Glass* we had to find a guitarist once again. John Carruthers had been fired for his slovenly appearance, turning up in stonewashed jeans and a T-shirt. There was a paradox at the time in that the Banshees' instability and internal tensions, especially between Siouxsie and Severin, worsened just as we were having our greatest commercial success. We were successful enough that our lives became a little monotonous: tour, record, tour again. We battled to find our place in a time of wildly evolving musical tastes and scenes, becoming more or less popular in America. This was the lot of a moderately successful post-punk group during the 1980s.

It was our moment to brush with fame, but we were always aware that there was a hierarchy, and we knew our place in it. In August 1987 we opened for David Bowie on his Glass Spider tour in Anaheim, California. The fedora-wearing Thin White Duke was backstage perched on a golfing buggy, with a huge pair of binoculars, watching the audience arrive. They were still arriving as we began our short set in the late afternoon sun, which was so uncool, so too hot, so un-night shift. Backstage in hospitality we mingled with an assortment of LA liggers, and Severin's old schoolmate Billy Idol. From somewhere close, a British voice announced, 'Ladies and gentlemen, we will be on stage in fifteen minutes. If you would like to take your places . . . have a wonderful evening, thank you.' Before the competition winners - and ladies of the 'blue-rinse brigade'- had had a chance to even squeak or squeal, Mr Bowie - for it was he - had disappeared. I never thought it impolite that Bowie didn't speak to us personally that day. It was our biggest gig to date, and yet it felt so insignificant - not playing with Bowie, but playing a baseball stadium in the California heat!

Sometimes the winklepicker of fame was on the other foot. Backstage at some European festival, Fish, singer from the band Marillion, approached Siouxsie. 'Hi, Siouxsie! Fish!' he said, holding out his hand. She only heard a Scottish accent. We were in Sweden, and Siouxsie assumed that he must be a travelling, die-hard fan. 'Well, you came a long way just to see us,' she said without a hint of irony. Neither Fish, nor his band Marillion, had made even a tiny blip on Siouxsie's fame radar. It appears that if you really have fame, you eventually only see yourself. Everyone else disappears.

We were infected by the mood of the times, the consumerism and ridiculousness of it all. Siouxsie and I would sometimes eat at the Hungry Horse in Fulham or Nikita's, a Russian restaurant on Ifield Road. Marc Almond lived around the corner. I say eat, but with the excuse that we loved borscht beetroot soup - which we did. We'd really go to Nikita's to drink vodka. We tended to order just a main course, 'dessert' simply an excuse for more vodka. I'd shop at Browns on South Molton Street and spend a small fortune on clothes. I was made up when I found a beautiful, dogtooth-patterned, loose cut, raw silk suit. The next day, the *Daily Mirror* had a photograph of Nick Rhodes from Duran Duran in the same suit. So henceforth it was either confined to the back of the wardrobe or I avoided Duran Duran. I loved that suit. But that's the risk you take shopping at Browns or around the corner at

Vivienne Westwood on Davies Street, splashing out on something you think is exclusive but isn't.

I'd spent my art school days creatively chasing Francis Bacon, who had way more of an impact on me than Marc Bolan or David Bowie. There I was in the 1980s, with my Harrods store card and my American Express card, going into the food department to buy a particular roast of Jamaican Blue Mountain coffee beans, and there *he* was. Francis Bacon was leaving as I walked in. I could say, 'Our eyes met as the doors opened,' but I flatter myself. His expression could have been one of inquisitive curiosity, but was more likely, caused by the sun being too bright for him to see anyone. I've since imagined many words of introduction. 'Hi Francis, Budgie,' would have been enough. I would have joined Francis for breakfast at Dino's near South Kensington tube station, where I would have accepted his invitation to help out at the studio. More likely I'd have been met with an incredulous non-sequitur, akin to that of Siouxsie greeting Mr Fish. Alas, no words were spoken. It wasn't exactly how I'd imagined it would be, but like all meetings with someone you've always dreamed of meeting, it rarely is.

It's fair to say that the excesses of the 1980s music business did little to discourage this mindset of adulation. Shortly before we left to start a Banshees tour, Geffen asked that we arrive a few days early to film an appearance on MTV in New York. The plan was to leave Heathrow early on Friday morning to reach the US by early evening. I took a cab to Siouxsie's, but she couldn't be roused, and then wasn't ready in time. Tim Collins (our longest-serving and longest-suffering manager) told the rest of the band and the crew to go ahead and get on the flight with all the gear. Much later, Tim got into a cab to Heathrow with Siouxsie and me. The only flight that could get us to New York in time for this MTV appearance was on Concorde, which, given this was a day-of-travel ticket, cost enough to make Collins look as if he'd just been drained of blood and blanched. Obviously, Siouxsie and I quite fancied going on Concorde, so we convinced him that we absolutely had to do this MTV thing. Tim took out his credit card, and we raced through the Concorde lounge, no time to say hello to Helena Bonham Carter (probably for the best) and onto the fastest plane in the world.

The interior was cramped, with ink-blue leather seats set in pairs either side of the narrow central aisle. Champagne was served in crystal, dinner on fine porcelain, and as the Rolls-Royce engines roared, the display behind the cockpit charted our progress - Mach 1, Mach 2. I felt like an imposter, squirrelling away the souvenir diary and pencil they handed out to all the passengers. I still have it.

We arrived in New York, checked into the hotel, and had time for a bite to eat before everyone else arrived. We were sitting drinking in the bar when they walked in. Nothing was said except a few mutterings of 'bastards'. Just jealousy of course, but there would have been more upset if they'd known that our tickets probably cost more than any tour of ours had ever made. We were told that Geffen ended up footing most of the bill.

Getting things paid for by the record company became routine, although it wasn't usually quite as decadent as using Concorde for a taxi. I needed constant attention to retain that bleached blond shock of hair that had become my trademark 'look' since I was christened with a toothbrush full of bleach, back in Liverpool. My trips to Trevor Sorbie's Covent Garden hair salon were all part of the Budgie maintenance ritual, all part of expenses. A process that was very of its time, it would take over an hour for the bleach to lift my natural colour out, and a bottle or two of Chablis was needed to subdue the pain of my scalp being stripped raw by 40 Vol. hydrogen peroxide. My whole head would scab over and my skin would be so tight it was like having a facelift. Having partied with the dancers of Arlene Phillips's Hot Gossip - yes, even the hairdressers served as a drinking club - I'd leave Sorbie's salon looking like a recently lit Swan Vestas match, bright pink with a burning shock of white on top. It had been the bane of my life since Liverpool, suffering for blond hair.

There was a little shop selling leather goods down the street from the Drury Lane Theatre in Covent Garden, full of fashion types and luvvies and, crucially, the person who supplied everyone with the eighties' magic powder. He wasn't the world's most successful procurer, committing the schoolboy error of getting too high on his own supply and acquiring a problem. He would cut the coke to make it go further, then realise that there wasn't enough, so he'd have to cut it a bit more, for which he used a laxative called Mannitol. I suppose it broke up all the inane conversations when everyone had to keep dashing to use the bathroom. The shop and its surrounding area was a mess of designer wannabes, all fuelled by illicit substances and champagne.

Siouxsie's look had become so much a part of her identity that she decided a change was needed. She'd had her shock of blue-black, crimped and back-combed hair imitated by so many – and if everyone wants your look, the hardest thing to do is change it. She decided to go for a cut inspired by the bob made famous by Louise Brooks in the 1929 Weimar German classic *Pandora's Box*. Siouxsie's version of the Brooks bob was more extreme, shaved high into the nape with a severe straight-cut fringe. It was very stylised, and soon to be immortalised in the video for our version of Iggy Pop's 'The Passenger'. Anton Corbijn shot the photographs of 'the Siouxsie Bob' (what a good name for a Siouxsie Sioux/ Robert Smith collaboration . . . or then again maybe not!), which would be given exclusively to the print media during the promotional campaign. This would be Siouxsie's first time playing the press exclusivity game, so we wanted to give it our best shot. But we had a dilemma.

Polydor CEO Richard Ogden had invited us to join Polydor's table at the BPI industry awards dinner at the Grosvenor House Hotel in London's Mayfair. Polydor were planning their own merry promotional scheme, which, without consultation, included introducing Siouxsie to West End musical mayhem-maker Andrew Lloyd Webber. We begrudgingly accepted our place alongside the luminaries of British pop with the knowing wink and nudge of inglorious infiltrators.

We had never been invited before and would never be invited again. We had just had our biggest success to date, but that was in the USA. We had to play the game, but what to do about the hairdo? Embracing her enthusiasm for a sitcom, Siouxsie announced in the voice of Baldrick, the fool of *Blackadder*. 'I have a cunning plan, I shall wear a wig!'

We were greeted into the belly of the beast by the flash of the flesh-hunting paparazzi, pecking and clicking at our arrival beneath the faux Parthenon portico of the 1930s Grosvenor Hotel entrance. We were resplendent in an array of silk and colour. My own two-piece was an electric-green rough-silk suit with a black rollneck sweater. Siouxsie wore my curated flamenco creation by Colin Swift of Monmouth Street. They snapped photos of us descending the staircase into the underground ballroom, which once housed an ice-rink frequented by a young queen of England.

We were so obviously in the right place for our own beloved ice queen. Our expressions looked like we'd been sucking lemons. I have rarely seen Siouxsie's cheeks look so scalloped and scowling. It was clearly going to be an interesting night. We had arrived just early enough to slip into the arena before our hosts arrived. There we found huge round tables, laden with crystal, cutlery, napkins and place-name tags, where world-weary luminaries would be quaffing and cajoling, greeting and slighting, laughing and grimacing. Our table was next to that of the '5 Star' family and far enough away from the stage to keep us separate from the proceedings: we hadn't been nominated for anything, and probably never would be. We quickly rearranged the seating arrangements so that Siouxsie was sitting between me and Severin, so the three of us could observe without being observed, rather than being stuck - as was the record label's plan - between Andrew Lloyd Webber and Tim Rice.

After the awards ceremony it was time to explore the faded glitz of the Grosvenor's corridors and find out where the Pet Shop

Boys' room was. They had won the award for Best New Group and there were rumours of Colombian delights in abundance. Alas, we couldn't find the Pet Shop Boys, so we headed out into the night for a jolly good romp at a nearby nightclub. Stallions was tucked away behind the Astoria, down a back alley off Tottenham Court Road, and was known for being a bit more hardcore than Heaven, but not as debauched as the infamous Anvil in NYC. It was a place where society's misfits, pop stars and children's TV entertainers could slip in to misbehave unnoticed.

Underground in every way, Stallions smelled of cigarettes, beer and something adjacent to urine, alongside the sweet and sour of poppers and steroids. Leather and rubber were the usual dress code, but tonight was less strict, and anyway Siouxsie was an icon, which always gave us access to the inner circles of deviance and degradation. The Pet Shop Boys hadn't made it, but Bananarama's Sara, Keren and Siobhan were already dancing. Screams from the boys announced Siouxsie's arrival. Humidity was rising as the Weather Girls' 'It's Raining Men' soaked the steamy dancefloor. At about half-past ten, Siouxsie and Siobhan had the spotlight. Darryl Pandy's multi-octave voice was rolling and booming out 'Love Can't Turn Around'. Siouxsie and Siobhan were gyrating, getting closer and closer. Like long lost nightshift sisters, they instinctively knew the routine; it flowed effortlessly, sinuously. It became a show. Aware of being watched, they knowingly toyed with a playful eroticism, arms swirling above their heads, entwining, almost touching, closer and closer, when suddenly, Siouxsie's wig got caught in Siobhan's fingers, and with a flourish it became airborne to a massed inhalation of, 'Oh, my God!'

Time seemed to stand still. Only the wig was moving, cutting an arc through the pulsating strobe lights, a stop-frame animation above our heads. Is it a bird? Is it a bat? Is it a spider? Is it a cat? Then it landed with a splat, on the dancefloor. 'Love Can't Turn Around' crashed us back to normal speed with a warm blast of bassline pressure. Trampled underfoot, and as flat as hairy roadkill, the wig was rescued and gingerly handed back to its owner.

The game was up, the bob was unveiled for all to see, and the paparazzi missed it. The secret was safe, and Siouxsie's bob was ceremonially revealed to the rest of the world the following week.

*

With Carruthers gone, and the 'get out of jail free' card of a covers album spent, we desperately needed to give the Banshees a mighty kick up the arse. Martin McCarrick had worked with us on *Through the Looking Glass*, and was brought in as a full-time member along with a new guitarist, Jon Klein. Martin and Jon were easy-going, creative musicians who enjoyed a drink and a laugh, though their initiation into the band was anything but. 'Song from the Edge of the World' had been written with John Carruthers, and we wanted to use the process of recording it as a way of bedding in our new members. It was recorded in tediously testing sessions with Wire's old producer Mike Thorne. We were all fans of Wire's first three albums, but it quickly became clear that the sound of those recordings was obviously more down to Wire's genius, than Mr Thorne's expertise. Siouxsie, who by now had developed quite the habit of commenting on attire, said he looked too stay-pressed, calling him the man with the coat hanger in his T-shirts. There was a lot of tension in the studio, both between Thorne and Siouxsie and between Siouxsie and Severin, and the resulting recording process was clinical and cold.

Desperately needing to move forward, we decided to reunite with Mike Hedges for what would be the band's first residential writing period. We began the writing period in Ardingly, West Sussex, not long after the great storm of 1987. Driving south from London we passed many fallen oak trees lying horizontal in the fields, damaged and exposed like ancient dinosaur bones.

On Bonfire Night, we went to the Ardingly village firework display, where a very loud Mike Hedges was clearly unimpressed. 'Call that a bonfire? What a load of rubbish!' he yelled, before almost falling into the flames. By contrast our manager Dave Woods was becoming increasingly uncommunicative. The man who had warned me to 'watch out for those London people' and had felt like an ally in the band was now remote and hiding away in a big new house he had bought in Islington, but I was more concerned about his health than his money. When I last saw him, he looked like a small boy in an anorak who wanted to go home. There was a lot of heroin around in London, and it was really shocking to see this man I'd respected like a brother turn into a shadow of his former self. I drove Dave to Ardingly railway station and said goodbye. It was the end of another chapter.

Dave wasn't the only one of us whose behaviours were being badly affected by drugs and drinking. I was trying to avoid it, but the habit had become more about the binge. Someone once described me as a functioning alcoholic and I never quite understood why, but that's what I was, carefully programming a drum machine one minute, losing my mind the next. All the same, we were hitting a musical peak, developing in a way that we hadn't experienced since the days of John McGeoch. One of us would often fall over and mess up, but we were finally writing as a band, trying ideas and working hard to bring them to life.

This was largely because Martin McCarrick and Jon Klein were such good collaborators. We'd fallen into the trap, without realising it, of becoming a big band who feel they don't have to do very much. We'd got there incrementally and were lucky, because by and large in the past we had pulled it off. But we were starting to lack that creative spark that you all need to share something that everybody believes in. It's essential to have that, or at least some semblance of it. I don't think three weeks of preparation in a rural retreat necessarily instils that in everybody. If it's not there, then you're risking endless nights in the country pub.

An escape of sorts came when Siouxsie and I went to Venice to film footage for what would become the video for 'Peek-a-Boo'. Banshees videos, Venice and my drinking did not have a good history, and lo and behold, everything swiftly went wrong again.

We were at the Mardi Gras festival, and our Italian promoter

Mauritio turned up with his girlfriend, whom I promptly hit on. If I was drinking there would be flirtation and attempted seduction, with a conquest in mind. If that's what I intended, and it usually was, I couldn't switch my focus off. Even with Mauritio and Siouxsie being in the same room, I carried on oblivious. I remember Mauritio saying, 'Budgie is not very happy, Siouxsie is not very happy, we go now, *ciao.*' The next day, I remember looking out over the lagoon and thinking once more, *Oh, not again. What did I do last night?* Venice had once again been a place of shame and alcoholic excess. Siouxsie and I had a row and nearly broke up. She had had enough.

Oddly, if I look at my diaries, each of these incidents hardly gets a mention:

Venice, 18 February - Had drinks with Italian promoter, up late, little sleep etc.
Friday, 19 February - Arrive home, sleep rest of the day in a hotel, Kensington. Salad.

Like nothing happened. Though I *was* in the hotel alone, banished for bad behaviour.

Siouxsie and I seemed to resume business as usual within a couple of days. Perhaps herein lies the cycle of addiction. I was falling from grace big time during the writing of *Peepshow*. The alcohol increasingly led to sexual compulsion, a removal of inhibitions. Siouxsie once kindly informed me that I masturbated in my sleep - which kept her awake. I said nothing, as any protestation would fuel further chastisement and accusations, which would always escalate: 'You were fucking the drug dealer', 'The fat ugly slut in the hotel bathroom', 'The brainless bimbo with no style'. I may have flirted with them, but if anything more happened, I don't remember.

This time, for the first time, I was forced to confront my drinking. The hospitalisations in Venice and Berlin had worried me, but not enough for me to make changes. My non-drinking periods were getting progressively shorter, and my falls from grace progressively worse. This pattern would continue until I met my nemesis in Sao Paulo – but that wouldn't be until 1995.

Cocaine had already started to push Siouxsie and Severin apart, a situation that only got worse when we went on the road with *Peepshow* after its release in September 1988, our biggest production to date. I'd quit drinking again after Venice, and had managed to stay dry throughout the *Peepshow* recording sessions and during the subsequent tours of Europe and America. I would be up early in the morning, rent a bike, and cycle around whichever city we were in. I'd bought a huge video camera, which I thought would be fun to bring to the party. This was, of course, not very popular with the rest of the band.

The cocaine use was getting out of control, especially one time before a gig at Le Zenith in Paris, late September 1988. Our dressing room was covered in the stuff, largely, it seemed, for the benefit of hangers-on and the usual suspects. Suspect was also the nickname of our new manager, Paul O'Reilly. I wrote a terse 'holier than thou' letter ticking him off for allowing the drug backstage, outlining a litany of errors and basically warning him to keep away from Siouxsie until further notice. It was the first time in my life that I'd taken control of a situation in that way.

Not drinking had given me a lucidity and confidence that I'd never known before. It also meant I spent a lot of time on my own in hotel rooms. I thought that as I had changed, so too would everything and everyone around me, but it didn't. I couldn't heal the band, and in fact things had deteriorated further. After our gig at the Universal Amphitheatre in LA on Bonfire Night 1988, there was an almighty row between Siouxsie and Severin, with the usual trigger of her displeasure being one of his girlfriends. Siouxsie recalls: 'I picked her up, threw her out of the room, then I began to strangle Severin with the cord of his telephone.'

This was the explosion of tensions that had been building for a while, something that had perhaps always been at the heart of the Banshees. I had stepped away from being Budgie for the first time since Holly had teased me back in Liverpool. It was a window into my behaviour as Budgie over the years. The drunken belligerence that had given me the confidence to survive and the ability to forget. Yet being sober was the loneliest period of my life. I wasn't drinking, but I wasn't present. I felt like I was living in a state of limbo, some liminal space between Peter and Budgie.

The Banshees never really recovered from that incident in Los Angeles. The rest of the tour was unpleasant, with a terrible tension between Severin and Siouxsie. She had felt utterly let down by his behaviour. After the tour ended in London in the middle of December, they could barely be in a room together and it was clear that the band, for now at least, was over.

We took this hiatus as an opportunity to reactivate the Creatures. Both being fans of the Miles Davis and Gil Evans recording *Sketches of Spain*, I drew up an itinerary for a road trip called 'Discovering Castles in Spain' - a fun if slightly ridiculous way of trying to find somewhere to record, driving around the country like we were doing a recce for film locations.

We stayed in Spain's Paradores, state-owned hotels set in renovated castles, monasteries, convents and fortresses. One was a thirteenth-century Arab fortress, sitting high on a hill above the town of Jaén in Andalucía. The locations were romantic, but we were on a mission. This involved talking to hotel managers in my extremely limited Spanish, animated with lots of ridiculous air-drumming movements trying to explain what we wanted, which was use of the hotel restaurant, ballroom, or any large interior space that could be used to record drums and vocals. We were not successful. Musicians from England with a recording contract needed no translation. It was all about money, money and more money!

We were very fond and caring of each other, even though we weren't sharing a bed. There are Polaroids from the trip. My hair is a blond candyfloss mess, and I could never dress for the sun. Siouxsie always looked composed, posing with the wild cats she found in the ruins of amphitheatres and ancient bullrings. Ironically, it was on the ranch of a former matador that we found a place to make music. With the help of the Domecq sherry family, an old adobe-style ranch was located on the road from Jerez to Arcos de la Frontera. La Penuela was steeped in the now familiar Catholic melancholy of the Iberian Southwest, and it was still a working farm and ranch. We were probably the strangest house guests that Carmen and her daughter Maria had ever laid a friendly table for. Isolated among the wheat fields, with the constant whining, buzzing and screeching of cicadas, bees and house martins, we set up on the stone floor of the bodega above the old oak wine barrels. The bittersweet aroma of ageing sherry, strangely familiar, wafted me back in time to the smells of the cellar beneath the Parr Hotel and late-night Cherry B kisses from Mum and Dad. Mike and his Abbey Road mobile desk joined us, and there was always ice-cold dry La Ina sherry on the table. I largely resisted temptation and held it together.

I wrote a lot of lyrics on *Boomerang*. 'Willow' has memories of a trip with some friends to the Isle of Man, not long after my mum had died. How it all felt like a play, perhaps with me already cast as an outsider, the role I would later adopt. 'Morriña', which closes the album, was a mood piece, with lyrics that I'd written years ago when living in Byam Street. I'd sit in the dark watching the moon rise slowly over the old Fulham Power Station. It was a lament for the lost physicality of our relationship, a lost feeling of being intimate, of being together. I realise now that the references to Christmas are part of a longing for the security and familial tenderness that were lost the moment my mum died.

What we had in common, just as we had in Hawaii with *Feast*, was trying to find songs together. It became increasingly clear to me that that was all we had left. We were not alone in struggling to sustain a loving writing partnership, and we wouldn't be the first to find that lustful beginnings and performance passions can, over time, turn malevolent behind the scenes.

18.
Twisted Honeymoons

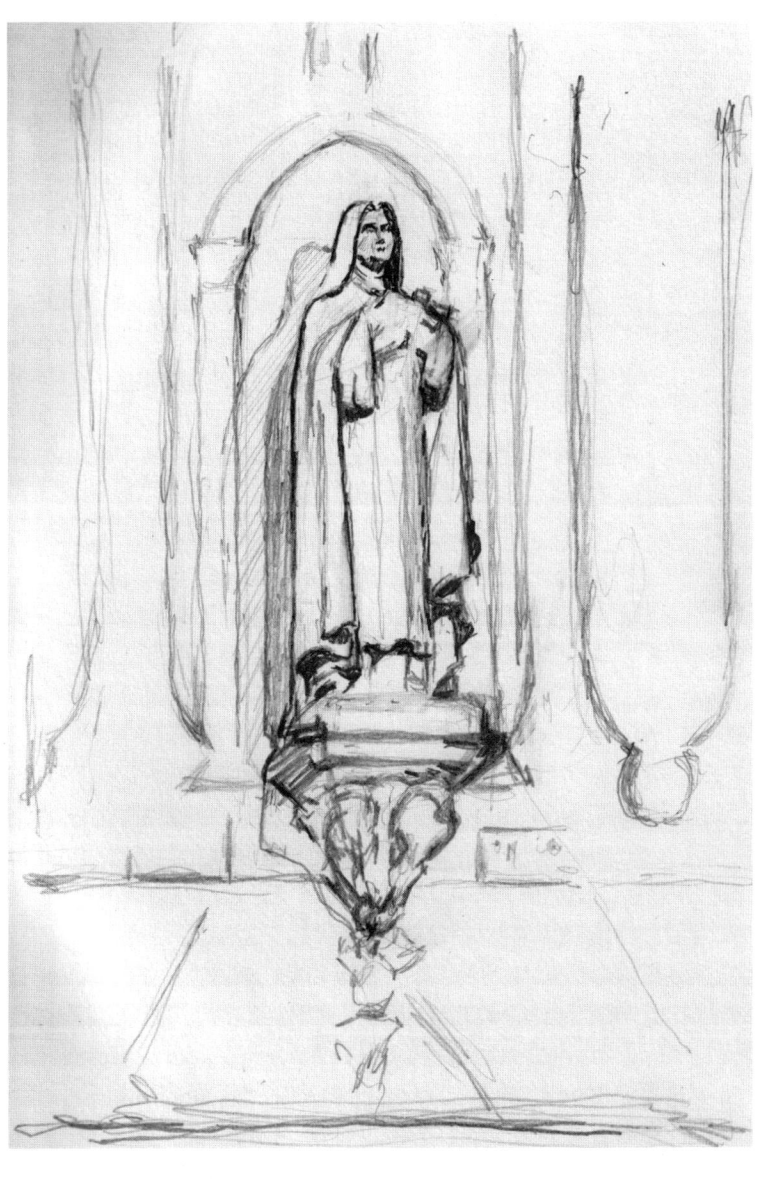

The Creatures was a breeze compared to the Banshees. In 1989 we wrote, rehearsed and recorded what would become *Boomerang* before going on tour for two weeks around the UK and Europe, and three weeks in America to promote the album with a skeleton four-man crew, our manager Tim Collins and assistant Viv. We travelled in two cars with a van for the gear. Tim was surprised to report that this was the first time any US tour of ours, including the Banshees, had broken even. Sober, I enjoyed the responsibility, embracing new ways of working using sequencers instead of a band onstage. We'd tried using musicians to play both the *Feast* and *Boomerang* material live, but it hadn't worked and it just didn't sound like us.

It was a functional, tightly scheduled tour, going from gig to gig by car, after the show to a motel for a few hours' sleep, then on to the next venue the following morning. Our stage dynamic was playful and relaxed, a far cry from the tension and studied seriousness of Siouxsie and the Banshees. Even though the Creatures was a lot of fun, I had responsibility for everything technical resting on my shoulders, which was stressful. And Siouxsie had to learn to get up early. Unfortunately, I hadn't worked out how to process my extra responsibility without relying on alcohol and drugs, and the spanner in my works arrived when we got back to London, and I had no idea how to decompress.

Steve Strange had opened a new nightclub called the Birdcage. Sober, I stepped right in. Boy George was there, being lovely, and I immediately fell off the wagon into a regular night of vodka and cocaine, a party atmosphere that rolled on to someone's apartment. I came to in daylight, in a strange room. It was clean and quiet, but odd, like a library without books. I was seated fully dressed in an armchair. I stood up, my legs steady as I looked out of a window. I was above street level, in what looked like London but *where*? I didn't have even the vaguest of memories about what had happened the night before, just the sickening feeling of dread that yet again my drunken lack of inhibitions had got the better of me.

The only door opened onto a landing above an empty stairwell, silent save for the muffled sounds of morning traffic outside. It didn't feel like anyone else was there, but I turned the handle quietly, closed the door behind me and stepped out onto the street, turning right towards the movement of cars and people. I soon realised that I was on the King's Road, somewhere between the World's End and Sloane Square. The café opposite looked open. I needed to think.

I checked my pockets. I had some cash, a credit card. I ordered tea, not as harsh as coffee, not as weak as water. My memory of the night before started to clear, slightly. I knew that cocaine had been involved, but I didn't have a cocaine hangover. I didn't have a hangover at all, which was bad, as it meant it hadn't started yet. Recollection started to swim through my mind, a slowly unveiling darkly erotic horror show.

There was a large-breasted woman sitting next to me, with Siouxsie and Severin sitting opposite and a periphery of shadows. The details were as ambiguous as a Francis Bacon painting. Were we wrestling on a hardwood floor, or on a shagpile carpet? Was she naked, was I naked, did we have sex? Was everyone watching, horrified, laughing? Was anyone there or had they left in disgust at my hapless, drunken foreplay? I had no memory of sound, voices, seduction, sex, rage, just a nothingness. But the guilt and shame were all too palpable, and very real.

Years ago, when I left home and went to Newquay for summer work before starting college, I went with a friend who was already well versed in sex and relationships, which I certainly wasn't. I was lonely and still like a child, trying to be poetic in writing, drawing balloons as the dots over the 'i's, working out how to drink and smoke, and feeling awful the next day. Sat in that café years later, I was drowning in the awful morning-after sensation that, once again, I had messed up, perhaps even more seriously than ever before. For some reason I decided that everything would be okay if only I went back to Newquay. I had the feeling that if I could return to the same spot, I could use time and the physical difference to unravel everything that had happened since, to get back to Peter, to myself, even to get back to the womb.

I arrived at Paddington station, bought a ticket with my credit card, boarded the train and, just as I did when I took the train to Italy to see Jeanette, sank into a fantasy world. A woman from Paris was sitting opposite me, and I pretended to be French. Another miniature whisky and I could have been from anywhere. I wrote down the name of every station we went through as we rattled down to the West Country. Of course, when the train pulled into Newquay the reverie had to end.

I walked through the tired old seaside town in my old tweed coat, with no bag, or anything useful. With my shock of blond hair and a general morning-after dishevelment, I must have looked in a terrible state. Newquay didn't look the same, and the illusion that I was going to be able to find my teenage self quickly started to fade. I wandered along Fore Street to the hotel where I used to work and knocked. I recognised the tall son of the old manager when he opened the door. I explained who I was, and he smiled and said that yes, of course he remembered me – he didn't need to add 'as a bright and cheerful seventeen-year-old'. They must have taken pity on me and let me have a room.

As the night fell across the sea, it became clear that this had been a desperate, futile exercise. The past was the past and the Peter who had slept under this roof all those years ago was long gone. I felt that I would never get him back, that this crazed flight from London to Cornwall had been a pathetic exercise in self-delusion. What was left but the next step? Which for many might well be suicide. The next morning, I found a telephone box, called my friend Philip in London and asked, 'What should I do?' They said they were worried, that Siouxsie was worried, and that I should come home. I got back on the train. 'Tail between my legs' doesn't come close to how I felt unwinding the miles back up to London.

Siouxsie and I never discussed what had happened: our mutual inability to communicate meant that what I had, or hadn't, done wasn't articulated or given oxygen. As the Banshees - that extension of Siouxsie and me in which still more people were utterly unable to communicate - we deluded ourselves that everything was better now. Siouxsie and Severin had an emotional reunion, and we started writing a new album.

Still smarting from the unresolved shame of the Newquay episode, I felt entirely out of sorts. When we started recording at London's RAK Studios, I would spend long sessions in a small room under the stairs. I even brought my recollections of Newquay to the band, writing the lyrics for 'Return' about the devastation at where I was, my Catholic guilt and drinker's remorse. When we recorded the song as the B-side to 'Kiss Them for Me', Siouxsie added the line 'when will you ever learn, the hurting it will return'. I wondered if she was expressing concern or contempt; what was clear was my uncertainty.

I had first proposed to Siouxsie in 1985, but the Berlin incident meant that marriage was definitely off the cards, which was in retrospect quite the right decision given how little passion remained in the relationship. Nevertheless, on Valentine's Day 1991, we announced to everyone in the studio that we were going to be married. The reaction was of some shock and no little confusion, but this being the Banshees, nobody ever really asked us, *Are you sure?* A couple of months later, Siouxsie and I had our wedding. I say 'had our wedding', as it felt as if it were something that happened to Siouxsie and me, rather than being *entered into* in the way you might normally expect.

Getting married was a bad idea, a means of protecting ourselves once the romance had died – and was long gone. Nothing fuels passion's flame more than the clandestine ruse, yet when everything becomes above board, as had eventually happened with us, the true commitment is revealed as superficial. On the surface, nothing conveys true love more than an open and public display of unity, but beware the sham of the marriage ceremony – its usage as a glue to prolong the agony of a waning affair, and as a show of pomp and ceremony to show the world that all is well behind the net curtains. We had the business to think of (it feels right to call the band that), and the business required stability. Therefore, a wedding was going to be good for business. We might have been subconsciously aware of this, which was why the ceremony, the dressing of it all, felt more like making a music video than anything romantic.

If this sounds cruel and cynical, well, it was. If marriage is a union of souls, then Siouxsie and I were certainly two souls entirely trapped by the Banshees, and to an extent the Creatures, with no sense of independence from our professional working lives. Marriage performs a function when you've been together for quite a while, and you feel like you've got to tell everybody: 'It's still okay. We're solid.' We were far from it. The romance had pretty much gone years before, but I knew how to fake it on the surface, which was ironic, given that the early years were spent hiding our relationship from the world. But while there was no longer any lust and love, I was still burning with a desperate need to be loved. It was what had brought us together. Once we had found that need in each other, the relationship was already doomed. Neither of us was giving anything back, and in any case, we wouldn't have known how to accept what was offered.

Covering up this void at the heart of the soon-to-be marriage took a lot of planning. What was the theme going to be? We were really into Indian music – we'd been working with Talvin Singh – and loved Indian food, so we went for an Indian theme. Siouxsie's friend Nassim took the role of lady-in-waiting, putting the bindi on Siouxsie's forehead. It was a very colourful spectacle: Siouxsie chose all the flowers to match the colours of her outfit, purples and yellows, the colour of an Indian royal wedding. I was dressed as an Indian prince in a gold brocade coat with cotton pyjamas underneath, and ceremonial shoes that were ridiculous and I'm quite sure that nobody seriously wore. It was all set off with the bleached blond hair, the whitest it had ever been, and an appalling hangover.

I wasn't really drinking at the time, but my best man, a QC in the Temple, had taken me out the night before. We'd known each other since I lived upstairs from him in my first flat in Byam Street. He had a cat called Jojo, a statue of Rumpole of the Bailey, whom he resembled, and he enjoyed a drink. We'd had a raucous stag night, and wisely he hadn't told anyone where we were, which of course was asking for trouble.

Come the morning of the wedding, I was in a terrible, terrible state, and he did what a best man does: took me for some Dutch courage. A large brandy was duly gulped down. Siouxsie was very late getting to the altar rails, but in that time hanging about, I was getting concerned about where and when I would find the next drink. I'd never had a brandy in the morning on an empty stomach before, and it hit me hard. What a day, your wedding day, to feel like 'I *need* a drink'. It wasn't even that I was in such a mess because I was afraid of the wedding and needed to wash away the doubts. I was very aware that this was a performance; that we were preparing a performance of a wedding ceremony that happened to involve us.

Everything was the wrong way around. At the reception, when my best man stood up to give his speech, he pulled a pair of horn-rimmed spectacles edged with flowers out of his jacket pocket, before putting on a Dame Edna Everage accent for the whole delivery, 'possums' and all. It was a little surreal. Anton Corbijn was there as our friend and our guest and as much as we'd have liked him to, he didn't take any photographs. He did do a little filming, however, as did Banshees guitarist Jon Klein, but we never watched the video footage. We never put photographs into a book, and we never held on to any documentation of what we had shared apart from the marriage certificate itself.

I just about managed to hold it together for the ceremony, but by the time we left the reception I was not quite with it. It was in moments like that that I realised how odd my adult life must have looked to my family. My sister Linda and her husband Brian came down to represent my family. My brother Mike had to look after his shop and my dad and my stepmother were too ill to travel. I've never really asked what they thought, but I suppose it was a step into the entertainment world that I'd always had a foothold in. I don't think they took any of it very seriously, thinking it was just me having one of those crazy days.

If marriage is the union of two families, our relations with the extended Clarkes and Ballions were not exactly harmonious. Siouxsie came up to St Helens once and it was a disastrous trip. My brother ran a small convenience store and had a Rottweiler called Rocky as a guard dog. Rocky wasn't socialised and spent a lot of time in the back yard. He was fine with the children and the family but nobody else, and Siouxsie got way too close. The dog-tooth check trousers she was wearing as she walked past Rocky must have vibrated in front of his eyes: he went for her, grabbing her thigh in his jaws. We had to take her to the hospital.

Siouxsie found my family too quiet. But, of course, my family never talked much about anything - all serious talking ended when Mum died. We didn't know how to talk as a family, how to discuss like a family, how to shout like a family, how to *be* a family. People who came into our orbit generally found us quiet. Of course, what Siouxsie had been through with her dad meant that she didn't have much to go on either. Are they a good family? Are they a quiet family? Her family argued a lot and were very dysfunctional while her dad was alive. This just meant that everything we seemed to try in the real world, things that most people would consider a normal part of a relationship, like getting married in a big fantasy wedding, seemed destined not to work out.

The Absence

We would occasionally spend Christmas with Siouxsie's family near Bromley in Kent. They lived in a 1930s art deco house that was cold and damp, especially in winter. Christmas with the Ballions always began with joviality and mirth. We played old-fashioned parlour games like the Minister's Cat, which would become more and more lewd as the clean adjectives got used up. But it didn't take much to disturb this game of happy families. Just like our wedding, it felt like another performance. There was an unspoken sense of blame that loomed above the dining-room table, like ectoplasm at a séance.

It is said that an alcoholic's drinking affects at least six people, usually their close family. This continues long after the alcoholic has left or has died. Maurice Ballion died in a chair in the room where every Christmas his family would argue, still furious at him for leaving them, angrily unearthing old conflicts and emotions. 'Dad' was rarely *mentioned* during Christmas with the Ballions, but the memory of him was always there, sitting silently in his chair, waiting for his cronies to arrive with more booze. Maurice was deeply loved and deeply missed, his absence leaving an appalling sadness. Siouxsie and I were still emotionally stuck in the rooms where a parent had died – mine in a two-up, two-down terrace in St Helens, Siouxsie in the semi-detached suburbia of London.

Siouxsie was quite suburban in her own way: in the lyric for 'Hong Kong Garden', her paean to the local Chinese takeaway, she sings of 'yens', not 'dollars' or 'pounds'. Singing about a Chinese takeaway in England, her currency faux pas reveals a young, naïve yet charming parochialism. But from the same period, her lyric for 'Suburban Relapse' reveals her incisive knowledge of what goes on behind England's twitching net curtains. Siouxsie's interest in obsession, breakdown, abuse and violence was ever-present throughout her writing. She experienced many of these psychological and physical events, both as victim and observer. Her lyrics and live performance could certainly be seen as an outlet and as tools with which to diminish their toxicity and exorcise their power. In music I was drawn to the expression of anger both lyrically and musically in the heavyweight riffs and beats of 1970s heavy rock music. I used this music to draw out my own anger and obsessions by physical expression on the dance-floor, and later by my primal approach to drumming. Siouxsie and I were not technically accomplished, our mutual need was for expression through performance. More than love and lust, this was the reason our connection was so strong and why we chose to secure that connection in May 1991, through the spiritual aspect of marriage.

After the wedding we went to Paris to stay in an old silver-service-style hotel called the Bristol, just off the Champs-Élysées. We had only been there a couple of days when the call came in to say that we had to return to London for a TV appearance on *Top of the Pops*. And that was it. The honeymoon was over before it had begun.

Superstition was released in June 1991, and a month later we were off to the USA for the launch of a new concept to the American market. Lollapalooza was a touring festival and featured mostly American luminaries of alternative music at the time, from the Butthole Surfers to Ice-T, Nine Inch Nails and Jane's Addiction, whose singer, Perry Farrell, was one of the idealist organisers. A few days into the tour, me and our guitarist Jon Klein got ourselves arrested in Chicago. There was an altercation and Jon was pushed over, at which point the only defensive option available to him was to bite the ankle that was nearest to him. After the incident in the Earls Court restaurant, there was clearly something about being a Banshee and a predilection for ankle biting. My hand caught somebody in the mouth, but that's as far as it went before the police arrived outside with a van, which we were thrown into, and then thrown again, into a prison cell, to be bailed out the next morning. This, of course, deeply impressed the American alternative rock royalty, making us heroes before the tour had even started. It also meant that they felt they had to push the boat out for the rest of the tour so as not to be shown up by these two crazy Brits. It set the tone for what ended up as an utterly debauched tour, and it quickly became very clear that Jane's Addiction guitarist Dave Navarro had primarily invited the Banshees along to seduce Siouxsie. His technique was very like Robert Smith's - *I'm out of it, I'm an artist*. At one point Perry Farrell said to me, 'David just wants to experience everything I have, but he never will.'

So, Siouxsie and the Banshees went off to join grunge and industrial, and I felt like a fish out of water because everyone was getting branded, pierced and tattooed. Bands like the Butthole Surfers seemed outlandish, but in reality they were just southern boys who enjoyed a drink. Half of Jane's Addiction were strung out on smack, the other two were all-round gentlemen.

At the end of the tour the accountants and legal advisors from the bands and the festivals all sat at the bar like the singing Scouse vultures in *The Jungle Book*, drinking champagne, splitting the cash. It was everything we thought we'd never do, and it was odd seeing how the Americans couldn't wait to get to the point where you had a management company getting your allowance for you to pay the mortgage. We just wished we had the money to be able to afford the accountant. It felt very careerist, not at all what we'd got into the band for, and not the counterculture it pretended to be.

At the same time, I was falling for one of the female camp followers around Jane's Addiction. Her lost 'Lady of Shalott' expressions felt so familiar. I was told later that most of those girls were in and out of drug rehabilitation centres. I felt there was a callous lack of care for them, and a cynical feeding frenzy from the vulture accountants towards the people responsible for creating the event. When we were at Lollapalooza, we saw all the little things that niggle you as a band, but they were just going on every day and at a far higher level. It was crazy, but we were all equally lost amid this well-oiled machine of industry chugging along, and if you got caught in the cogs, well, tough.

Everything came to a head at the huge hotel we stayed in when the tour rolled in to Santa Monica. Navarro had 'gone missing' and

Siouxsie had left some clothes for me outside our firmly locked bedroom door. Very sweet. But where was I supposed to sleep? The 'Lady of Shallot' lookalike and her friend put me up until morning. Nothing happened, but it was so strange - if you'd grown up in Californian drug culture, perhaps 'crashing' like that was very normal. But it was very alien to me. I was caught between lapsed Catholicism, caretaking, and everyone else's cocaine addictions. There were a lot of lost people on that tour and around that scene. It was all very sad.

I tried taking Navarro's girlfriend for a picnic, a wicker basket with food and wine, something nice. It was clumsy and odd. I didn't know about courting or romance. Emotional development stops when alcoholism begins, and I was still very much a teenager, mentally. We all stepped over the line during that tour, and I'd been no angel sexually. But anything that happened was steeped in shame and confusion. There was the American culture of the strip club; for a tour that was supposedly for artists who were in opposition to the mainstream, it was oddly popular on Lollapalooza. I couldn't cope with strip clubs - too much, too close up.

Siouxsie's exalted position on the tour was perhaps the first time she'd realised that she could *exist* outside of the group and our marriage and just do what she wanted. Perhaps it became a roleplay. There are many images of her in roles from famous films. Siouxsie so loved the promotional image of Charlotte Rampling in Liliana Cavani's *The Night Porter* that in 1982, she asked Anton Corbijn to recreate it for the front page of the *NME*. She also dabbled with the role of the Hollywood diva. She adored Carolyn Jones as Morticia in *The Addams Family*, and was simply 'divoon' channelling Jayne Mansfield in the video for 'Kiss Them for Me'.

During the shoot and in one of our rare conversational moments, Severin told me that I had no self-respect when I was drunk. He had a point - self-esteem is the first thing that the alcoholic loses. He later recalled: 'I was hard on Budgie because he was supposed to be a Banshee, and when I saw him drunk and behaving like an idiot he wasn't wearing the right suit as far as I was concerned . . . I wasn't nearly as hard on him as Siouxsie was. She would publicly demolish him. That was the nature of their relationship . . . Budgie would always take over and play the fool until Siouxsie would cut him to shreds or physically attack him and put him in his place.'

The absence of a script to guide interactions allowed me to turn a blind eye to what I assumed was going on with Siouxsie and Navarro. My apparent lack of concern for the evaluations of others was perhaps me keeping quiet to avoid the risk of rejection. Self-appeasement masquerading as low self-worth.

The Banshees returned to the USA in November the same year, to play the cities that the Lollapalooza tour hadn't visited. Navarro flew down to see Siouxsie in Austin, Texas. It was the oddest thing. I was having dinner at one table with the rest of the band, she was sitting at another with him, having a heart-to-heart discussion. He had obviously flown down to woo her, it was so blatant. As usual we all had separate rooms, and they left the restaurant together. It was obvious what was going on. I called Siouxsie's room several times but got no answer. I drank the night away with Martin and Jon. Nothing was ever said about it between Siouxsie and me.

My diaries reveal periods of loving and caring intimacy in our relationship. These periods could be sometimes lengthy, away from familiar temptation, or brief, between increasingly frequent bouts of me, her or us both drinking to excess. When a therapist reported a repetitive cycle of addictive behaviour in our relationship, I presumed that this cycle referred only to the periods of drinking and non-drinking. I now see that our cycle was behavioural and ran far deeper than a solely chemical addiction. Our intense love was real, as was our intense anger and disgust. This was the foundation upon which we perpetually destroyed and rebuilt the relationship.

19.
My Black Hole of Calcutta

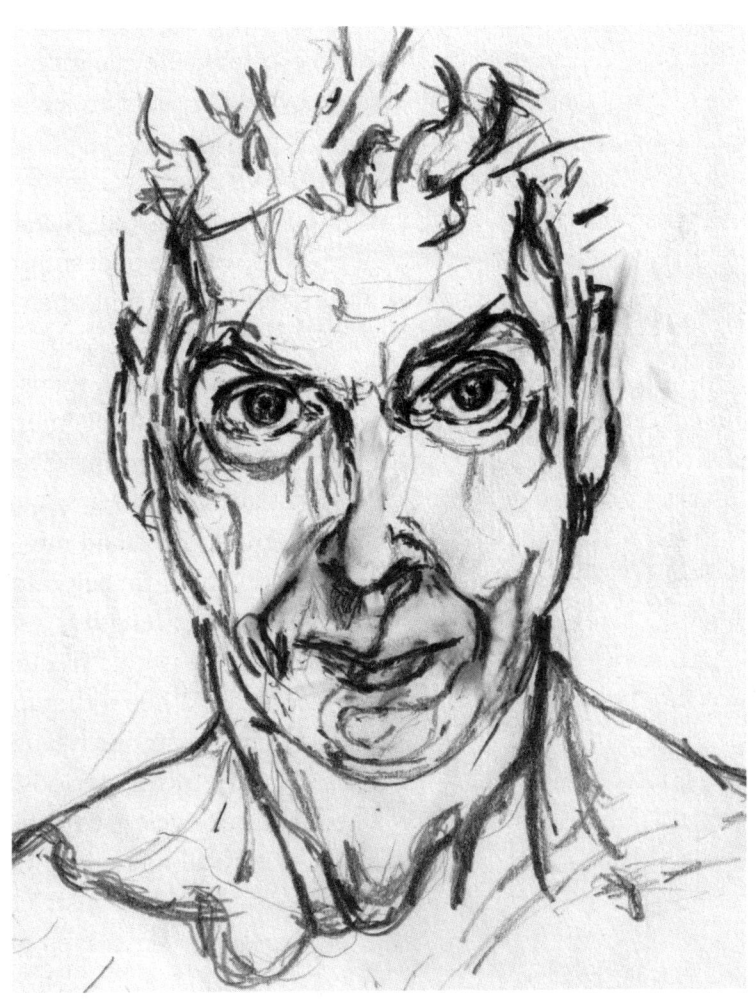

We had only just survived the tawdry, manufactured tryst and partner-swapping antics of Lollapalooza. It was nothing short of a miracle that Siouxsie and I could still tolerate each other afterwards. At the end of that year, Severin with his then girlfriend Cricket spent Christmas and New Year with Siouxsie and me in Los Angeles.

And so 1992 began with a week-long fresh-juice fast. Together we also quit nicotine, caffeine and alcohol. We visited Disneyland where it poured with rain, so there were no queues and all the rides were empty. We spent a few nights in the desert at Joshua Tree, and together we got high on life. Had it been possible to step back and view this apparent bliss in context, it would look like the 'calm before the storm' in the ongoing drama. We remained in North America for a twenty-date tour, during which I desperately tried to retain my new healthy ways. Though physically sober, bright and breezy by day, I became a neurotic nighthawk. A gig-analysing, diary-keeping, travelling-minstrel photographer with insomnia. I have a suitcase full of photos of late-night city junctions, aerial views from high-rise hotel rooms.

Did I mention getting bored or going crazy? This tour's opening act were Polydor stablemates the Wonder Stuff. They often borrowed our tour-guest Talvin Singh for tabla parties on their bus. The tour ended on 29 February in Frankie 'Thrill Kill' Mann's hometown of Chicago, with Frankie running a real onstage tequila bar. Our crew were mixing the cocktails backstage and had compiled a 'best of' setlist, comprising only singles. If proof were needed that the only requirement for a great show is everyone having a good time, then that second night at the Riviera Theatre was it.

Siouxsie and I arrived back in London and checked into what would become our new home from home, the Regency Hotel, 100 Queen's Gate, London. We had left our last real London home in September 1991, after the Lollapalooza tour ended. We had been living out of suitcases for nearly six months. After a further two weeks of restaurants and room service, any semblance of luxury had lapsed like a limp lettuce leaf. It was time to finally leave. On Sunday, 15 March 1992, Siouxsie and I left England and moved to France. This was an attempt to restart our lives - in some circles it's known as a *geographic*, a change of location which hopefully begets a change in fortune. It rarely works.

Less than a month later we were back in Los Angeles to meet and talk with producer/director Tim Burton about 'Face to Face', a song for his new film *Batman Returns*. It was on a return visit to London to rehearse and record 'Face to Face' that I found myself back at the Regency Hotel. After a long day in rehearsal, I went to bed, couldn't sleep and got up at around 6am. I went downstairs for breakfast but was too early.

I walked out over Queen's Gate and onto Manson Place. I had passed the entrance many times but had never entered the cul-de-sac with the high window in the wall at its closed end. I had always assumed that this window was at the rear of 7 Reece Mews, Francis Bacon's studio. I stood there in the pouring rain, looking up at the window. It was Tuesday, 28 April. Later, the news broke: Francis Bacon had died at 9 o' clock that morning in Madrid.

Our move to France was not entirely based on a whim. Mike Hedges had already moved to Domfront, an hour and a half south of the port of Caen by car. The steep pitched roofs of Normandy, reminiscent of Scotland, were perfectly suited to a big man with a red beard. Mike bought a chateau and installed a recording studio. If Mike moved to France, we'd all move to France. All for one and one for all!

Siouxsie and I had toyed with the idea of leaving London for a while. Siouxsie once told me that she felt she had to get me out of London to keep me out of trouble. Drinking took away the few boundaries I possessed. When I was drinking, I would always be looking for love in all the wrong places. In my own way I was seeking a fix for the perceived absence of intimacy in my life. Siouxsie's genuine concern for my sanity was coupled with an apparent need to keep me under lock and key. The influence of the residential studio sessions we had done with Hedges led us to believe we could turn a French house into a studio, thus saving the band money. It was all to serve the Banshees, or maybe to serve Siouxsie - I doubt that Severin had any intention of travelling to a rural French town whenever we needed to work.

We spent little time planning or doing the things you're advised to do, like 'spend a year living in your new country to see if it works out'. Like everything else in our lives, we never looked too much before we leaped. I had contacted a French estate agent, and on a whirlwind tour of the region around Bordeaux, Biarritz and Toulouse, found a big house in a small town. Condom, located on the River Baïse, is central to many small rural communities that still seem to belong to another, older world. From a stone balcony above the front door could be seen the spire of St Michel and the cathedral tower of St Pierre; one for my brother, one for me.

Old French chateaux tended to be big rambling wrecks with an elderly couple shuffling around, living in just the kitchen watching television as the grandeur decayed around them. The house we bought was well preserved and in good order. What set it apart from other much larger houses was that it had retained many original features, unique to what estate agents call a *maison bourgeois*. It had been built at the end of the eighteenth century for the Catholic Monseigneur of the Gascony area. We bought it from the Germain family who had probably updated the electricity in the 1960s but little else. Those original features included beautiful wood parquet floors, wrought-iron banisters around a central stone staircase, floor-to-ceiling windows and marble fireplaces. I noticed similar workmanship during a visit to Paris and Napoleon's apartments in the Louvre. Apparently, teams of artisans travelled around France offering the same fashionable work, wherever it could be afforded. The entirety of 138 Morley Street would have fitted into the house's *grand salon* twice over - most of it would have fitted into the kitchen . . . in which there was only a two-ring electric hob to cook on. Madam Germain employed a *femme de menage* who cleaned and apparently cooked for the entire family. The buying procedure was long and protracted, but we had made up our minds and the deal was eventually done.

We arrived at the house but had to spend the night at another hotel, Les Trois Lys on Rue Gambetta, to wait for the house keys to be delivered and for our furniture to arrive. Well, it was mostly Siouxsie's furniture - except for my Habitat sofa. While we were on the Lollapalooza tour, our flat in Notting Hill Gate had been cleared, its contents crated and everything put into storage at Heathrow Airport. On moving day everything was shipped over in a semi-articulated truck and trundled off to Condom. There was barely enough furniture to fill even two of the rooms; their grand volumes with high ceilings swallowed everything.

So, there we were, sitting in the *salle à manger*, at a white Formica-topped table with gatefold legs, drinking large bottles of *vin de table*, the six-franc basic stuff. It was a bit like a sitcom. One time when Pam Hogg came to visit, she and Siouxsie gave a wonderful impersonation of Edina and Patsy in the episode of *Absolutely Fabulous* in which they drink the wine-tasting dry.

In November 1992, with major renovation work producing a daily cacophony of hammering and drilling, I received an invitation to join Amy Ray and Emily Saliers, the Indigo Girls, on a tour around Europe. This enabled me to escape the renovation work, but left Siouxsie alone in the house with the cats and the electricians. She was not pleased to hear that the tour was continuing to the USA in December, so I suggested to Amy and Emily that Siouxsie come along as a guest and sing a couple of songs. Indigo Girls fans were treated to Siouxsie performing with an all-female band, comprised of Amy and Emily, Sara Lee on bass, Jane Scarpantoni on cello, Scarlet Rivera on violin, and little ole me. Siouxsie was very relaxed and slotted in perfectly, though dressed a little differently to what the audience were accustomed to. They screamed with delight to see Siouxsie walk onstage resplendent in a skin-tight shiny-black vinyl catsuit. She performed 'Strange Fruit' and 'Something Wicked This Way Comes'. A lovely run-up to Christmas, and a much-needed distraction.

But two weeks later it was back to rural France, to the cats, the quiet and the isolation. We didn't know it then, but I don't think either of us were in a good way – a lot of stress had been building up. This came out most shockingly not long after we returned from a promotional trip to London. Siouxsie had given a 'one-off exclusive' interview to a newspaper in which she revealed things she had never spoken about in so much depth before. Mostly to do with her father, his alcoholism, the violence at home between him and her older sister, and his death in the house. Apart from a brief talk, we hadn't mentioned this again, but it must have been bothering her since then. In the centre of the French house kitchen was a marble breakfast bar, and we were sitting facing each other on high tubular steel barstools. Suddenly, she stopped talking, her face froze, lips losing colour. I leaped up, the barstool clattering behind me, and just caught her before she hit the deck. She was having a seizure, like she was holding her breath. I held her and thought of my dad, and that fateful night, the familiar fear of helplessness. It was only moments, then she relaxed and slowly recovered, breathing returning to normal. Isolation can be scary.

The press at the time loved the idea of Siouxsie and Budgie living in a French chateau with their cats, with an air of gothic pop domesticity. It was sadly less romantic than it seemed. We would often be drinking in separate rooms in this huge house. Siouxsie in the *grand salon*, watching movies by the open fire, while I listened to music in the *salle à manger*. One night, perched on a window ledge, drinking merrily from a bottle of Poire William schnapps, I reached down to pet one of our cats. I lost my balance and head-butted the hard tiles of the kitchen floor. I must have been lying there, not moving, for some time, before I felt someone trying to pull me up. My blood was so thickly congealed that my hair had stuck to the cold ceramic tiles. I'd lost so much blood that my blue denim jacket had turned purple and was also stuck to the floor. Siouxsie was probably in shock when she phoned the doctor. They arrived, scraped me up, put me into their car and drove me to the hospital. My eyebrow took my full drunken weight and had split open. It was neatly stitched up without anaesthetic, the Poire William providing excellent pain relief. Until the next morning.

I woke up to a scenario I now knew only too well. An intravenous catheter, feeding my body a glucose solution to counteract the elevated levels of alcohol in my blood. The two female nurses were giggling when they came to see how I was. I had turned up without any underwear on, which apparently had provoked great mirth when they had whipped off my bloodstained trousers. It was another return to consciousness loaded with shame: *Oh God, not again, and this is where we live now, it'll be all over town.* The humiliation was far outweighed by my need for something to relieve the tightening grip of my hangover. The bag hanging from the hook above my head took forever to empty itself. Drip, drip, drip after endless, silent drip. Nothing to do, nothing to think, nothing.

She didn't visit me. What could she have said? 'Oh, you poor thing, what happened?' or, 'Here, I brought you a pack of your favourites - *Fruitgums.*' It was late evening when I discharged myself. Walking the long way back to the house, the catchphrase from an ancient TV commercial offered some long-lost home comfort.

'Don't forget the Fruitgums, Mum, threepence and sixpence.'

Things were not going well. They got even worse when we made an attempt at recording the next Banshees album, one of the main reasons why we had moved to France. When we did the deal on the house, the exchange rate was a healthy 10 French francs to the British pound. After Black Wednesday, and Britain opting out of the European Exchange Rate Mechanism, the pound crashed in value. The monthly pound sterling transfer to repay the French mortgage was suddenly devalued by half. This huge investment was now costing double, and it was touch and go. Our only option was to continue with our plans. We first used the house and its many rooms to dream in, and then to write and rehearse for the record that would become our swansong - *The Rapture.*

By January 1993 the rewiring of the house was almost complete, and in February my drums arrived in preparation for the first band writing period. I picked up the boys from Toulouse airport in our old Saab 9000. But I also had an older Swedish car standing on bricks in the *orangerie* at the top of the garden. A 1968 Volvo 1800 needs a good mechanic, and as I was not one, I had a Volvo engineer travel all the way from South London to the house in France to fix my car. Old car expertise was hard to find, as were parts, so he would be staying with us too. After a couple of days the car was fixed and he could relax. I then discovered his penchant for whisky: I had a new drinking buddy. I rarely drank whisky, but I couldn't leave him to drink alone.

The house had a series of rooms, which were admittedly confusing to navigate, because there wasn't the usual corridor separating the rooms, just adjoining doors. Martin McCarrick the keyboard player and his girlfriend Jill were woken from sleep by the sound of running water. They jumped out of bed and screamed at the stranger standing in their room - the car mechanic. He seemed a bit worse for wear: his wig was hanging off and he was peeing into the wardrobe all over their shoes. Siouxsie came storming into the room where I had drunkenly passed out, screaming, 'Get that arsehole out of here!' She was brandishing a candlestick, like the one Wee Willie Winkie carried in the Scottish nursery rhyme. It was like a particularly bleak cartoon, and something that had become a twisted theme to our relationship.

There are a couple of photos that I took during the late eighties of Siouxsie, always with the mask on. There's one where she's just popping out to the shops in the snow with a fake-fur hat on and full make-up, looking for all the world like the Queen from *The Lion, the Witch and the Wardrobe*. In the other, taken backstage at New York's Radio City Music Hall, she's wearing a coat of fake Dalmatian fur, modelled on the one Dodie Smith's Cruella De Vil desired. She also loved the theatricality of Disney characters and was obsessed with *The Aristocats*. She imagined herself as a playful cartoon character, but there's a lot of violence in cartoons. It's all make-believe when the characters are chased around a kitchen with a breadknife, little feet pattering on the floor, cats and mice cut up into a thousand pieces that become little biddie-bodies running around. But it's less fun in real life when you're woken up with a Wee Willie Winkie candlestick crashing against your head. The brass candlestick was forever dented, my constant reminder of the Night of the Pissing Wig. It was typical of the bleak humour that used to surround us; it was all a bit like the board game *Cluedo* – 'I suspect Miss Scarlett with Budgie, in the Ballroom with the Candlestick'. The next morning, I had to unceremoniously escort the car repair man to the train station. His wig was straight, but he was mortified, a regular guy who had landed in this other world with all these crazy people.

On Sundays, I would cycle along the River Baïse through the local vineyards of the Gers and stop by the old watermill to phone my dad. Dad and I could imagine ourselves as we were before everything changed, it was a connection to the simpler, innocent times when we could just be ourselves. I could still be young Peter and he could have a body that wasn't debilitated by Parkinson's disease. Together we recalled our Sunday morning walks to visit his mother in King's Moss, pausing on the way to collect bunches of chickweed from the roadside, vital greens for the budgerigars at home. We would arrive at Pimbo Road around midday, always in time for Dad to have a pint in the Colliers Arms. I would sit outside in the sun, with crisps and pop. Then it was over the road to Grandma's house and her homemade pie for lunch. Dad usually had a sleep upstairs and I would wander off through the magical names of the surrounding countryside, Black Brook, Red Cat Lane, Crow's Nest and Hangman's Wood. These were the days when the clock face of Beechams tower remained high above my imagined flood level. Home was safe, and life was simple. I made that space for him. It was a regression, so that he could be talking to his little boy. I would tell Daddy I loved him, but I always had to leave that magical place we had created together, end the call and cycle back to the big house, away from Peter and back to the growing complexity of Budgie and Siouxsie's relationship, and an increasingly dysfunctional Banshees.

When we were working, it was so vital to get things done. Everyone mostly put the effort in. It was a productive time, despite us often not being in the same room together. Either Severin was up in his bedroom, Siouxsie was writing, or I was riding my bike in the countryside. I was feeling more and more like I couldn't be in the house. My uncertain positivity felt like it was being countered by a determined negative energy.

It was May when we relocated to a recording studio in Léon, just north of Biarritz on the Bay of Biscay. Despite being so far away from the record company, we had more interference than ever before. Maybe people liked the idea of a trip to France? But the writing was on the wall; the music business was changing, and they were worried. The A&R guy was dropping large hints that all was not well.

We had no producer, so it was our overworked engineer, Charlie Gray, who tried to hold us all together. I was going off the rails with drinking, having terrible hangovers at the studio. My pitiful pendulum swinging ever harder between self-righteousness and self-loathing. I was still able to be present and function, but I couldn't stop drinking. It was sometimes similar for the rest of the band, especially Jon Klein, but I was overindulging in the extreme.

Oddly, those recording sessions were the first and only time that Severin ever asked me for musical advice, specifically about the bassline for a song I had written, 'Sick Child'. It was also the only album session when my demons got the better of me. We were so close to nailing the guitar theme for 'The Double Life', so close that I exploded at Severin from behind the kit, 'If you haven't got a bassline yet, just get out of here!' I wasn't drunk, but I was recovering from an almighty, crippling, two-day hangover. It wasn't my proudest moment, and perhaps it wasn't just about that moment. In our usual uncommunicative way, we were willing each other to stick together. We were ploughing on, creating the record that only we knew how to make.

After tracking the album we finished the record in London, relocating to Wessex Studios, where Siouxsie and I had recorded 'Right Now'. My memories of Wessex were only positive, but we arrived into a very different atmosphere. Doing new songs with John Cale was a bit of a dream come true; we were all fans of his writing and productions with Lou Reed, Nico, Patti Smith, and his solo work. The rehearsals were intense, the music simple and raw, but when we got to Wessex he seemed disinterested. His attitude had changed. Sitting at the mixing desk, occasionally looking over his copy of the *Financial Times*, he would say things like, 'Don't close your eyes in the studio, you have to concentrate.' It all felt a bit 'nine to five', and we were lucky if we rolled in at three o'clock, granted a bit slovenly, but ready to work. Maybe John found our recording process tedious, especially the one that we now employed. He wanted us to record as a band but Severin also seemed to be losing interest, or motivation, or perhaps both.

We hadn't recorded in the same room together for some years, so it felt strange and uncomfortable. For the first time I didn't feel in the least bit connected to the person I'd worked with for well over a decade. I had sworn off drinking, then I'd weaken and go for a pint, and it would be tough. During one session at Fred's, a cocktail meets cocaine bar in Soho, Jon Klein and I were drinking pints with chasers, me morbidly apologising for the financial state of the band, which was affecting Jon's own finances. My old Liverpool mate Pete Burns turned up. We were reminiscing, but the conversation got personal when Jon realised it was his sister who

Pete was slagging off. Jon saw red. I tried to calm things down, words were exchanged, and when Pete got up to leave, Jon emptied a pint over the head of Pete's wife Lynn. There was a scream, Jon was pushed in the back and fell outside onto the street. His head hit the pavement, Lynn straddling him and attacking him with her stilettos – much like Siouxsie with the sailor at Pearl Harbor. The stiletto was obviously a weapon of choice for the ladies of the post-punk era. Jon was bloodied and bruised, with a nasty puncture wound in his *derrière*. I had to take him in a taxi to the nearest A&E to get him stitched up – I knew how he felt. Another Banshees guitarist had begun their downward trajectory.

It was perhaps not surprising that the tracks we did with John Cale were lacking the edge we were hoping for. They needed the kind of treatment that somebody like Mike Hedges had always given our rough material. Rather than glorifying the inconsistencies, John assigned an engineer to smooth out the roughness, and any remaining edginess was gone. We had never worried about being out of sync with the mainstream, but we began to feel that this record wasn't sitting well within our own musical world – but that was also a feeling we were familiar with whenever we finished a new project. My shuffle beat on 'O Baby' became a saccharine-sweet shuffle rather than the something incongruous I was aiming for. It wasn't John Cale's fault, it was ours. Siouxsie and the Banshees' juju magic was fading away.

The Rapture received good reviews, but Jon Klein, fed up with how he felt he was being treated and the endless petty arguments over who had written what, jumped ship after its release. Yet again we had to find a new guitarist. I had the number of Iggy Pop's current guitarist Eric Schermerhorn, and Eric put me in touch with ex-Psychedelic Furs guitarist Knox Chandler from New York. Knox and I talked on the phone for about four hours, after which I said to Siouxsie, 'Knox is our man. We'll never get bored on long drives again, he's a storyteller.' The tour started off with a vengeance in the UK in January 1995. Back in the same routine, as intense as it had ever been, it was quite possible that our agent was aware that this could be our last tour. We played across Britain and Europe, before undertaking an exhaustive tour of North America. By May we were heading over the border into Mexico.

After we played Mexico, we were set to carry on travelling down through South America. They were big shows, we were playing well, and I felt I was hitting a new high in my own playing and that the band was getting better and better. It always did me good to be playing that much; it was what I loved to do. Nothing caused what was about to happen, nothing special, anyway. There was a hint of wife-swapping going on with an old friend, who had turned up with some ecstasy. He got fruity with Siouxsie, which his wife didn't like very much, but I got fruity with her, so any objections faded.

The problems really started in Mexico City. After a day of promotional TV and radio interviews at the hotel, we went out to a local club, where I was introduced to a special fourteen-year-old tequila matured in oak vats. It was the most powerful and magical drink I had ever experienced, almost hallucinogenic. Drinking continued into the early hours, and I was still chatting and laughing with the crew in the hotel reception as it neared the time for us to leave for the airport and the flight to Sao Paulo, Brazil. I was not looking forward to the guaranteed arrival of the mid-morning hangover, so as I grabbed my luggage from my room, I also grabbed two small tequilas from the minibar, one for each eye, just as a precaution. The drive to the airport felt much too long. I'd never drunk in the morning before, but as the bus picked up speed I sipped the first tequila and felt immediately better. I downed the other one and became immediately drunk.

At the airport I hit the bar for a couple more beers. Then my drunken delusion took over - move over Peter, here's Budgie.

I first imagined myself as James Bond, and the female flight attendants as Bond girls, then I became the doomed alcoholic played by Albert Finney in the film version of Malcolm Lowry's *Under the Volcano*. I had first stepped into this role, complete with soiled linen suit and Panama hat, on a day off during 1991's Lollapalooza tour. The outcome was tame then; I just sauntered into the tour hotel after spending all day getting completely drunk in a bar only a block away. The third drink was always free, and I managed to win a lot of booze for myself, and all my new friends – whoever they were. But flying to Brazil took a lot longer than my addled brain had thought it would. I assumed a short couple of toasts with champagne, a quick flirt with the 'trolley dollies' and then we'd be coming into land in time for evening caipirinhas.

Unfortunately, the flight took ten hours. I wouldn't sleep, couldn't sleep. I read my *International Herald Tribune* upside down, bought a multi-coloured compact powder that I thought would hide a multitude of sins, took the phone numbers of most of the female crew members while drinking champagne with them in the galley. To top it off, I insisted on visiting the cockpit to slur my appreciation to the pilot. After this, Knox came and sat down next to me. I eventually collapsed just before we landed. Knox was amused by my bouncing around with no seatbelt. 'That'll teach him.' Severin and Siouxsie were sitting together and had had a talk. I wouldn't have blamed them and I wouldn't have heard them; I had more pressing concerns.

My mile-high party ended in the fluorescent glare of Brazilian immigration. I was shunned by everyone, except bass-tech Kelly who was my companion at the airport bar and had retrieved my make-up. I had my own queue at passport control, and on the drive to the hotel I insulted the promoter and their assistant, and no one would talk to me except the lady driver, whom I assumed might like to go dancing with me later. I was by all accounts pathetic, laughing loudly at my own bad humour, and basically being a complete tosser. This was Budgie at his most extreme, but behaviour that had become increasingly normal. For Siouxsie, band, crew and friends, this was to be the final straw.

My black hole of Calcutta had been waiting for me, and it even had room service. In my hotel room I tried to eat but couldn't. I shivered and shook the whole night through. The walls buzzed and vibrated into black coiling swirls. Lights flared out of dark corners. The room was a vortex, everywhere was buzzing and crawling with insects. If I slept, I was sure I would die. I did sleep and I didn't die. I woke up terrified, deeply embarrassed and feeling incredibly guilty. I phoned Severin to apologise for my behaviour. I assured Siouxsie that normal service would be resumed as soon as possible. I crept out of my room into the huge hotel atrium that I had no memory of. I saw Knox sitting in the café area. We sat and talked for what seemed like hours.

I told him, 'This feels like me hitting an all-time low. This is all wrong, I just want to stop.'

'You said it,' was his response.

A few days later in Rio de Janeiro, I wandered out of another hotel and bought Siouxsie a ring from H. Stern on my Amex card. A birthday gift, a wedding anniversary, an apology offering. She never wore it. Who can blame her? Nice ring, but the gesture was all for my own benefit. The receipt, I posted to myself to remind me of my last crash-and-burn drinking binge – 21 May 1995.

The window of my hotel room looked out onto the Sugar Loaf mountains and the boiling ocean waves. I vowed never to forget that vision. The housemaid had left an orange silk ribbon on the table. It was a metre long, with a card explaining that the ribbon was the same length as the outstretched arms of a statue of the Virgin Mary in a small village just north of Rio. Written along the ribbon's length in black script was a prayer in Spanish; the card's instructions said to loop the ribbon around the wrist three times, tie with three knots and seal with three wishes. I wished for health, happiness and prosperity. I thought the ribbon would stay there for a few weeks or maybe a couple of months. Silk is very durable. It stuck with me for three years, becoming a frayed twist of dark thread. This was just long enough for me to get over the anger and resentment of not being able to be like the others.

Once we got back to Europe, gigs started to become lacklustre, audiences diminishing and venues downsizing. Siouxsie spent most nights at the bar getting very drunk, watched over by Knox, who found her entertaining, even though he wasn't drinking.

We ended up playing our final set at a beach festival in Belgium, alongside Faith No More and Oasis, younger bands playing music so derivative that we as a band from the late seventies, viewed as old punks, could only despair. Is this it? Old goths fading in the sunlight? It was a hot, sunny afternoon gig and I was still feeling ashamed after my antics in South America. Still out of sync with reality, it felt like I'd landed on 'Just Visiting' outside the jail on a *Monopoly* board. After our performance, a festival-friendly set, we retreated to one of those white backstage tents with folding tables and plastic chairs, wine and beer, and cold cuts sweating in the heat. I was still licking my wounds, the others were still drinking. And then everyone said goodbye and returned to London.

Siouxsie and I took a taxi to the airport and returned to France. Previously, we might have talked about everything that had just happened. But there was no discussion. It was such an ignominious end, but abundantly clear that on 21 July 1995, Siouxsie and the Banshees was over.

20.
The Constellations are Upside Down

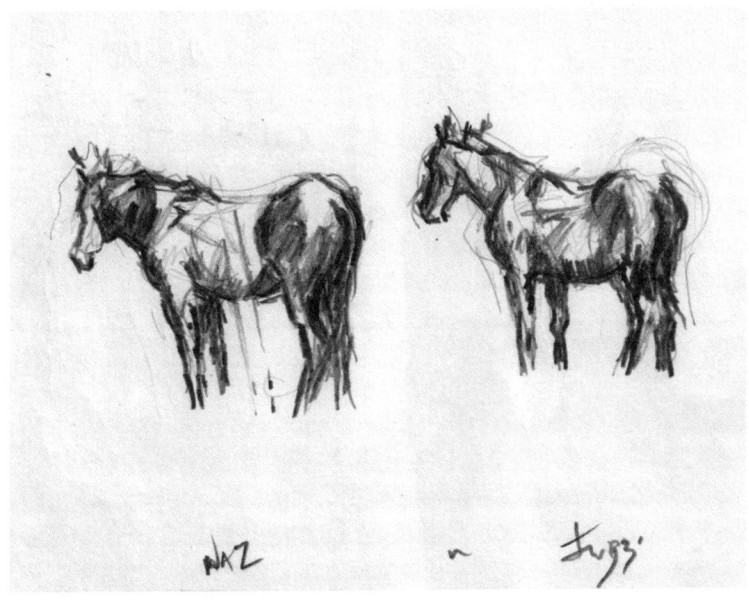

It was New Year's Eve, the end of 1995, not long after I had stopped drinking. The silk prayer ribbon was still clinging to my wrist - the colour had faded but its significance remained strong. It was a small party at a friend's apartment in the Pigalle district of Paris. The people were relaxed, conversation was light and flowed as freely as the Bison Grass vodka. Newly sober, I was still sensitive to drinking, counting the number of drinks others were consuming, not to be judgemental but to gauge how the evening was going. I soon relaxed and gave up on that. It didn't seem like anyone had overdone it, and I was happily chatting quietly, eating canapés. Why would I be counting units? After midnight, the celebrations outside in the streets began to quieten down. We said our goodbyes and headed out into the Parisian night. I didn't think to call a taxi. I'd just hail one on the street. It would only be a short ride back to the hotel. But there were no taxis.

Walking to what looked like a main avenue, I wasn't sure which direction to go in. She was already struggling to stay on her feet. Then the intense cold hit her like a mainline general anaesthetic. She slumped down on the pavement comatose. Her breathing was becoming shallow, and I was shaking with tiredness, cold and fear. I could neither lift nor move her, and the few passing revellers were of no help. How was I going to get her off the street? This cold could kill.

I then became aware of a large shadow looming over me. Without speaking, the shadow slung her over their shoulder and began to walk. I may have said the hotel name, but I don't recall speaking. The large figure moved silently and steadily through the twisting streets of Montparnasse until they came to the hotel.

The room was several flights above street level, but the big figure didn't stop until they had safely laid the body down on the bed. Then they turned to leave. 'Wait, please, who are you?' The figure replied, 'I work for an airline company.' Where else would an angel work?

It was not hard for me to believe that this was a celestial visitor. Especially recalling how the aftermath of my flight to South America had me knocking on death's door, pleading to be allowed in. The constant question that gnawed like a hungry rat: *Who am I?*

I spent a lot of time dwelling on what might, or might not, have transpired at the end of the Banshees, and how much was my fault. The incident on the plane was a useful scapegoat. I wondered why there had been no conversation about Siouxsie and Severin continuing as a two-piece - they had, after all, been the enduring core of the Banshees. Perhaps I really wasn't expendable. Siouxsie certainly kept me around, so I must have had my uses.

Once I quit drinking there was obviously a big change to our lifestyle in France. An alcoholic in recovery can develop a nurturing need. I would walk around thinking, *I know exactly how you feel. I'll do that for you.* When out at restaurants together, I pretended to drink, even lifting the glass to my lips, because I didn't want people to think she was drinking alone. We would still order a carafe of wine and would still stay behind for a *digestif* with the owner. Siouxsie seemed to be angry that I was sober, and I was angry because I was sober, angry because people annoyed me. They jostled me or pushed me in busy bars, which was rather hypocritical given what I would get up to when I'd had a few too many. But I couldn't stand unpredictable drunken antics - they really scared me.

It's a common misunderstanding that it's not the first drink that gets you, but the second, or the sixth or seventh. My alcoholic radar for spotting 'real' drinkers in a crowded bar was always accurate. I became just as adept at knowing when the first drink was leading to a bender. I didn't mind being the 'nominated' driver; I had, after all, taken control of driving duties. It was knowing how difficult it would be to get her out of the bar and into the car. The responsibility emphasised my sobriety, and only added to my growing plea of 'woe is me'. I was alone in my self-pity.

We quickly sank into a pattern. On Saturday morning I would drive thirty minutes to the industrial-sized supermarket in the next big town to buy wine and food - but also simply to have something to do. I tended the garden, made the fire, carried in the logs. I'd not see Siouxsie until maybe two o'clock in the afternoon. After that I'd try to stay out of the way, keep a safe distance, not because I felt in any physical danger, but to avoid the discomfort of engagement - having to talk about the situation, or worse, some form of cross-examination. Any chat would often get darker as the day progressed. On a good night, I would cook dinner, we'd play backgammon, there'd be wine, more wine, and then the phone calls would begin. I could handle this routine, as it also meant that my morning would be quiet. But on a deeper level an unhealthy co-dependency was developing.

When we moved to France, Siouxsie had mostly given up driving. I chose and bought the cars and chauffeured her around. I began to feel guilty that I had disenfranchised her from driving and decision-making, rather than seeing it as a way of me being controlled. It's a form of willing self-sacrifice, putting oneself in the role of victim while being the perpetrator. It's assuming that when things went wrong it was primarily my fault - overcompensating for their lack of engagement, empathy or just laziness. I've recently discovered that this behavioural pattern is called 'passive dependency', most common in a relationship involving two people who have been traumatised, where one has grown up with a lack of love and the other has had too much love.

Siouxsie and I fitted these patterns. She used to have a wind-up musical box, its brass lid a model of a twin-spired church. It played a nostalgic German tune called 'O Mein Papa'. She took the melody and lyrics (originally about a young woman remembering her beloved father, a once famous clown) and rewrote them for 'Mother/Oh Mein Papa', a song on the Banshees' second album, *Join Hands*. Siouxsie wrote about an evil mother who gave life, and who both gives and sucks away vital energy, and ends up smothering her children. Yet she concludes with a translation from the original German, 'Oh my papa/To me he is so beautiful/Always the same'. Perhaps somewhere in that lyric and in that juxtaposition is a clue to the Siouxsie persona – the father who died a sick alcoholic and was valorised, and the mother who survived and, despite loving and caring for her brood, was demonised.

This came out when she was drunk: the switch was flipped, and the anger was unleashed. (Jon Klein recounts witnessing Siouxsie switch personalities within the blink of an eye: 'She's Gemini and there's definitely two of her.') It wasn't always aimed at me, but it was an anger that I could feel. It was a litany of 'men are awful, doctors are not to be trusted, how dare my dad die', and then the inevitable accusation, *'You're just like my dad!'* That's what manifested when she got drunk and angry; the rage came up and she lashed out. It was then that I understood what had brought Siouxsie and me together, a rage at the world for taking a parent, an absence that neither of us had ever dealt with except through alcohol and the intoxicating power of our co-dependency.

When I wasn't cooking and cleaning, I'd be calculating every franc, looking at the exchange rate and wondering how we could keep this ship afloat. Workahol replaced alcohol as my new addiction. It was a way of keeping my brain going in times when there wasn't much music happening, perhaps a new form of compulsion in which I suddenly got interested in numbers and figures. I spent hours checking back-catalogue sales to make sure everything was adding up.

The trouble was that income from the back catalogue was our lifeline. The Banshees had stopped and those last gigs on *The Rapture* tour had not been well attended. It knocked our self-confidence. We could have been dropped much sooner than we were; we had already run out of steam. Yet however fraught the ending of the band and my part in its downfall was, it was perhaps a blessing in disguise and should probably have happened after the *Peepshow* tour. When Siouxsie and I made *Boomerang*, which was very well received, we should have said that it was no longer time for the Creatures to be just a side project, but to focus on it, just the two of us. It might have been the right thing to do, but loyalty, record-company pressure or managerial pressure always forced us back to the mothership. There was a lot of legacy there to protect, and a huge weight to pull. The Creatures, on the other hand, had no baggage. *Where shall we go? We can do anything. Okay, we'll do a big-band session tomorrow.* Whereas by the end, the Banshees were taking three months to organise a track and a year to actually do one. Letting the Banshees run on too long made us lose our self-esteem. We didn't know what was going on out there, and Siouxsie and I being isolated in France didn't help things. Reports were that the music industry had changed, but we didn't believe it could change that much. Unfortunately for us, it had.

The Banshees and the Creatures felt completely out of place with what was going on back in Britain. The mid-nineties had seen acid house, then rave, jungle and the rise of mainstream clubs. We had taken ecstasy back in the early eighties, but it was now clearly a different drug, fuelling a very different scene. We had no idea about Britpop, hearing bits of it in France and thinking, *What is all this?* Our last ties to major-label music business were cut when Geffen Records became part of Universal Music.

With nothing else to do and no management, I took charge, and we started doing everything ourselves, writing and recording demos of new songs on a little Roland 8-track Portastudio. Knox was also involved, making loops on the guitar. Then the Cure's producer Steve Lyon came over to France after recording *Wild Mood Swings*. Steve had unknowingly adopted Robert's mannerisms, his accent and even those characteristic pauses Robert has

269

when speaking. It struck me that that's what happened in and around the Cure - everyone ends up speaking like and adopting the mannerisms of Robert.

By the end of 1996 we had recorded enough material for an album, so the following year Siouxsie and I moved back to London to reconnect with the music business. We were hoping to find someone who would be interested in releasing our new music. We met with all sorts of people, but nobody wanted the record, or us. Meanwhile, we were spending everything we had left on the extortionate rent of a penthouse flat above the Toy Museum in Craven Hill, the streets below full of Lamborghinis and Porsches. 'It's lovely! Look where we're living. Come around. We'll do an interview. Yeah, we've got an album. It's all going great!'

It was all going wrong. Sanctuary Records gave us the feeling that they were interested in our new music, but it transpired that they really wanted to get their hands on our back catalogue. They put us in touch with their music manager, who seemed keen but proceeded in a traditional way, offering us to major labels. They renewed our publishing deal, pocketed their commission on the advance, and that was that. They were probably the first generation of what is now the domain of hedge-fund investment companies: buying up the rights to TV programmes, books and characters like Rupert Bear. The music business had indeed changed; it was now primarily concerned with buying and selling intellectual property rights, with little interest in the actual music.

Sanctuary had an old-fashioned boardroom with a dark wooden oval table surrounded by green buttoned leather chairs and cricket memorabilia on the walls. We had one meeting there with dub maestro Adrian Sherwood. Adrian was going to help us with remixes to try to integrate us into the new electronic music culture - but he was tired and seemed uncomfortable. Sorry, Adrian, so were we. We even asked an old friend to ask around record-company contacts in America, but they too came back and said, 'Nobody's interested.'

Against the indifference of the music industry, we opted to

release the album ourselves. We had poured all our money into it, there was nothing more to lose. A temporary salvation arrived in the form of Doug Hart, son of a plumbing dynasty and the boss of a label called Hydrogen Jukebox. A cheeky barrow boy, zipping around London on his Lambretta scooter, he'd meet up with us at Café Rouge (France was never too far away) and we'd talk about how we could release music again.

In 1996, I had also bought my first computer and I was enthusiastic about this new thing called the internet. We formed an internet forum called the Gift Horse. I would log on, drop in on discussions, post answers to questions, and share anecdotes. We had subscribers who for a small fee were sent a fold-out magazine and a CD called, wait for it, the Gift Horse CD! The first CD featured four demo versions of what became our ode to Don Luis Buñuel, 'Exterminating Angel'. It was a limited run of a thousand, complete with handmade covers. That number doesn't sound like a lot until you see a thousand white cardboard CD covers laid out side by side, ready for you to get creative. Through Doug, we were able to set up our own label, Sioux Records, finally releasing a track called 'Sad Boy' (Doug renamed it 'Sad Cunt' and a new design agency called DED went to town with a Y-front-wearing skinny figure as the cover star).

Doug and Hydrogen Jukebox were operating out of a little shed on the banks of the River Thames. There was money floating around, but most of it was on the river. We lacked the clout of a major label and the support we'd been accustomed to for so long. The Creatures became like a little cottage industry. Very cute.

We thought that the best way to try to promote the record and get ourselves re-established would be to get back out on the road, so I booked the smallest rehearsal room I could find in North London. The Verve had the biggest space in the Depot complex, packed with all their gear. The crew would turn up, but rarely the band. This was exactly how we behaved in the heyday of the Banshees, and it really emphasised just how much had changed. My room was tiny and up on a mezzanine level, only accessible by a lift pulley system and a set of stairs. It was cheap! I needed cheap, but I had flight cases of drums and equipment and no crew. The staff were saying, 'What bus were you in? When's your crew coming, Budge?'

'I haven't got any crew. I thought I'd wheel them all in, but could you give me a hand, please?' They were very nice and looked after me, though it did all make me feel rather old.

As I worked, the luminaries of Britpop seemed to be all over the place. Elastica's drummer Justin Welch with his pal Dave Bush from the Fall came into the café while I was having my cup of tea and an egg sandwich. They bowed down giggling, 'We're not worthy! We're not worthy!' just like Wayne and Garth in *Wayne's World*. They were so nice, saying, 'Oh, the Slits' *Cut*, it's the best album!' They didn't mention the Banshees, or Siouxsie, just *Cut*. For a moment, I thought, *Hmm, maybe I need to reappraise myself,* to see more value in what I had achieved . . . but the moment passed. I had work to do.

I had to learn how to be a musical director. Preparing loops and samples, using technology and a way of performing that we really hadn't done that much of before. I had set up in that big rehearsal room, when the Verve left, so I could blast my Akai samplers through the big sound system. Sampling the loops that Knox had prepared, I'd get hypnotised sitting there, as the loops played, loving how they resonated in the room. Every now and then a person from the studio would put their head in the doorway and say, 'Hey, that sounds great. We thought there was a band in here.' I'd say, 'Well, there is, but I'm it!' It was mesmeric. I knew that this could work because it was such a great sound. But we were unsure of going out again as the Creatures, just the two of us, the way we'd done after *Boomerang*. Was I confident enough to pull it off? Did I have enough belief? We chose to have two female bassists, thinking it would be a strong statement and make for an amazing sound. We worked out the arrangements and parts with Clare Kenny, from Sinéad O'Connor's live band, and Anna Piva, Tricky's live bassist, and this was the band we debuted with at

London's Garage on 30 May 1998, just three years after the end of the Banshees.

John Cale's manager got in touch to ask if we would consider a double-headliner tour of America. Obviously, we had worked with John on *The Rapture*, and as the Creatures we had written and performed together for an orchestral show in Amsterdam earlier in the year. The Velvet Underground and his solo career meant a great deal to us. It was a way to build on that collaboration and relieved the pressure of it being solely our show.

For the tour with John we were joined by Susan Stenger from Band of Susans. Tricky's bass player couldn't make it, so we had to quickly rejig things in rehearsal in San Francisco. John's guitarist Mark Deffenbaugh learned our missing bassist's parts, and Susan quickly learned John's setlist, either on bass or violin. I sat centre stage on drums watching the changing of the guards as John and Siouxsie exchanged positions during what was an unusual show. A trusted friend said, 'When John came on it was like watching the tide go out, everyone went to the bar – when Siouxsie came on, it was like the tide came back in.' The performance ended in togetherness with us all performing the cutely titled 'Murdering Mouth', written with John for the Amsterdam orchestral show.

Our third album, *Anima Animus*, was released in 1999, and our little band, now with Jane Pickup on bass and violin and Rob Holliday from Curve on guitar, toured and toured for the whole of the year. The album's title referred to Jung's ideas of the duality of genders within an individual, which was a loose theme of the record. In the photoshoot to promote it, Siouxsie appeared confrontational with a cigarette between her snarling teeth. She was wearing a pinstripe suit with shiny slicked-back hair, which I always felt was her strongest look. I wore a little black dress and high heels, my hair silver-white. I looked more feminine than I ever had, arguably my strongest look. I threw myself into the theatre and fantasy of it all.

'Exterminating Angel' was based on the title of a film by Spanish director Don Luis Buñuel, who worked with Salvador Dalí on the surrealist classic *Un Chien Andalou*. It was the death of the first-born, blood on the doors, the big cross, and I pummelled away, *Kodo* style, on this big bass drum set-up on a big X-frame, stage left. I wore a sparkling mini-skirt and a slinky little sequinned top. For years I had worn dance tights and oversize T-shirts, which was all a bit too eighties. So, I thought I should get a bit dressier, and the only way to do that was to wear a stretchy short skirt that would allow me to sit down and spread my legs to play - like Kenny Everett, all done in 'the best possible taste'.

Billy Chainsaw, one of my dearest old friends and right-hand man to every manager of the band from day one, had a very perceptive take on why my relationship with Siouxsie had endured, and why it had worked. He said that she always had a masculine energy, and that her hard masculinity complemented and balanced against my softer feminine side. If this is true, it could be that this role reversal replaced or became love. The Creatures' struggles in the mid-nineties didn't strain our relationship. They were probably what held it together. We knew how to do the Creatures, jumping off the cliff with complete confidence knowing we wouldn't hit the rocks. We always had each other's back. But giving 110 per cent to a relationship *and* an artistic endeavour was too much to sustain. I just couldn't deliver that any more.

Perhaps we didn't give each other the validation that we needed. 'That's a great drumbeat', 'I love that melody', or simply, 'What a great song'. It was noticeable that she'd 'forget' to mention me on stage during Creatures gigs while thanking the band - you can hear it in her faux-surprised, 'Oh yeah, Budgie!' on the *Zulu* live album from 1999. It became a comedy routine that had worn thin, like Peter Cook and Dudley Moore when Cook didn't know when to stop and Dudley was clearly hurting. But did I ever say to Siouxsie, 'That's a great vocal. That's the best thing I've ever heard you do'? The coldness had become mutual, our devotion to the project functional.

The greatest imbalance came because I wasn't drinking, and

she was. Nothing particularly bad was happening, but every now and then the door to the dark side would creak on its rusty nails. It would take just a few words from the tour manager for it to swing wide open.

'Okay, everyone, we've got to get going now. All the gear's packed, and we've got a show tomorrow.'

'But the party's *here*. Just one more for the road.'

For years I'd been the one never wanting to leave, but now I was trying to be sensible without being boring, and that was tough.

I always saw the dark side as the funny side that plays too hard, the funny side that wants to strangle everyone with affection. 'Booboo' was my pet name. She might tickle me under the chin, and coo, 'Oh, Booboo.' It felt a little patronising, and that affectionate humour was always the first sign of the emerging dark side. It was like a horror film werewolf transformation. The eyes are always the last to change; the eyes that are beckoning and pleading, still shining with love, suddenly get taken over by the demon. There's still a smile, but physically they get stronger and clumsier, and suddenly dangerous. As the love flickers out of the eyes, anything can take its place: accusations fly, disrespect and bile follow. It appeared like a whirlwind and could blow deep into the night. As Banshees' guitarist Jon Klein vividly remembered, 'On *Nocturne*, she says something like "Roses are red, violets are blue, I'm schizophrenic, and so am I." On big drinking nights, you'd see her nod and her eyes would shut. But when they opened again, there would be someone else inside. Siouxsie was a cross between the lovely big sister I never had and the worst headmistress you could imagine.'

It was such a different feeling touring with the Creatures compared to the Banshees. The crew were different, the fans were different. The Gift Horse project had gone from strength to strength, and in retrospect we were quite pioneering in using the internet to connect so intimately with fans. When in France, rather than being on my own or wondering what to do, I would go online into the forum and speak to the fans. The Gift Horse releases, a magazine that we hand-wrote and decorated and folded around a CD, were incredibly popular, although it took a lot of work. The Gift Horse devotees became the 'Exterminating Angels', they'd get together and follow us on tour.

The Creatures' logo, of the male and female symbols that you'd find on a toilet door, reflected the gender interchangeability between Siouxsie and me during this period of the band, and would be adapted for each release, with different expressions. The 'Exterminating Angels' would turn up at gigs wearing red T-shirts featuring the two figures, one with devil horns and the other with a halo and angel wings, evil and good in one. They followed us to Scotland or Surrey, even to America and Australia. It was unheard of for us to have such an ardent following, a nucleus who enjoyed the trip as much as being with us. We would let them into the club early, helping us to load our gear in. It really was like being back to the way it had all started, your friends helping, getting in for free and everybody having a great night.

These interactions allowed us to be the compatible version of ourselves and pretend to be the magic couple. As soon as I finished playing, I was packing the gear away. We had a crew, but I'd be interacting with all the people that were following us around as well. Siouxsie was drinking with them. She was the 'Queen of Court'. I thought, *That's good. She's happy that way.* Maybe she wasn't. Maybe that was the perfect screen for what was going on between us and not going on, that and perhaps the whole switching of roles.

This meant that through 1998 and 1999, Siouxsie and I started to occupy different orbits. We were trying to do the same thing that we'd always done, but getting further apart all the time. I was getting further away from the last drink. Because I didn't understand why just not drinking wasn't improving our relationship, work took over. Throwing my addictive personality into work meant that I didn't get to the core of what was wrong with me. I had stopped drinking, but I still hadn't grown up. If I was lonely because my musical partner and wife was still doing things in the same way as she always had, then Siouxsie must have been lonely too because we *were not* still doing things in the same way as we always had. If a mutual dependency has replaced love, then what can sustain you?

Sobriety hadn't stopped my wandering eye. It didn't take much for me to fall in love, or to think that I had, and start rearranging my life around foolish, pseudo-romantic notions. I was desperately trying to make connections, to find a sense of intimacy, somewhere. That was a part of the untreated alcoholism, a grandiosity, no grasp on reality. I had no idea. Not drinking alcohol meant that everything felt better and in fact seemed brilliantly clear, but the problem was that I had nowhere to hide from the set-up and the play, the routine of a musical career that was everything I had dreamed of.

As the millennium approached, the self-treated alcoholism that I had never got to the core of had a dry hold over me. I felt I was losing my sanity. I wasn't drinking, but I wasn't 'sober' for a minute. I had every other hang-up going on. The internet had provided the Creatures with a lifeline, but it was also the route to another addiction.

I tried to fix myself with porn, online forums, chat rooms and webcams. I would go through the charade of 'not being able to sleep' in what was supposed to be the marital bed, and then sneaking off to look at porn and sleep in my own bed, which was really where I felt safe. Safe and sad. I was in awe of the internet connection, feeling it had a power over me, that when I was online someone was tracking me - as ever, overcome by guilt. Yet porn became a way of trying to untangle a sexual identity that felt as confused as the gender one projected during *Anima Animus*. After the initial lust, experimentation was always prompted and fuelled more by alcohol than by desire or curiosity. It was never a physical, loving relationship - there was no holding hands or demonstrations of togetherness in public, but there wasn't that much behind the scenes, either.

Perhaps most people have a period in their adolescence when they are confused by their sexuality. The death of my mum during mine seemed to have flipped a switch that created a slight change in my adolescent trajectory. That change, at first imperceptible, became more exaggerated as I moved further and further away from the night of the trauma. In St Helens in the 1970s nobody was going to be aware of what was happening to me, I certainly didn't know. The trauma affected my core being, rewiring me, my thoughts, my desires, and what little I knew of my sexuality. While alcohol and performing as Budgie might have covered that up for years – as a non-drinking person I was suddenly confronted by it all. It was getting more and more difficult to call this a life.

This confrontation resulted in my being drawn to the possibilities of other people during the time when Siouxsie and I were spinning so far apart. In 1995, on the last US tour as the Banshees, a pretty young girl came into our circle, chewing gum and wearing purple John Lennon shades. She was working as a stripper and invited us all down to the Hollywood club where she gave us a private dance. She was so close to me that I was overwhelmed by her scent. I just found it too much, utterly over-stimulating, making me feel nervous and shaky. I was entranced and yet repulsed. Siouxsie appeared to be infatuated.

The next night, Siouxsie, Severin and I were at the Viper Room in West Hollywood. Kate Moss and Johnny Depp were there, as was Charlotte Rampling and the usual hangers-on. It promised to be an interesting night. Severin was talking European cinema with Johnny; I was talking British TV adverts with Kate. The girl in the John Lennon shades arrived and Siouxsie whisked her off into the night in the back of a long black limousine, leaving me thinking, *Is this really happening?* Everyone was staring at me, their eyes asking, 'What's going on, Budgie? What's going on?' She just left, obviously a prearranged pick-up. It wasn't hidden. She said some time much later, 'I was losing my mind.' She could well have been. We both were.

I spent hours alone in coffee shops whenever we were in the US, drunk on insomnia. I'd met someone we were working with professionally, and there was a spark. For the first time I was able to respond physically and sexually, but only briefly. I instantly realised I'd never felt this way before, but it ripped the roof off the house, a huge freak event, a crack opening in the fabric and then closing again. It was different from previous indiscretions, my embarrassing flirtations during long sessions of drink and drugs. For the first time I was quite within my own skin, calling the shots; but this was sex with somebody who was asking questions as well. 'Are you sure? Shall we . . .?' Even in the intensity of it. I remember it very clearly. It was a first time. I had never experienced that mutual generosity and care before. I remember saying to them, 'I never thought this would happen.' It wasn't a one-night stand, but the culmination of something with a person I'd known over several years. This meant that it felt oddly mature in many ways, a glimpse of how intimacy could be. I was, so briefly, there with another person, in the moment. I called them when I got back to my hotel: 'Are you okay?'

They laughed quietly: 'Yeah, I'm still shaking.'

'So am I.'

When I got home to France, I wandered the countryside, picking wild flowers, a hopeless gesture of immature romance. I didn't even dry them, just put them in an envelope and posted them to the US, so they must have arrived as a dull, liquid mush.

The International Olympic Committee invited the Creatures to perform at a concert as part of the 2000 Sydney Olympics. Around the show we even had some time off together for the first time since we'd gone on a holiday to the Canary Islands in the early nineties. I was still drinking then, we argued for hours in the hotel car park, car headlights were smashed, and I woke up in an empty room. As ever, nothing was said. In Australia, there was nothing like that. There was so little passion left that we'd even given up fighting. On the Gold Coast, with the blue mountains in the distance, there was every opportunity for us to just hold hands, to talk. We'd given up asking what was wrong with one another. We were there as a couple but had given up on being one. A rut can have a strange comfort and be hard to leave.

I still called my dad every week to let him know where I was. I told him that from Australia the constellations appear upside down, and I confirmed that water does indeed go down the plughole anti-clockwise. Dad loved silly jokes and sharing useless information. I returned from the Australian summer to the European winter. My dad died between Christmas and the coming New Year; he was seventy-nine years old. His death didn't come with the same shock as my mum's; his was a merciful release from a long illness. I had had some chance to prepare, to say goodbye, to share grief without ever speaking its name. If I had voiced my feelings, he would have heard me say as I left, 'I'm going to carry on running away if that's okay.' (I was always leaving.)

21.
A Girl Like You

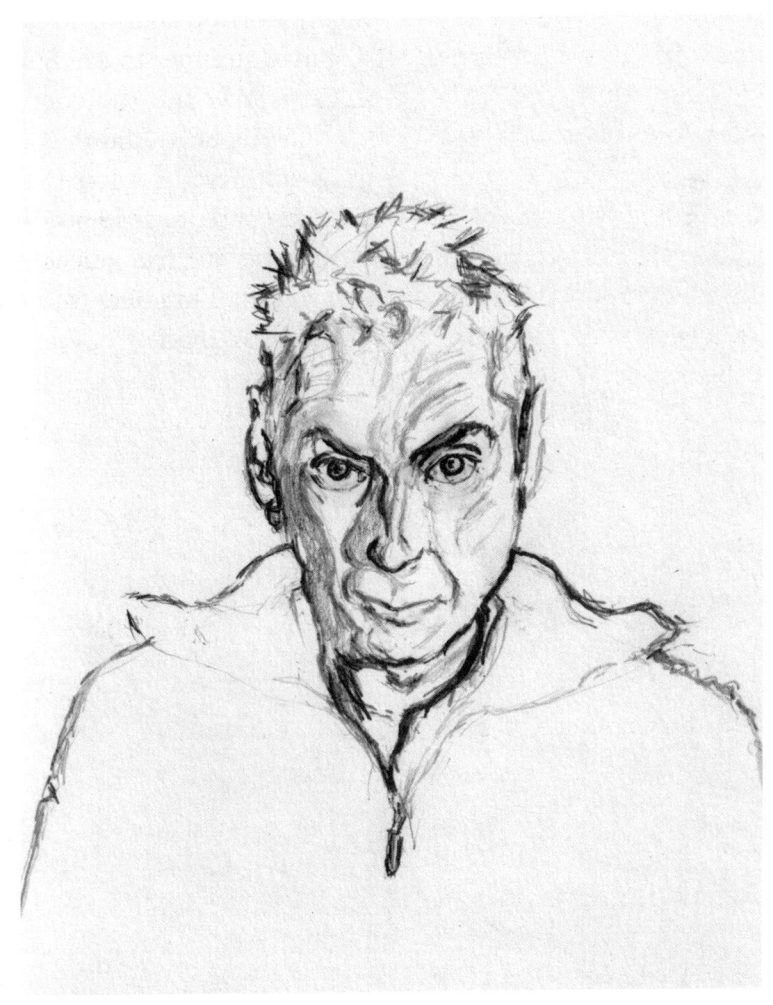

Pick a night, any night, look at it, don't show it,
now replace it, is this your night?

Night-time, 2002. Frank Sinatra's 'Witchcraft' segues into John Leyton's 'Johnny Remember Me' and then the non-stop cycle of Edwyn Collins' 'A Girl Like You'. Louder and louder, playing over and over, a cacophony of music in our very own wretched dreamhouse.

It would begin like any other evening. I may have been pruning shrubs in the garden, then preparing dinner in the huge kitchen. The smell of fresh shrimp from the morning market, freshly squeezed limes for the vodka gimlet. The tang of lime always reminded me of a salted glass of tequila – my last ever drink. These foolish things remind me of the times when we used to share everything. With dinner done, the evening backgammon session would commence. Backgammon over, the phone calls would start, usually to her friend back in the UK, affectionately known as 'Fuzzy Bull-Dyke'. The wine was usually flowing freely by now, the cackling laughter and the music, getting louder and louder. Though still sober, I would always be aware of how much wine was going down. I would eventually turn in and try to get off to sleep. The stereo would be blasting a mix of dance music or Bowie or Charles Mingus, but after a certain time it always followed the same pattern. Frank Sinatra's voice sounding lost in the old stone house, like some incidental music looking for a scene in a bad horror film. It would sometimes go quiet as dawn crept over the house, sometimes louder in the dark, with cackling laughter as an accompaniment.

I would tell myself I was happy that she was having a good time; that this just wasn't something I could provide any more. I'd listen for the music to stop, but not from the old marital bed that we once shared. When Edwyn stopped crooning his best Iggy Pop-ness, the house fell silent. Even the dawn chorus was mute. I could hear footsteps, and from the time it took for the adjoining bedroom door to open, I could calculate roughly how unsteady those footsteps were. If the door closed and quietness returned, then I was okay. If I heard the door to my room being opened, I could be in for a tongue-lashing or an ear bashing. It would not be a goodnight kiss or cup of cocoa.

Daytime was a different world. I would cycle to the shops, do odd jobs, some cleaning, some cooking. I grappled with music production. She grappled with Marcel Proust. We had started working on new material when Severin got in touch to say that the Banshees had been offered a huge fee to play the Coachella Festival in California. It all sounded very positive and, unlike after all our hard work as the Creatures, there would be a nice chunk of money at the end of it, as well as the distant possibility of a new future with the Banshees. As the Creatures, we had re-established a connection with our US audience and thought that rather than going cold into a big reunion show, we should do a little tour from the East Coast to the West, playing seven shows – calling it 'The Seven Year Itch'.

It's interesting that the Seven Year Itch for the Banshees was the same seven years since I had given up drinking. I felt like I was straddling two worlds, being part of the Banshees again, but also established as the Creatures, where I'd worked hard learning new skills, becoming the musical director, and through the late nineties making a success of the band against all the odds. How I played live had changed, I was having to be a conductor from behind the drum kit. In the Creatures I'd never felt like I was just the drummer in the band, whereas in the Banshees I was there to hold my corner, play the role. This had all changed. As I took on the weight of the organisational aspect of it all, I became the musical director of the Banshees, trying to bring everyone up to speed.

The tour started in Washington DC on 17 April 2002, before heading to New York's famous Roseland Ballroom on the nineteenth. Rehearsals had been good and, after the ignominy of the band ending in the sun on a Belgian beach with a bunch of frisbee throwers, it was exciting to feel that we were playing well and to appreciative crowds. My confidence levels had increased, and there was now more of the gregarious Peter coming out of the knackered shell of Budgie. Unfortunately, old problems began to resurface.

Washington, New York and two nights in Chicago had all gone well, but in San Francisco, Severin introduced his new girlfriend. She was a lot of fun with a lovely smile, but what was he thinking? Given Siouxsie's long-standing aversion to girlfriends on the road, we can only assume he had forgotten what had happened the last time. To bring a girlfriend on any tour, especially unannounced on a tenuous reunion tour, could only have been love. She was obviously elated to see him and got very happy very quickly. The dynamic of the tour immediately changed. What could have been a build-up to a long-term reunion had sadly lost its flavour on the bedpost overnight.

After the US tour we played a run of UK dates, recording the *Seven Year Itch* live album, before flying to Japan for the 2002 Summer Sonic Festival, held in Osaka and Tokyo. The Banshees had been supported through much of the Seven Year Itch tour by a Japanese band I had found on the internet called eX-Girl. I loved Keikos, Fuzuki and Kirilola for their amazing playing and strange compositions, but also for their unbelievable lust for life, their incredible smiles and their unbridled generosity. Fuzuki also played the drums standing up, Moe Tucker style, looking very cool. Siouxsie and the girls immediately hit it off, and through them I finally met my hero of the Japanese 'taiko' drum, ex-Kodo drummer Leonard Eto. Siouxsie and I stayed on in Tokyo after the

Banshees and crew left, and on 19 August we entered Gok Sound studio in the centre of Tokyo. Joined by eX-Girl, their manager Hoppy Kamiyama, and the studio's owner, Mr Kondoh, Leonard and I began our spontaneous drum conversation. We drummed together for over an hour and a half, which laid the percussive foundation of a new project. Returning to France, Siouxsie added her words and vocals, and I pushed myself to mix and produce what would be the final Creatures album, *Hái!*.

Once the album was done, we spent time in Los Angeles, where I started working on our plans to get back out on tour again, talking with some of the old Banshees crew and the sound engineer, setting up rehearsals with Knox and a keyboard player, keeping things simple but expanding the palette. We decided to use backing vocalists for the first time, and asked Leonard to bring his taiko on tour with us so that we could properly replicate the sound of *Hái!*

It was hard for Siouxsie to be involved with the tour preparations and rehearsals. She had been having major sinus problems and was still receiving treatment during the rehearsal period in LA. During the last Banshees dates she had been making regular trips to ENT specialists, always trying to find the right treatment. She was already tired and frustrated, but this wasn't the only issue. Unlike the Creatures' late-nineties tours that had been such a DIY success, this line-up was struggling to gel. I was sitting on the drum kit, singing, directing and trying to get some routine into the nucleus of the band. Siouxsie was absent. By the time we got into production rehearsals, things were not going well. My long-time friend and drum-brother Walter Earl told me it was like watching a boxing match, with a team in each corner of the ring, and me in the middle as the referee. I was quickly losing my mind.

During the rehearsals, we had an invitation to meet the photographer David LaChapelle, who was keen to work with Siouxsie. We met at the infamous Chateau Marmont hotel, a faux-castle folly and a beautiful fantasy world of four-poster beds in which luvvies read scripts in their dressing gowns. Tim Burton's dog was in the penthouse suite. Even at the time, it felt like a sign that we had 'arrived'. We met around a long table, like the scene of the last supper, surrounded by lots of young celebrities that I didn't recognise, and Christina Aguilera and her entourage. Siouxsie was busy being Siouxsie down at the other end of the table with some close friends, some new friends and lots of shooting stars. Not drinking for nine years had given me this false sense of clarity, that I was okay and everyone else was crazy. Yet I was fully aware that the stress of the *Hái!* tour rehearsals and the undiscussed emptiness at the heart of our relationship meant that I was heading for a crash or a crush. And there she was on the other side of the table at this ridiculous dinner at the Chateau Marmont. Almond-shaped brown eyes, pale skin, and the smile and face of a Modigliani painting.

We were sitting opposite each other and everything peripheral went out of focus. I was mesmerised. *Wow. You're special,* stuck on my lips, and the thought felt reciprocal. The dry-drunk puppy that Budgie carried within him panted and yelped. I fell instantly in love. She was there with a publicist whom I knew was not a partner. We chatted over sparkling mineral water. Mutual feelings of lost happiness and sadness barely concealed beneath polite conversation. There was an unspoken understanding that we both simply *understood*.

As everyone was leaving, I caught her eye again before she vanished into the night. Sometimes a strong connection can be made without words. 'Our eyes met' is such a cliché, but I knew *I wanted to see her again.*

I was jolted back to reality almost immediately, with the usual struggle to get a reluctant Siouxsie into a taxi and back to the hotel.

The tour brought us back to LA and the House of Blues. Afterwards, I was working the room, speaking to all the friends and acquaintances we had gathered there in the city over the years. I caught a glimpse of the brown-eyed woman from the Chateau Marmont and, as the room whirled us together and we said hello, she touched my hand. It was like being zapped by a high-voltage cable. Everything came alive. It was as if I had taken truth serum with an honesty tab. I was convinced that everyone had watched me change. I was no longer the same person that I'd been a second before. If I was feeling something this intensely, it must have been written all over my face. I was scared. But I wanted more! We exchanged numbers and spoke constantly for the next few weeks. I was working eighteen-hour days keeping the tour going. These surreptitious calls were a glimpse of another life, another way of being. I always had my own room on tour. We talked at every opportunity. It was wonderful, but excruciatingly stressful.

At the same time, it was another secret being nurtured, and it was pulling me apart. The real dilemma was that we were due to fly to England to play gigs at London's Royal Festival Hall and at the 100 Club where, in 1976, it had all started for Siouxsie and the Banshees. There was no way I could remain silent. It wasn't honourable or courageous. To say I chose my moment for maximum effect would imply that I had some smart sadistic skill. I had none. I simply didn't think about the consequences. The tour entourage had left Los Angeles – Siouxsie and I were finally alone, sitting in a West Hollywood hotel bar, a somewhat dubious romantic setting more reminiscent of Hopper's *Nighthawks* than Manet's *Folies-Bergère*.

I waited, sanctimoniously sober, until the second or third vodka gimlet had subdued the underlying tension. Then I let her have it: 'I don't love you any more.' From the silence erupted a voice of anger and contempt, then a moment of sadness, then nothing. I was shocked, as much by my own bluntness as by her reaction. 'Well, isn't it better to be honest?' I could have *thought*, but I didn't *think*. Twenty-five years of intense entwinement, undone in less than one second. But had I ever said 'I love you'?

I was surprised at her reaction. I wasn't ready for the numbness, rage and upset all in one. 'But why?' screamed my sober, clean brain, 'Isn't it obvious, that it hasn't been right for years?' But that's the way it was. I didn't know how to react to the reaction, so I offered to get her another drink - I was tactless. We returned to where we were staying. She fell heavily into the bed and into a deep sleep. I decided to go and do the laundry, not in the hotel laundry room, but at the home of the woman who had turned my world upside down. She answered the door and welcomed me in. We didn't even take our clothes off; I just sat on her sofa and cried as she embraced me. It wasn't bursting into tears, just a deep unleashing of emotion. I was feeling love, a love that superseded all logic. Yet even then I had to deny it. She suggested we go to bed, and I said, 'I'd better put the dry cycle on first.'

For the first time in so long I felt a connection with Peter, with who I really was. I wasn't pretending to be Budgie the drummer or rock star, or whatever cliché anyone might have thought I played into. It was Peter. It was me. The little boy who was lost when his mum died. That aspect of me: the innocence, the love that needs every molecule to be present to be felt, had been trapped and bottled up for so long. That evening I realised that it was all intact. I was not a manipulative person. I was a caring, loving person, if I only allowed myself to be.

Even months before, I would have responded to that situation by thinking I could go home, pack the bag, ditch everything, naïvely having impossible dreams that she and I could both sort out our messes and everything would be great. *'No, really, Budgie. It's fine. You go, leave it all to me. I'll sort everything out. You just go off and be happy.'*

Of course, that's what the insane person would think, and many have. I couldn't just walk out of the door and never look back. It wasn't *only* because of an allegiance to the person I had married. I realised that I needed to sort myself out, otherwise I would be doomed to repeat the whole situation over and over again.

The opportunity was presented, and I was able to take its hand - not the hand of the person in LA, though that was part of it, but the hand that says: *Just believe it can get better. You can be more than that.* I could no longer hope or expect the person

I'd spent half of my life with to suddenly grasp the situation, and try to move forward with me. So, I didn't go out beating my chest and screaming. It was more a case of, *What on earth do I do now?*

I took the clean laundry home the next morning only to discover that for once she had woken up early. She had been sitting in a rage for hours, furious that I'd disappeared for the night when I wasn't even drinking. '*How could you?*'

How could I? I really thought I was in love and that's what I told her. She recovered herself quickly. '*How could you do this to me?*'

As always, I allowed myself to believe that she was unaware, or uncaring. As always, I thought I could deny everything, thinking, *It's just me being out of control.* This excuse had replaced, *It's just me being drunk.* This time I realised that my actions required a decision. That I had to see what needed to be done with me.

Siouxsie was already ill and exhausted from the long Banshees and Creatures tours. The resulting stress and anxieties were affecting her performance. She wasn't looking after herself, not recognising the warning signs, and we were both emotionally worn out. I was trying to be musical director, chaperone, partner, husband and, despite the bombshell, still trying to support her in every way that I could.

After the final Creatures gigs, we had nothing planned, an ominous feeling that obviously had deeper, undiscussed roots. We went back to France. It was very painful to go back to that big house and simply sit down together. She was furious. I had taken a Polaroid photograph to send to LA. In it I am clearly trying to give off a charming air, a casual 'please love me' look. It had taken me ages to perfect it. She had found the photograph and wrote on it with a Sharpie, 'BARRY MANILOW or WANKER?' It was typical of her, a mixture of piss-taking humour and rage, and as usual I was on the sharp end of it.

I still had the same off-road bike I had rode around London. I now used it to ride out into the French countryside to escape from the house. It was the bike I rode to keep fit, good for meditation, but it did nothing for my delusional dilemmas. I cycled along the river, stopped, sat down by the old water mill and rang LA. It was a difficult conversation, full of tears, of how both our marriages seemed to be falling apart, of dreams of a new life. I told her that whatever the outcome, it alone would not make things better. This much I knew. I told her that if I came out of the situation feeling that I understood and could trust myself, I would call her. If not, I wouldn't be in touch. This would be the last time we spoke. I went home and told Siouxsie that it was over with the lady in LA. She thrashed me around the head with a spiral-bound diary as I cowered like a whipped dog. I didn't even feel guilty or ashamed. I felt inhuman.

The next day I found her sitting at the little garden table inside the conservatory. She said she needed to tell me something. I fetched a pot of coffee and sat with her. She lit a cigarette with a pink BIC lighter; I used to use a Zippo - I liked the smell of lighter fuel. She exhaled as she said, 'I can't stand this any more. We should get a divorce.'

I didn't need to think, and I wasn't surprised. I simply said, 'Yes, I think you're right. We should.'

She drank some coffee, put her cup down and held her cigarette - a breeze from the garden caused the smoke to drift my way. *Why does it always go away from the smoker?*

'Well, don't you want to think about it?' she said finally.

I was watching the smoke, but fully aware of the deeper meaning beneath her question. 'No, no,' I replied. 'There's nothing to think about. You're right.'

This obviously wasn't in the script, and I had no idea whether she was processing any of it calmly. How could she be? I was scared to be around her later in case she took a drink, because then she could become angry and unpredictable. She didn't. We carried on talking and decided to find out if there was something to salvage. I started talking about getting some help with a therapist. She had already found a marriage guidance counsellor in London.

Our first joint session didn't go too well. Siouxsie stormed out of the room, out of the building and into the bustle of Marylebone High Street. I chased after her, as usual. I tried to pacify her, as usual. To no avail, as usual.

I soon realised I was living under a state of surveillance. She went through my mobile phone calls and messages, noting down date and time. I'd joined an all-male therapy group that focused on issues around sexuality. The meetings took place at a facility near London's Regent's Park. Sitting outside waiting to go into the first session, I knew that I would have to introduce myself with a name - just one, no surnames. Would it be Budgie or Peter? I knew it had to be Peter. Part of the group therapy process was writing. Writing about anything and everything in our lives that had caused us to seek help. Disclosing incidents and concerns that we might not be comfortable with, writing about everything, no matter how dark it might seem. I started putting to paper things I'd barely even thought about, and certainly never written down before. Admitting my part, taking responsibility for my actions, looking at aspects of my behaviour that I was ashamed of. I had to go further and include everything I was keeping secret. I wasn't sure about this and was transported back to the fear of young Peter, sitting in the dry air, the woody smell of the Catholic confessional booth in Lowe House church. Leaning into the grille, muttering that I had said bad words, that I'd had lewd thoughts, that I'd stayed out late with older boys and hadn't gone home. Into my notebook went the adult version of confessional disclosure, my acting out and seeking comfort in all the wrong places as Peter, as Budgie. I shook for us both as one. It was terrifying, but the more honest I could be, the more powerful the healing effect. Writing not just about actual events, but thoughts and desires, no matter how perverse or delusional they might have seemed. Everything we could reveal went into the notebook, and the notebook went into a private briefcase padlocked with a key.

When everything was on paper, the plan was that we would read out what we had written within the safe space of our small group. Many men left before they got to that stage; they left still hiding in fear and shame. It was a daunting task, but it would ultimately prove to be extremely cathartic. I travelled to London every week for two months, a huge commitment. I would keep my bag locked and hidden between sessions. But towards the end I became complacent, or perhaps just comfortable with my fears. I do believe it was a test of trust leaving my bag unlocked.

Siouxsie found my unlocked bag, opened it and read my writing. It would have provided her with much circumstantial evidence to back up anything detrimental. But these were thoughts and feelings that I had barely even started to articulate to myself, that were there in the context of therapy. The therapist had assured us that these words and thoughts were not who we were, they were not a character blueprint to be read and analysed. But that was what she did, as she read what I had written. What was intended as a process of healing, she used as a stick to beat me with. There was no way back from that.

How do you explain to someone you have spent half your life with that you just met someone who blew your world apart? Even that isn't true. They were just the catalyst. I was completely lost and there was no empathy coming from the one person I had sworn my allegiance to. I know that that's because I usually pushed them too far. When two people meet and come together, each of them brings some undesirable baggage, but neither lets the other see it. It's locked away until the day a key or a clue is found. Then the questions begin. 'What's this?', 'Who was that?', 'When did this happen?' It could be anything. It's all too easy to say, 'Hey, ignore all those twisted things you found, they aren't who I am. Can we please just carry on playing let's pretend?' Maybe an honest relationship is one where you show your hand. All the stuff you've been carrying around, all the dark secrets. Look at it all together, acknowledge and accept it. We never did that. We didn't do it as a band. We didn't do it as people. We certainly didn't do it as a couple. Perhaps it would have helped and maybe could have changed the course of what happened. The brutal irony is that if we had, Siouxsie and I may have realised that the deaths of our parents could have been our strongest bond. But instead of forging a deeper understanding, that shared trauma is what tore us apart. Alcohol, drugs, disgust and distrust all played their part. There was cruelty, too. I think she had a sadistic streak that pushed the boundaries of 'black humour', and which didn't sit so easily with me. I don't find humour in cruelty. Not unless I'm pretending to be someone who does; in my core I don't. And yet I know that Siouxsie loves animals and loves innocence, but perhaps she can't tolerate innocence. Though her dark lyrical imagery was often delivered in the first person - songs like 'Obsession', 'Night Shift', 'Head Cut' - any enactment of Hitchcock frenzy was usually confined to that lyrical world. Maybe the sources of her rage - her father's death, the not-so-innocuous suburbia - are all now safely in the past. Perhaps alcohol opens up a conduit to the present, and the 'furies', of anger, rage and destruction, are released. 'I'm sorry that I hit you, but my string snapped', that line from 'Suburban Relapse' again. (In her own words Siouxsie explained, 'With me, I just explode and smash something.') Siouxsie never apologised to anyone for anything. Isn't that what was expected of the Ice Queen?

In therapy, I remember saying that I felt there was an important part of me, a vital essence of me, and that there was only one tiny drop left. That tiny drop was safe inside a small glass vial, sealed with a tiny cork. I desperately wanted to make sure that it was still there, but I realised that if I uncorked it, my vital essence would simply evaporate, and I'd be gone forever. It was the largest real metaphor for me that I could envisage. I felt I had vanished, having been constantly told that I was worthless. And that hurt. Of course it hurt. But I accepted it all - malicious and evil - because we were in such a bad place, or everything had gone wrong in the music. I could justify it all to myself by saying,

'It's okay, they didn't mean it', or, 'They wouldn't say that', or, 'They had a bad night last night', or, 'They had too much to drink the night it happened', or, 'They didn't mean to almost take my eye out', or 'leave gouges in my flesh like I've been branded'.

Some people might give anything for that dubious privilege. But not me. No. I wouldn't. I might have kicked a door in or smashed a car's headlights. I broke windows when I was frustrated as a child. But no. Instead, as our marriage fell apart, I rattled around in a big French house feeling like I'd lost the will to live, a blubbering fragile mess, a few tears and no substance. Desolation – and not an angel in sight.

Epilogue

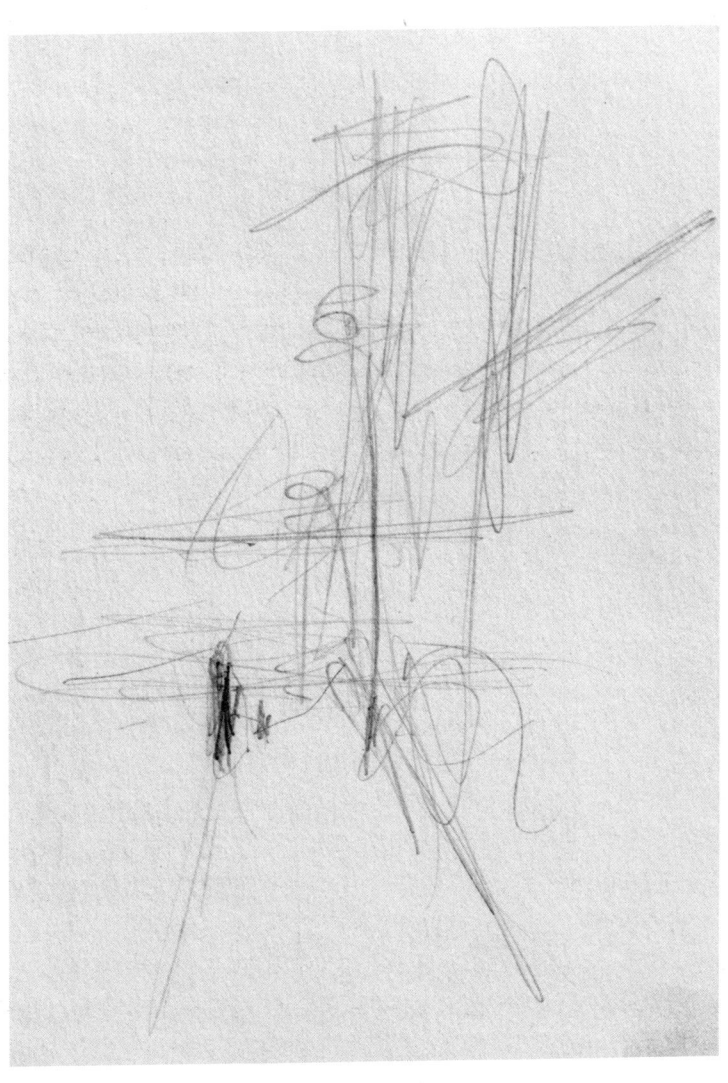

'WHY are you not wearing your wedding ring?'

And before you can answer . . .

'How long have you not been wearing your ring?'

Then the accusations.

'You're cruising meetings to pick up women, no ring says you're available - this is what men do!'

You attempt to talk, to explain, but quickly stop.

You know that your words only add fuel to the fire of their growing rage.

You clear the dinner things away, taking care to hide anything that could be used as a weapon. You go to your bed, leaving them in the kitchen, cackling into the telephone, smoking cigarettes, exhaling noisily, and drinking. You have been sleeping in separate rooms for years, but tonight you bolt the old door latch from the inside and lie awake in bed, waiting and listening. At 4am the disembodied growl of an angry voice demands to be let in. A reversal of The Exorcist *possession scene puts you in the bed beneath the crucifix - and the thing possessed prowling behind the bolted door.*

When you were a little boy and scared, you pretended to be asleep. You are scared now. A nightmare?

Laboured breathing and a doleful moaning quickly builds into a rage of verbal abuse and bile and then - BANG! - the door flies open and slams hard against the stone wall. The impact forces the lock clean out of the door jamb. You see a steel spike impale itself into the floorboards, then a moment's silence. From nowhere, a faceless figure lunges down at you, fists punching, strong fingers gripping your neck. Sharp, hard nails digging deep into your skin. Then a scream from the darkest depths of somewhere bad:

299

'I'll fucking kill you!'

You try to protect your head against the fury of the attack. Like someone drowning, you panic and thrash. You break free and crash out of the bed, out of the room and out onto the landing. You're at the top of the staircase; they try to kick but nothing connects. You try to restrain them, grabbing their wrists as they struggle to pull away. You realise that if you release your grip, their momentum will carry them backwards over the banister and down onto the stone steps below. You are being attacked yet are concerned for their safety. Manoeuvring them back into the bedroom, you stumble and fall into a corner. Trapped and beat, you cower down, until their rage and anger subside, until their malevolence is spent, and they slither away silently to their bed.

Shaking, sad and empty, you stay in the corner barely breathing, not moving until the pale light of dawn creeps up through the louvred shutters; it seems to hesitate before slowly revealing a mess of carpet, clothes and twisted bedsheets. The door hanging awkwardly like a broken wing reveals the ferocity of a violence it could not contain. Your neck is bleeding, but you'll live. You go downstairs to the kitchen, and as the clock on the cooker blinks 6am, you decide to leave. Not just the house, not just this situation, but this marriage. Life as it has been is over.

I shower in the bathroom furthest from their bedroom knowing that I must get out of here, but first I feel compelled to clear out and clean a small room above the kitchen at the far end of the house. The carpet fitter is due to start work later today, and the house is being readied for sale - this is my reasoning, though I never did need a reason to clean. Cleaning has always been a substitute for feeling. As a child complaining of being bored, my mum would hand me a polishing cloth and invite me to clean her brass ornaments. The smell of Brasso always made me hungry for bread and cheese. The Hovis TV ad made me sad.

The attic room has never been lived in; it smells of emptiness. Floor to ceiling cupboards, labelled in faded French script, *'Linge de lit et couvertures'*, from a time when everything in the house was cared for. I will never spend any time in this room. I feel as if I have never lived in this house at all. Feverish, exhausted and running on adrenaline, I begin picking through the past. Along with the usual broken lamps, chairs and unopened wedding presents are several brown cardboard boxes, sealed with that shiny caramel-coloured parcel tape that sticks to everything it touches. Our move to France coincided with the band vacating its London office in Notting Hill Gate; these boxes followed us to our new address. They contain old tour programmes, posters, pictures, cassettes and records, plus folders, faxes, memos and hundreds of receipts, all impregnated with the pervasive smell of cigarette smoke. Our manager Tim, like Siouxsie and Severin, was a devout smoker. Leaving this life will not be easy; these boxes only hint at the many years of emotional baggage to be unpacked. They are like ticking time bombs, primed to detonate emotions in an unguarded moment.

Without any idea of where I'm going or for how long, I pack a few things into a small old suitcase that my grandmother gave me. A floral-patterned suitcase with purple leather corners and fasteners, I always thought it would be perfect for an overnight trip. It's where I've kept mementos from a time before I left St. Helens: a broken alarm clock, empty Camel cigarette packets and a book-sized tin that once contained chocolates, a prize won in a school essay-writing competition. The suitcase conjures up many memories that for years I would attempt to find, using alcohol as a magic potion. If I could just get statues to open their eyes, to move like the lions in Eisenstein's *Potemkin*, life's secrets would be safe with me. I wouldn't tell. Honest. Scout's honour. Hope to die. I decide to drive south to meet friends at an English-language meeting in Gaillac. There, just as in the London group therapy sessions, I introduce myself not as Budgie, but as Peter. No more hiding.

The clock on the cooker says it's nearly 10.30am. I'm about to leave the house when the kitchen door opens and the trauma returns. Like a dark cloud passing before the sun, it moves across the kitchen towards the fridge. Her rage reignites and begins to boil over: 'Running away as usual? You're pathetic, you make me sick.' And as she disappears up the back stairs, bottle of water in hand, I hear her shout, 'I pity your next victim!' As I turn to go, everything spins. I feel sadness for her, and some hope for me.

Today the only ticking sound is that of the car's direction indicator - I tap in time on the steering wheel and remember how tapping in time got me here. With some physical distance between us, I gain a semblance of clarity. It's all still hazy, but as summer turns to autumn's fall, I often admire the horses in the paddock. Naz and Twigs, standing like glistening black statues, stoically facing the driving wind and rain. I hear these two mares galloping up from the lower field when I arrive back late at night. Stopping abruptly, their proud heads raised high above the paddock fence, they snort a steamy greeting into the cold night air. I feel in awe of their power and dignity, and I feel loved.

She maintains contact via phone message. I tense with each alert; incoherent, shouting texts, which always arrive well after midnight. She maintains that she can control herself by willpower alone. I know that my own attempts at restraint while still drinking failed miserably. I must keep my distance if I'm to have a chance of surviving. To make progress, I must let go of our past, all the bad and all the good of it. I don't reminisce about the good times; I don't dwell on the bad. If we're both willing to address our issues, then perhaps we have a tomorrow together. But today, it's safety first. If I stay and try to change them, I only prolong this limbo. I can easily slip into my old caretaking ways and be of no use to anyone.

Four days before my forty-ninth birthday, I'm sitting at a small table in the kitchen of my two-room refurbished pigsty refuge; the French *porcherie* makes it sound somewhat sweeter and cosier. I've covered the TV with a drape - other than the Arte channel, I find most French TV unwatchable. Unplugging the TV and covering the screen prevents me from losing sleep, waiting for late-night softcore temptation. In a more creative attempt to make changes,

I've set up a still life in a small attic room. With a plumb-bob and line, I am revisiting Euan Uglow's measuring technique; those long analytical days in the art college Life Room return as support and knowledge. Painting again now, there are no nagging doubts, no noise in the head; I know what I'm doing. This long-lost activity distracts me from the nauseating feelings of sadness, anxiety and fear. When not painting, I drive to meetings. Cahors, Gaillac, L'Isle-Jourdain, Vic-Fezensac, Mirande. My route to recovery is lengthy, but it takes me through beautiful landscapes.

She has left our old home for England, where she will file for divorce. The next few days will be difficult, but I enjoy the sanctuary of my little pigsty, even though I'm feeling tired and alone. I miss the house, but I can only visit when she is not there. As I drive along the familiar twists and turns of the French countryside, I see everything as if for the first time. Roads rise and fall like a gentle rollercoaster, each curve mirrored by the next. Napoleon's plane trees still shade the Roman roads as they cut like lasers across the wide river valleys of Aquitaine. I now know, and more importantly acknowledge, that all verbal and physical abuse, no matter how much I instinctively try to justify it, is unacceptable. Thinking of the imminent end of my marriage brings up feelings of loss from my childhood that I've never attempted to deal with. I have always avoided those thoughts and emotions. I now need to embrace them and come through this with some dignity. I can't help her; I can only pray for her. Prayer is another long-abandoned, recently rediscovered source of comfort, from a time before I began to harden against a world that hurts.

A letter from her solicitor arrives - her petition for divorce. Though I knew it was coming, it still hits me hard. Emotionally winded, self-pity follows, but I don't dwell and time alleviates the worst of the dull, aching, sick feeling. I take positive action, copying the letter to my solicitor, and seek advice. I then dutifully take photos of the car she wants to buy when she returns from the UK. This will be the first time in fourteen years that she will drive herself, because I, the chauffeur, caretaker, cleaner and enabler, will have left. I email over the photos, determined not to offer any advice. Caretaking has been what I do to cope with uncomfortable feelings. I think of all I have tried to hide, feeling abandoned, unwanted, unworthy, guilty, ashamed, the list is endless. I seem to think only of how she is. I hardly seem to matter - but then that's the way it's always been.

One night, I kneel by my bed and try to say some prayers, like I did as a little boy. I can't speak, my body is wracked with loud, uncontrollable sobbing. I cry for my mum, I cry for my dad; I cry for the little boy, and I cry for me. I have never cried like this. When I stop, the bedspread is soaked and I am exhausted, but I think, *Is that it? Is that all there is to grief?* If this is grief then it's not enough. I could never have enough. I always wanted more, until the day came when I placed my hand on my brother's coffin and finally felt the full force of what it is to grieve.

The ghost of the boy I used to be was waiting for me when I got home. This was the house the little boy was born in, the house he had been unable to leave until I returned to let him know that it was not his fault. This is our story. The little boy and me.

Acknowledgements

Without whom this book may not have happened:

Jane Ram, for patiently transcribing my early memories.
Lol Tolhurst, for reading my first pieces and for putting me on the right path.
Bobby Gillespie, for graciously and selflessly introducing me to his friend and publisher.
Lee Brackstone, who persisted with endless encouragement and introduced me to my agent.
Clare Conville, who understood and who gave me a title and introduced me to my editorial guide.
Luke Turner, who conducted and compiled long conversations and helped me dive deeper into the dark places.
Elizabeth Milne at C&W for support and meticulous proofreading.
Natalie Dawkins at Orion for laughter and guidance with visuals and layout.
Sarah Fortune at Orion for her judicious overview and eye for detail.
Sophie Nevrkla at White Rabbit for holding the fort.
Kasimiira Kontio at Kontio Comms for amazing liaising.

-: in time at the right time :-

Selwyn Jones-Hughes, Mike Knowles, Pete Griffiths, Dave Littler,
Paul Rutherford, Holly Johnson, Jayne Casey, Ian Broudie,
Bill Drummond, Jeanette Sabo, Clive Langer, Frank Silver,
Glen Matlock, Danny Kustow, Steve New, Viv Albertine,
Ariane Forster, Tessa Pollitt, Paloma McLardy, Nick 'Topper'
Headon, Dennis Bovell, Nils Stevenson,
Billy 'Chainsaw' Houlston, Siouxsie Sioux, Steven Severin,
Ray Stevenson, Clive Richardson, Joe Lyons, Anton Corbijn,
Tony Selinger, Jos Grain, Kenny Morris, John McKay,
John McGeoch, John Carruthers, Jon Klein,
Robert Smith, Martin McCarrick, Talvin Singh, Knox Chandler,
Ben and Norma Watkins, Joseph Brooks, Lydia Lunch,
Marcy Blaustein, Kid Congo Powers, Annie Bandez,
Boris and Helen Williams, Liz and David Fox, Monica Sutcliffe,
Lucy, Nick, Robin and Boe Donovan.

For giving me important dates again and again and again, and for
sharing her own memories, I thank my sister Linda.

For her unending patience and encouragement, I thank my
wonderful wife and first reader,
G.

In loving memory of Bill Rieflin (1960-2020)

and for all the Angels past, present, and future.

Notes

'He was with three or four other people...': Mark Paytress, *Siouxsie and the Banshees: The Authorised Biography* (Sanctuary Publishing Ltd, 2003), p.84

'determined to get fuelled up...': Paytress, p.116

'I picked her up...': Paytress, p.185

'I was hard on Budgie...': Paytress, p.230

'She's Gemini and there's...': Paytress, p.183

'On *Nocturne*, she says...': Paytress, p.183

'With me, I just explode...': Paytress, p.84

Illustration Credits

Frontispiece: *In the mirror in the bathroom 2.00am Friday* (Verlhac-Tescou, France, 28 July 2006)

Prologue: *Galway Bay* (Galway, Ireland, 27 June 2006)

Chapter 1: *Self-portrait* (Ampthill Road, Liverpool, 1977)

Chapter 2: *On the Bus* (Edge Hill, Liverpool, 1976)

Chapter 3: *Self-portrait* (Ampthill Road, Liverpool, 1977)

Chapter 4: *Life drawing - Sue Lee* (Art college, Hope Street, Liverpool, 1977)

Chapter 5: *Self-portrait with Tie* (Ampthill Road, Liverpool, 1977)

Chapter 6: *Laundrette* (Edge Hill, Liverpool, 1976)

Chapter 7: *Self-portrait* (Ampthill Road, Liverpool, 1977)

Chapter 8: *Metropolitan Cathedral* (Mount Pleasant, Liverpool, 1977)

Chapter 9: *Self-portrait with Roll neck* (Ampthill Road, Liverpool, 1977)

Chapter 10: *Coq et poule* (Verlhac-Tescou, France, 9 November 2006)

Chapter 11: *Self-portrait 12.00–1.00am* (Ampthill Road, Liverpool, 1977)

Chapter 12: *Canning Street* (Canning Street, Liverpool, 1977)

Chapter 13: *Self-portrait* (Galway, Ireland, 25 June 2006)

Chapter 14: *Life drawing - Sue Lee* (Art college, Hope Street, Liverpool, 1977)

Chapter 15: *Self-portrait* (Condom, France, 1 January 2006)

Chapter 16: *Shinto Shrine* (Chiyoda, Tokyo, Japan, 20 August 2002)

Chapter 17: *Self-portrait* (St Helens, 26 December 2006)

Chapter 18: *Église St-Valier* (Saint-Girons, France, 20 November 2006)

Chapter 19: *Self-portrait* (Verlhac-Tescou, France, 15 August 2006)

Chapter 20: *Naz and Twigs* (Verlhac-Tescou, France, 24 March 2007)

Chapter 21: *Self-portrait* (Verlhac-Tescou, France, 4 October 2006)

Epilogue: *The Everyman* (Hope Street, Liverpool, 1977)

All drawings by Budgie.

All plate section images from the author's personal collection, with the exception of:

Page 3: Beecham's Clock Tower - Mirrorpix; The off-licence on Morley Street - via *St Helens Star*

Page 5: Happy House - Ray Stevenson; Spitfire Boys, Siouxsie and the Banshees and Big in Japan - Hilary Berg

Page 6: Yucca and Nils Stevenson, Phil Oakey, Siouxsie - Ray Stevenson

Page 7: Siouxsie and the Banshees - Michael Grecco

Page 8: Getty Images